Parents and Toddlers in Groups

This book explores how psychoanalytic principles can be applied when working with parents and toddlers in groups. Illustrated with lively observations, it discusses how these parent-toddler groups can be an effective medium for early intervention during a period which is critical for the negotiation of a child's central emotional issues.

Parents and Toddlers in Groups demonstrates the particular challenges of the toddler phase and its contribution to an individual's future development and relationships. Focusing on an approach developed by the Anna Freud Centre and comprising chapters from a range of expert contributors, topics include:

- the history, theory and practice of parent-toddler groups at the Anna Freud Centre
- how this approach has been adapted and applied across a wide range of settings and cultures
- the findings of research projects carried out on parent-toddler groups.

This book will be a valuable resource for practitioners wanting to reach parents and young children in community, educational and a variety of other settings. It will also appeal to child psychotherapists and psychologists working in CAMHS teams.

Marie Zaphiriou Woods, F. Inst. Psychoanal., is a child psychotherapist and psychoanalyst working with children, adolescents and adults. She was the psychoanalytic consultant and then manager of the Anna Freud Centre Parent-Toddler Group Service from 1999 to 2008. She teaches and supervises for a number of training schools and is a training analyst for the British Association of Psychotherapists.

Inge-Martine Pretorius, PhD, DPsych, trained as a Child and Adolescent Psychotherapist at the ⸺⸺⸺⸺⸺⸺⸺ (AFC). She started working in

the AFC archives in 2001 and became manager of the Parent-Toddler Service in 2008. She is a Clinical Tutor for Psychoanalytic Developmental Psychology at University College London and the AFC where she organises and teaches the MSc Child Development course.

Parents and Toddlers in Groups

A psychoanalytic developmental approach

Edited by Marie Zaphiriou Woods and Inge-Martine Pretorius

Routledge
Taylor & Francis Group

LONDON AND NEW YORK

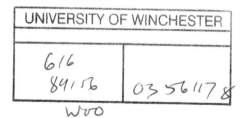
First published 2011 by Routledge
27 Church Road, Hove, East Sussex BN3 2FA

Simultaneously published in the USA and Canada
by Routledge
270 Madison Avenue, New York, NY 10016

Routledge is an imprint of the Taylor & Francis Group, an Informa business

Typeset in Times by Garfield Morgan, Swansea, West Glamorgan
Printed and bound in Great Britain by TJ International Ltd, Padstow,
Cornwall
Paperback cover design by Andrew Ward

British Library Cataloguing in Publication Data
A catalogue record for this book is available from the British Library

Library of Congress Cataloging-in-Publication Data
Parents and toddlers in groups : a psychoanalytic developmental approach /
edited by Marie Zaphiriou Woods and Inge-Martine Pretorius.
       p. cm.
   Includes bibliographical references.
   ISBN 978-0-415-48639-2 (hbk.) – ISBN 978-0-415-48640-8 (pbk.) 1. Parent
and child. 2. Social groups. 3. Child psychology. 4. Child development.
5. Child analysis. I. Woods, Marie Zaphiriou, 1948– II. Pretorius,
Inge-Martine, 1960–

   BF723.P25P32 2010
   616.89'156–dc22

                                                            2010038415

ISBN: 978-0-415-48639-2 (hbk)
ISBN: 978-0-415-48640-8 (pbk)

This book is dedicated to Alexander and Roxana (MZW)
and to Nathan and Matthew (IMP).

Contents

Contributors

The editors

Marie Zaphiriou Woods is a Child and Adult Psychoanalyst. She was the psychoanalytic consultant and then manager of the Anna Freud Centre (AFC) nursery from 1986 to 1997. She also ran a parent-toddler group, and became psychoanalytic consultant and then manager of the Anna Freud Centre Parent-Toddler Group Service from 1999 to 2008. She works privately with children, adolescents and adults, and teaches and supervises for a number of training schools. She lectures for the joint UCL-AFC MSc in Psychoanalytic Developmental Psychology, and is a training therapist for the British Association of Psychotherapists. She is the author of published articles and book chapters.

Inge-Martine Pretorius, PhD, DPsych, trained as a Child and Adolescent Psychotherapist at the AFC. She started working in the AFC archives in 2001, became a toddler group leader in 2002 and manager of the Parent-Toddler Service in 2008. She is a Clinical Tutor for Psychoanalytic Developmental Psychology at University College London and the AFC where she organises and teaches the MSc Child Development course. She works part-time in the NHS, running a Consultation Service at the Randolph Beresford Early Years Centre. She has published in the fields of molecular genetics and psychoanalysis.

List of contributors

Elizabeth Allison is a member of the British Psychoanalytic Society and Publications Editor at the Psychoanalysis Unit at University College London. She has a DPhil in English Literature and teaches on psychoanalysis and literature and Freud's views on femininity in the UCL Masters courses in Theoretical Psychoanalytic Studies and Gender, Society and Representation.

Kay Asquith is Course Tutor for the MSc in Psychoanalytic Developmental Psychology (UCL/Anna Freud Centre) and the MSc in Psychodynamic Developmental Neuroscience (UCL/Yale/AFC) and has taught quantitative and qualitative research methods at the Anna Freud Centre for the last six years. Her research interests are attachment, adoption and parenting and she has co-authored a number of articles in these areas. She has also developed a parenting skills programme specifically for adoptive families in conjunction with Coram Family.

Ana María Barrantes is a psychoanalytical oriented child psychotherapist. She has run a nursery school for children aged 1½ to 5 years, since 1977. In 2000 she co-founded Grupo Carretel and started running a parent-toddler group with Elena Piazzon. She is co-founder and representative from Peru of the Latin American Reggio Emilia Association (Red-Solare). A member of the APPPNA (Asociación Peruana de Psicoterapia Psicoanalítica de Niños y Adolescentes), she works in private practice with children and adults.

María Luisa Barros is a psychoanalytically oriented psychologist. A graduate of the MSc in Psychoanalytic Developmental Psychology at the Anna Freud Centre and University College London, she now lectures in Developmental Psychology at the Universidad Del Desarrollo in Chile and works in private practice with children and adolescents.

Lesley Bennett trained as an Educational Psychologist at the Child Guidance Training Centre (Tavistock Centre) and has worked for many years in Local Education Authorities. During this time she held several specialist posts for Early Years services that offer support to families with children with medical and/or developmental difficulties. She joined the Court Assessment Service at the AFC in 2004 and became the Leader of the outreach community toddler group in 2005. Lesley is also a Professional and Academic Tutor at the Tavistock Clinic, teaching and supervising on the doctoral course in Child, Community and Educational Psychology.

Carolina Camino Rivera, MSc in Psychoanalytic Developmental Psychology (University College London and the AFC), is a psychoanalytically oriented psychologist working with children, adolescents and adults in private practice, interested in attachment relationships and eating disorders. She currently teaches at the University of Lima, and works in a programme sponsored by the university which promotes emotional development in children, adolescents and parents from a deprived community.

Peter Fonagy, PhD FBA, is Freud Memorial Professor of Psychoanalysis and Head of the Research Department of Clinical, Educational and

Health Psychology at University College London; Chief Executive of the Anna Freud Centre, London; and Consultant to the Child and Family Program at the Menninger Department of Psychiatry and Behavioral Sciences at the Baylor College of Medicine. He is Chair of the Postgraduate Education Committee of the International Psychoanalytic Association and a Fellow of the British Academy. He is a clinical psychologist and a training and supervising analyst in the British Psychoanalytical Society in child and adult analysis. His work integrates empirical research with psychoanalytic theory, and his clinical interests centre around borderline psychopathology, violence, and early attachment relationships.

Joshua Holmes, BA (Geography), MSc (Psychoanalytic Developmental Psychology), was a play assistant at a baby clinic as part of the Anna Freud Centre's Parent-Infant Project. He has published papers on the links between agoraphobia and attachment theory. He now works as an English teacher in Lima, Peru.

Valentina Ivanova, PhD, is a psychologist and Parent-Toddler Group leader. She is also a consultant for the parents and children in the nursery school. She is a lecturer in St. Petersburg State University.

Annabel Kitson is a Child and Adolescent Psychotherapist. She works at the Marlborough Family Service, working with infants, children, adolescents and families, as well as being a core member of an assessment team carrying out specialist assessments for court. She also works as a Specialist Clinician in Luton and Bedfordshire Parent Infant Psychotherapeutic team, an early intervention and prevention service. She has over 20 years' experience working with under fives, children and adolescents in a variety of settings and roles in the UK and abroad.

Fátima Martínez del Solar, MSc, a Psychoanalyst and associate member of the British Psychoanalytical Society, works in private practice and in CAMHS in South London. For eight years, she was the Head Teacher of Little Villa Nursery School in Lima, Peru. At the Anna Freud Centre, she was a toddler group leader, before starting a toddler group following the AFC psychoanalytic approach in a deprived, multicultural area of South London.

Nick Midgley is a Child and Adolescent Psychotherapist and Head of Programme for Children and Young People at the Anna Freud Centre, London. He is the author (with Eilis Kennedy) of *Process and Outcome Research in Child, Adolescent and Parent-Infant Psychotherapy* (NHS London, 2007) and joint editor of *Child Psychotherapy and Research: New Directions, Emerging Findings* (Routledge, 2009).

Evanthia Navridi, BSc in Psychology (University of Athens), MSc in Psychoanalytic Developmental Psychology (University College London and the AFC), is a Research Associate at the Child and Adolescent Unit of Vironas – Kessariani Community Mental Health Centre of the University of Athens, where she has organised and co-ordinates a toddler group service.

Elena Piazzon is a psychoanalyst, a full member and training analyst at the Sociedad Peruana de Psicoánalisis, where she teaches at the Institute and has been the Co-ordinator of the Infant Observation Seminar for six years. She has been teaching Child Psychotherapy to psychiatric residents, at the Universidad Peruana Cayetano Heredia, since 1983. Co-founder of Grupo Carretel – a group that promotes psycho-emotional development of infants and their families – she has run a toddler group since 2000. She works as a psychoanalyst in private practice with children and adults.

Anna Plagerson trained as a Child and Adolescent Psychotherapist at the AFC. Previously, as an Early Years teacher, she worked in inner London schools for five years. While completing the MSc in Psychoanalytic Developmental Psychology at the AFC and UCL, she worked as an assistant in the AFC parent-toddler groups. She is currently working in the NHS, based in a CAMHS in South East London.

Elspeth Pluckrose is a Child and Adolescent Psychotherapist and a former Parent-Toddler Group Leader at an Anna Freud Centre outreach toddler group, based in a hostel for homeless families. She also works in the NHS and is currently working as Principal Child and Adolescent Psychotherapist in a tier-two early intervention service in South London. She has published articles in the *International Journal of Infant Observation*.

Anna Prützel-Thomas is a trainee Child and Adolescent Psychotherapist at the BAP and in the NHS. She previously worked at the Anna Freud Centre, co-supervising qualitative and quantitative MSc research into the Parent-Toddler Groups and worked as a Toddler Group Assistant for three years.

Jenny Stoker is a psychoanalyst working with children and adults. A former toddler group leader at the Anna Freud Centre, she also ran a group for toddlers with special needs and their parents. She is the author of *You and Your Toddler* (Karnac, 2005), a book aimed at helping parents understand their young children better. She has taught and lectured for academic and professional courses and she has contributed to academic journals as well as to magazines for parents and allied professionals. She also works privately.

Mary Target, PhD, is Professional Director of the AFC and Professor of Psychoanalysis at UCL. Her first training was in clinical psychology at Oxford University. She practised for some years in NHS adult and child mental health and medical liaison roles. Her PhD at UCL and the AFC was on the outcomes of child psychoanalysis. She trained at the Institute of Psychoanalysis where she is a Fellow. She carries out research on child and adult attachment, social cognition and psychotherapy outcomes. She has a half-time psychoanalytic practice.

Nina Vasilyeva, PhD, is a psychoanalyst (direct member of the IPA) working with children and adults. For eight years she worked for the Early Intervention Institute in St. Petersburg with families and parent-infant groups. She is a Professor in St. Petersburg State University.

Julie Wallace is a Child and Adolescent Psychotherapist, and a former Parent-Toddler Group leader at the Anna Freud Centre. She is currently working full-time within the NHS in South and West Wales.

Foreword

Peter Fonagy

The past two decades of developmental research, both behavioural and neuroscientific, have underscored the importance of the early years. As we learn more, particularly from rodent models, we cannot but be impressed by the ingenuity of nature in creating multiple mechanisms for adaptation and adjustment to specific environmental conditions. Michael Meaney's work in Montreal has shown how genetic mechanisms respond to early stress, affecting not only an individual's responsiveness throughout their own life but also the life of the next generation through transmission of these genetic characteristics (e.g. Meaney & Szyf, 2005). The importance of early experience is also underscored by a veritable plethora of intervention programmes created to enhance wellbeing in infants, increase a sense of security and ensure a genuine reduction in antisocial behaviour in adolescence and earlier adulthood (Olds, Sadler, & Kitzman, 2007). More specifically pertinent to this volume, developmental studies are increasingly pointing to the second and third years of life as particularly significant in the acquisition of social cognition and mapping the child's developing understanding of what it means to be a person.

Psychoanalysts have focused on toddlerhood as developmentally critical, but historically not everyone was convinced. Kleinian writers, particularly in the 1950s and 1960s, prioritised the understanding of infancy and had little apparent concern for the toddler who was neither a viable subject of observation nor, for the most part, a potential patient. Indeed, the great developmentalists of psychoanalysis, Donald Winnicott, Daniel Stern, Robert Emde, and John Bowlby, had focused on the first year as the formative period, even though they extended their models into later childhood. Anna Freud's and Margaret Mahler's insistence on observation as a key part of psychoanalytic inquiry led them both to studying the emergence of selfhood out of a two-person unit. Both these giants of the psychoanalytic observational method created images of toddlerhood as the root of subjectivity, although their models were different and in most ways complementary.

This tradition finds a fitting heir in the work of Marie Zaphiriou Woods and her brilliant colleagues. With Inge Pretorius, she has put together a quite wonderful testament to the richness of psychoanalytically oriented study of human interaction. The book itself represents a superb summary of what we can learn from a modern psychoanalytic perspective about the development of a toddler in the parent–child relationship and the emergence of social understanding through peer interaction. The book is solidly rooted in psychoanalytic understanding, with several chapters offering eloquent and lively contemporary theory and research on the second and third years of life. In addition to psychoanalytic and neuroscientific theory there are beautiful illustrations of toddler behaviour and its psychoanalytic understanding.

The book would be a worthy contribution if it rested here. But it offers far, far more. The central contribution of the volume is in an intriguing model for therapeutic early intervention, evolved over years in a tightly-knit group of committed clinicians which has enabled Zaphiriou Woods and her colleagues to offer assistance to these parents using Anna Freud's, Dorothy Burlingham's, Hansi Kennedy's, Anne Hurry's and many others' framework of developmental help. This construct, which runs through the spirit of this book, is rooted in a clear conceptualisation of developmental process, from which arrests and deviations can be readily identified, and progressive movement facilitated. The process of change is where the science of observation turns into the art of engagement with the toddlers and their caregivers' fantasies, anxieties and constitutional limitations. The book offers marvellous illustrations of how the difficulties that parents encounter in promoting a child's play can be overcome through subtle yet enormously powerful, meticulously placed brief interventions. Jenny Stoker, for example, writes beautifully about how play, which has such an important role in the creation of the child's representational world, can be promoted through facilitating the parents' seriousness about the internal world of the child. However, it is the work with more severe disability that brings out most clearly how much psychoanalytic understanding can achieve for a parent–child couple. In two chapters the book movingly demonstrates how the toddler groups can help parents to protect their child from some of the psychological challenges which the child's 'specialness' tragically can bring with it in our society.

As if this was not already offering enough, the book takes us to where it is hard to reach, the world of social disadvantage. Epidemiological research has shown us just how profound the impact of inequalities can be in terms of physical health, general wellbeing, and psychological disturbance. As the toddler groups move into homeless hostels and council estates, we glimpse some of the roots of long-term social disadvantage (e.g. Marmot, 1998; Marmot, Bobak, & Davey Smith, 1995). Although the book resists blaming parents or social conditions, it is clear how the normative processes outlined in the first part of the volume are regularly compromised by the deprivation and accompanying stress which parents experience. It is exactly those capacities which the authors have drawn our attention to in the first part of the book, those relating to recognising the child's unique subjectivity, which are the first to go when the going becomes tough. It is a remarkable testament to the readiness of these parents to do the best for their child to see how much a brief non-intensive intervention which nevertheless is well-crafted and subtle can achieve in facilitating social development in the toddler through enhancing effective parenting in mothers and sometimes fathers.

By the time the reader reaches the second section of the book they will not be surprised to learn that the model has quickly achieved recognition and popularity, as it is taken up by a number of talented clinicians in places as far apart as Russia, Peru and Greece. These experiences are intriguing for a number of reasons. They illustrate just how readily the project can fit into cultural environments quite different from its Southern England origins. While each application is unique, its transportability illustrates cross-cultural uniformity in the developmental processes that are at the heart of this book.

Finally, the book can also boast of major methodological advances. In bringing qualitative and quantitative research methods into the toddler groups we have a perspective beyond narrative description on what happens in this process of developmental facilitation. This kind of integration of research and practice was of course Anna Freud's lifetime ambition, although she would not have been familiar with the methods described here, but moving developmental science forward by the best available methods of psychoanalytic inquiry would surely have met with her approval. In these chapters the book also does much to show how education, research, clinical observation and psychoanalytic insight can be woven into a single immensely rich tapestry of understanding.

Beyond its declared aim of describing developmental process and therapeutic intervention in a range of contexts, the book provides a paradigm for how creative clinical interventions can and should be carefully described, integrated in theory, translated into well-illustrated practical recommendations, disseminated across a range of sites and contexts to demonstrate translatability and researched in all these settings to understand how they work, what they achieve and how they could do more. Zaphiriou Woods and Pretorius have provided the field with a hallmark volume that illustrates an innovative and powerful clinical paradigm, one which demonstrates the generativity of psychoanalytic thinking in providing solutions to the most important problems of our time.

Acknowledgements

Thanks are due to many people who contributed to this book in various ways. First and foremost, we wish to thank the toddlers and parents who have attended our groups and taught us so much about playfulness, passion and conflict. We are indebted to past and present members of the parent-toddler group teams, for their enthusiasm, commitment, observations and insights. We wish to thank valued colleagues, Nancy Brenner, Viviane Green, Jessica James, Wilhelmina Kraemer-Zurne, Angela Joyce, and Jenny Stoker for helpful suggestions on drafts of chapters. Liz Allison's invaluable and thoughtful editing helped us through the final stages of this book. John Woods' unwavering support and encouragement helped MZW through every stage of the book.

Extract on page 19 from "Walking Away" from *The Complete Poems* by C Day Lewis published by Sinclair-Stevenson (1992) Copyright © 1992 in this edition The Estate of C Day Lewis. Reprinted by permission of The Random House Group Ltd.

Introduction

Marie Zaphiriou Woods

This book is about psychoanalytic parent-toddler groups (PTGs) – how they are run at the Anna Freud Centre (AFC), in various outreach settings around London, and in other cities abroad, where colleagues have taken our approach as a model and introduced it to different populations and cultures. It shows how such groups can be an effective medium for early intervention during a period which is critical for the negotiation of central emotional issues to do with intimacy, autonomy, aggression, separateness and sexuality. The accessibility and ordinariness of the groups make it possible for many parents, who may be suspicious of mental health services, to attend with their toddlers. Whether they are struggling with typical toddler behaviours (e.g. negativism, tantrums, battles over eating and sleeping), more specific difficulties, or merely looking for company for themselves and/or their toddler (consciously, at least), they place themselves in a position to receive professional help which is informed by an under-standing of developmental needs and psychoanalytic processes. The parent–child relationship is supported during a period which is crucial for future development, difficulties may be identified and addressed before they become entrenched, and, where necessary, appropriate referrals may be made to clinical services, on the basis of the trusting relationships that develop in the groups over time.

The groups are led by trained professionals, meet weekly and last for 1½ hours. They are for toddlers and their parents or close relatives. Despite the fact that, nowadays, most parents work, it has proved possible for them to come to the groups with their toddlers. In some countries (Greece and Peru), the PTGs meet outside working hours, so that both parents often attend. In England, where the groups are held during school hours, parents may organise their work in order to bring their toddler to a group, or postpone returning to work till their children are old enough to go to nursery school. Asylum seekers and refugees in England, or orphanage graduates in Russia, may attend a conveniently situated group during the difficult period of transition and adjustment, while they organise housing and/or take courses which may enable them to gain employment.

The "excursions and returns" (Winnicott, 1966, p. 136) of toddlers using the groups to explore their internal and external worlds, and to separate and individuate from their parents, have been paralleled by the journeys of students and colleagues who have observed, assisted, and sometimes led PTGs at the AFC. After attending our seminars and team meetings, or coming for individual consultations, they have taken our ideas and methods into their worlds, maintaining contact by email, and sometimes returning for further consultations or the annual toddler symposium. Alternatively members of the AFC team have gone to their countries, giving talks and offering consultations. Just as toddlers encounter a painful tension between subjective and objective reality (ibid.), so have we all had to struggle with the tension between the AFC approach, and the exigencies of the very different settings and cultures in which we have found ourselves. We commonly encountered the privileging of a medical over a psychological approach to early difficulties, the delegation of child care to the extended family or professional carers, rivalries between professionals, and splitting and projection within the host organisation. The ways in which these were understood, the creative solutions found, successes and failures, are chronicled in the second section of this book.

I first conceived of this book when I began to think of retiring from my post as manager of the parent-toddler service at the AFC – evidence perhaps that the process of separating and individuating can stimulate creativity throughout life. It seemed to me that our way of working had become sufficiently refined to be written down, and that, although there are of course many other ways of running successful psychoanalytic parent-toddler groups around the world, our approach had shown itself to be sufficiently flexible to be helpful to families with special needs and vulnerabilities in a variety of settings. Firmly embedded in a psychoanalytic theory of child development, constantly tested and enriched by observations of toddlers and their parents, and evaluated by research projects arising from the AFC-UCL MSc, the parent-toddler groups fulfil Anna Freud's vision of combining training, service and research (Kennedy, 1978). They also carry on her tradition of reaching out into the community and offering psychoanalytically informed support to very young children (and parents) suffering from deprivation, trauma, and loss. I was very glad when Inge Pretorius, who took over as manager of the toddler service in 2008, agreed to edit the book with me. We both hope that this book will prove useful to practitioners working with toddlers and their parents in both similar and diverse settings. Our understanding and approach to the complex developmental challenges of toddlerhood may be relevant to work with older children and their parents who are still struggling to achieve autonomy and positive relationships.

The book is divided into three sections. The first section (chapters 1–6) describes the parent-toddler groups at the Anna Freud Centre – their history, theory and practice. The second (chapters 7–13) shows how adapting the Anna Freud Centre approach for toddlers and families with specific needs and in a range of settings has raised a number of issues, which required modifications of technique. The authors explore these, drawing from a variety of theoretical sources and traditions (group analytical, systemic, and Kleinian as well as Independent and classically Anna Freudian). The final section of the book (chapters 14–16) summarises the findings of three research projects carried out on the AFC parent-toddler groups. A brief introduction places them in the context of the joint AFC-UCL MSc in Psychoanalytic Developmental Psychology.

Chapter 1 shows how our current toddler groups grew out of Anna Freud's lifelong endeavour to link psychoanalytic theory, observation and practice, to build a theory of normal development, and to intervene early to prevent later disturbance. Chapter 2 sets out the theory of normal toddler development that underpins our approach to working with parents and toddlers. It draws on classical psychoanalytic texts by Anna Freud, Winnicott, and Mahler while also incorporating contemporary psychoanalytic and developmental thinking and attachment and neuroscience perspectives. Observations from the groups bring the theory to life and highlight the centrality of the relationship between toddler and parent. Chapter 3 describes how the toddler groups work – their structure, their aims, and the sorts of interventions carried out in the groups. It uses vignettes from the groups to show how the group setting and individual interventions can support the development of those attending. Chapter 4 explores the nature of play and playfulness and extends our understanding of their role in toddlers' development. It explores some of the difficulties that parents have in playing with their children, and shows how the groups encourage playfulness in both. Chapter 5 is an example of a toddler observation paper written by a student observing fortnightly in one of our groups. It shows the student's struggle with difficult feelings as she observes the impact of the toddler's growing autonomy and aggression on a previously idealised mother–toddler relationship. She uses her observations and countertransference to reach a deeper understanding of the complex fluctuating nature of normal toddler development.

Chapter 6 is a longitudinal study of the relationship between a partially sighted father and his daughters, both of whom were born with floppy baby syndrome, who attended two groups successively. Using observations spanning a period of four years, it shows how, with the support of the groups, he was able to differentiate the frustrations arising from his progressive disability from his daughters' more benign condition, and to use his experience to be particularly empathic and supportive in finding ways to assist their development.

In chapter 7, an experienced member of the AFC team outlines the background, aims and development of a toddler group for children with special needs. With the help of portraits of three children attending the group, she shows how the uncertainties and ambiguities arising from difference and disability impacted on the toddlers, the parents, and the professionals working with them, giving rise to intensely painful feelings of helplessness, frustration and ambivalence which were then enacted or avoided in the group. In chapter 8, another member of our team details the challenges of running an outreach group on a run-down council estate. She shows how the design of the estate reflected and compounded the experience of the families on the estate. Their traumatic experiences of dislocation, invisibility, rejection and intrusion were then repeated in the group, requiring firm management at the boundaries, to protect the parents, toddlers and staff, and to process and understand intense feelings that paralleled those of the toddlers in the group. Chapter 9 reviews the gradual modification of expectations and technique required to run a successful toddler group in a hostel for homeless families. It shows how flexibility regarding boundaries was combined with holding in mind the group frame to create an ongoing therapeutic group. Mothers and toddlers were helped to negotiate core issues of separation and aggression, made more complicated by the families' previous experiences of helplessness and loss, and everyday living in a hostel. In Chapter 10, expectations and technique are differently modified to reach another vulnerable group of parents in a deprived part of London. Here the emphasis is on reaching out to families preoccupied with day-to-day survival, showing them that they are held in mind, and creating a sense of belonging. An example of three years' work with one mother and daughter shows how, by providing a flexible group experience in which the mother was allowed to regulate closeness, she was helped to tolerate her toddler's aggression and bids for autonomy and to build a stronger relationship.

Chapter 11 takes us to Russia where a long-established service of integrated toddler groups brings together mothers who grew up in orphanages, toddlers with special needs, and other parents and toddlers struggling with the developmental challenges of toddlerhood. Although special efforts are made to reach out to and engage particularly vulnerable parents, the authors stress that, within the groups, attention is distributed equally between all members with the focus on shared issues rather than special needs. Chapter 12 describes the painstaking process of introducing the professional and local community to the idea of toddlerhood and its unique challenges, before setting up a toddler group in a community mental health centre in Athens. Drawing on group analytic theory as well as Winnicott and Bion, it explores the many levels on which sharing takes place within a toddler group, and uses vignettes to show how this process can strengthen attachments and promote separation and autonomy. Chapter 13 shows how the authors were able to start a parent-toddler group in Lima, within a culture where early child care is traditionally delegated to others, and excellence of performance is privileged over emotional development. By meeting on Saturday mornings and offering an alternative innovative model which valued spontaneous play and reciprocal communication, they were able to engage working parents and foster the recognition of their children as unique individuals with minds of their own.

The final chapters describe the research and evaluation of the groups. Chapter 14 provides an account of parents' experience of attending an AFC toddler group, and confirms how important it is for early interventions to address and support the needs of both parents and children. Chapter 15 measures the reflective functioning capacities of 12 mothers who attended an AFC parent-toddler group. It concludes that attendance at a psycho-analytic toddler group may positively influence the mothers' capacity to reflect on their toddlers' behaviour. Chapter 16 uses microanalysis of video footage to extend our understanding of the developmental processes involved with social eating, linking it to affect regulation and the process of separation-individuation.

Part I

The Anna Freud Centre parent-toddler groups

A historical background of the Anna Freud Centre parent-toddler groups and the use of observation to study child development[1]

Inge-Martine Pretorius

> People no longer remember who led the way in the methods they now use.
>
> August Aichhorn

Introduction

The Anna Freud Centre's parent-toddler groups embody Anna Freud's consistent endeavour to link psychoanalytic theory, observation and practice in the field of child development. The history of the groups is rooted in her lifelong interest in the applied field of psychoanalysis and her many attempts to build bridges between different professional disciplines concerned with the wellbeing of children: education, paediatrics and family law.

This chapter offers a historical overview of the work of Anna Freud and her successors with toddlers, from the Jackson Nursery in Vienna to the current parent-toddler groups run at the Anna Freud Centre and in the community. It shows how Anna Freud's first tentative attempts at direct observation became a crucial component of her "double approach" which integrated observation and psychoanalytic reconstruction, in her quest to build a psychoanalytic theory of normal child development.

Die Kindergruppe (1927–38)

Writing about "Little Hans", Sigmund Freud (1909) called for use of direct observation of children to complement psychoanalytic investigations:

> Surely there must be a possibility of observing in children at first hand and in all the freshness of life the sexual impulses and wishes which we dig out so laboriously in adults from among their own debris.
>
> (1909, p. 6)

Anna Freud's own interest in direct observation emerged when she gave four lectures on the "Introduction to technique of child analysis" (1926–27), at the newly-founded Vienna Institute of Psychoanalysis. Regular seminars on child analysis followed and became known as "die Kindergruppe" (the children's group). Held on Wednesday afternoons, these seminars were the forerunner of the Wednesday Meetings at the Anna Freud Centre (Kennedy, 1995). They were attended by Dorothy Burlingham, Erik Erikson, Hedwig and Willi Hoffer, Anny Katan, Margaret Fries, Edith Jackson and others (A. Freud, 1966). While doing analysis with verbal children and observing babies (often their own), these analysts began to think about the importance of the mother–infant relationship for the child's future development. The longitudinal observations that took place within the context of a training analysis were regularly recorded, in special columns of the psychoanalytic journals of the time (A. Freud, 1967; Young-Bruehl, 2004).

During these early years, the Viennese school of child analysis (led by Anna Freud) explored the adaptations to classical technique required by the child's developing mind. They believed that the aim of child analysis was to prevent arrests and inhibitions and undo regressions and compromise formations, thereby "setting free the child's spontaneous energies directed toward the completion of progressive development" (Freud, 1967, p. 9). Anna Freud became convinced of the need for child analysts to build up "a psychoanalytic theory of normal development" (Freud, 1978b, p. 276) in order to recognise and assess psychopathology.

The Jackson Nursery (1937–38)

Anna Freud's interest in observation and normality, together with her awareness of social deprivation in Vienna, motivated the opening of the Jackson Nursery. As a Jew, she was not allowed to be in charge of an institution, so the nursery was officially run by her American friends, Dorothy Burlingham and Edith Jackson, who also funded the venture (Edgcumbe, 2000). They rented part of the "Haus der Kinder" from the Montessori Society and shared some of their toys. Twenty toddlers aged 1 to 3 years were selected from the poorest section of Vienna. Anna Freud explained her interest in directly observing pre-oedipal children:

> Our wish was to gather direct (as opposed to reconstructed) information about the second year of life, which we deemed all important for the child's essential advance from primary to secondary process functioning; for the establishment of feeding and sleeping habits; for acquiring the rudiments of superego development and impulse control; for the establishment of object ties to peers.
>
> (Freud, 1978a, p. 731)

Considered an "experimental nursery group" (Freud, 1978a, p. 731), it offered an opportunity to learn and to test some of the developing theoretical ideas in a day-care setting. Anna Freud immediately introduced recorded observations when the nursery opened in February 1937. She visited regularly as an observer and attended the once-weekly staff meetings where the individual children were discussed. She also convened monthly seminars to discuss theoretical issues arising from the nursery work. The first meeting took place on 1st March 1937 and was attended by Anna Freud, Dorothy Burlingham, Josefine Stross (the nursery's paediatrician), Grete Bibring, Berta Bornstein, Edith Buxbaum, Heinz Hartmann, Hedwig and Willi Hoffer, Anny Katan, Ernst Kris, Hans Lampl, Jeanne Lampl-de Groot, Richard Sterba, Robert Wälder, Jenny Wälder-Hall and Wolff Sachs (Kennedy, 1988).

They discussed the methodology of data collection and debated whether they should try to make objective behaviouristic observations or use the "analytic method": gather material to confirm or contradict impressions gained from their psychoanalytically informed, first impressions (Kennedy, 1988). The possible pathology of the children seemed to be of less interest than establishing a sound methodology. No observations survived when the nursery was closed by the Nazi government in 1938.

The Hampstead War Nurseries (1940–45)

When Sigmund Freud and his family fled to London in June 1939, Anna Freud anticipated the direction of her work in London, by including ten little children's stretcher beds in her luggage. Most of the furniture and toys from the Jackson Nursery followed soon after (Young-Bruehl, 2008). With the outbreak of war, Anna Freud realised the need for shelters for children and their families who were rendered refugees or homeless by the war. Together with Dorothy Burlingham, she opened the Children's Rest Centre at 13 Wedderburn Road in North London, January 1941. In the summer of 1941, two additional residential nurseries were opened; the Babies' Rest Centre at 5 Netherhall Gardens, in North London, and New Barn, an evacuation home in Chelmsford, Essex. Freud and Burlingham were pioneers in establishing the three residential homes that became known as the Hampstead War Nurseries (Hellman, 1983), in that they sought not merely to provide for the physical and educational needs of young children, but also for their psychological and emotional needs.

Anna Freud and Dorothy Burlingham ran the London homes and required a supervisor for the country home. Hearing reports about Alice Goldberger, who had established a nursery school on the Isle of Man, where she was interned as an "enemy alien", Anna Freud set about enlisting Alice's expertise. Through her intervention, Alice was released and became the superintendent of the country home, New Barn. After the war, she joined the first cohort of trainees on the Hampstead Child-Therapy Course (Friedmann, 1986, 1988).

Although repairing and preventing physical and psychological damage caused by war conditions were the two most important aims of the nurseries, they also offered a tremendous opportunity for research and teaching. In particular, the work offered an opportunity for longitudinal studies of child development (Burlingham & Freud, 1942). Children aged from 10 days to 6 years were admitted (191 children in total). Approximately one fifth came with their mothers, who remained in the nurseries for periods ranging from several days to several years. This made it possible to observe children, almost from birth, in contact with their mothers or deprived of maternal care, being breast- or bottle-fed, being separated or reunited with their mothers, in contact with mother substitutes and developing relationships with peers (Freud, 1951).

All staff recorded detailed observations as part of in-service training. Apart from six highly qualified people, the staff comprised younger workers – many refugees themselves – who had not been analysed or exposed to psychoanalytic theory. Anna Freud described them as, "young people, eager for an adventure in education and observation, untrained for this type of work, but also untrained in methods hostile to it" (Freud, 1951, p. 20). She described the early observational work and stance:

> Emulating the analyst's attitude when observing his patients during the analytic hour, attention was kept free-floating and the material was followed up wherever it led.
>
> (Freud, 1951, p. 19)

Recorded mostly in English, the observations were classified under English and, occasionally, German headings, like "Einfühlung" – a word that encompasses empathy and insight. Hundreds of observations recorded on index cards remain in the AFC archives. These observations were integrated within the overall theoretical framework, which was continually being modified and developed by information gained from new observations. This process highlighted how important the child's earliest relationships were for the child's later development. Anna Freud and her staff began to show that early intervention could mitigate the development of later emotional and behavioural difficulties. This preventative work is central to the parent-toddler groups (Zaphiriou Woods, 2000).

The monthly reports on the war nurseries gave examples and summaries of observations on various themes (Freud & Burlingham, 1940–45). The first major summary was published as "Infants without families" in 1944 (Freud & Burlingham, 1944). Although in Anna Freud's opinion these early observations were unsystematic, they were nonetheless the immediate forerunners of her subsequent advocacy of direct observation, a method that continued to be frowned on by many analysts (Solnit & Newman, 1984).

Anna Freud revealed her initial scepticism about the direct observation of children, writing that "the observations of manifest, overt behaviour mark a step which is not undertaken without misgivings" (Freud, 1951, p. 18). Anna Freud hoped – but was doubtful – that observations would prove useful in validating or refuting psychoanalytic reconstruction, thinking in 1951 that "it will not break new ground" (Freud, 1958, p. 93). However, by 1958, she realised that she had been overly pessimistic about the value and power of observation. She noted that – as she had hoped – direct observations confirmed some psychoanalytic assumptions, such as the overlapping of libidinal phases. She highlighted the value of direct observation for children subjected to trauma; these children often showed regressive and repetitive behaviours that were easily recognised during observations (Freud, 1958).

Anna Freud eventually came to value the "double approach" to gathering data – observation and reconstruction – and the way in which direct observation and psychoanalytic insight could reciprocally enrich each other to create a psychoanalytic child psychology (Freud, 1958). Such became her appreciation of this approach that she wrote:

> While observing the coming and going of the manifestations of pregenitality in their inexorable sequence, the observer cannot help feeling that every student of psychoanalysis should be given the opportunity to watch these phenomena at the time when they occur so as to acquire a picture against which he can check his later analytic reconstructions.
>
> (Freud, 1951, p. 21)

Anna Freud's concept of developmental lines epitomises the synthesis of data gathered from observation and analytic reconstruction, as does the Provisional Diagnostic Profile (Freud, 1965). While the developmental lines give an external picture of the child from which psychic development is inferred, the Diagnostic Profile includes the child's subjective, inner world. Essentially a developmental assessment instrument, the Profile drew on and reinforced Anna Freud's quest for a greater understanding of normality and pathology. Her written work during the last 20 years of her life showed her preoccupation with both, as well as her awareness of how much remained to be learned about how to treat disturbance (Freud, 1983; Solnit & Newman, 1984).

The Hampstead Nursery School (1957–99)

When the War Nurseries were closed at the end of the war, Kate Friedlander and Barbara Lantos encouraged Anna Freud to organise a formal course to train "child experts" (Freud, 1965, p. 9). The Hampstead

Child Therapy Course began in 1947 with seminars held at the teachers' homes and at 20 Maresfield Gardens (Kennedy, 1995). Friedlander and Lantos served as teachers and training analysts (Young-Bruehl, 2008). With the acquisition of 12 Maresfield Gardens, The Hampstead Clinic opened in 1952 and the organisation became known as the Hampstead Child Therapy Course and Clinic.

The nursery school was founded to provide the students training at the clinic with an opportunity to observe and study normal development, to bring the two disciplines of education and psychoanalysis together and to offer a nursery service for children. Anna Freud chose Manna Friedmann to run the nursery school that opened in May 1957. The two women had met in 1946 when Manna was Alice Goldberger's co-worker at Weir Courtney in Surrey: the residential home for the youngest survivors of the concentration camps (24 children aged 4–16 years) (Friedmann, 1986, 1988). The nursery school rapidly became Anna Freud's favourite project and many delightful anecdotes survive from her playful interactions with the children. Friedmann recounts one little boy asking Anna Freud where she lived. Anna Freud replied "I live in Coco's house" (Coco was Anna Freud's dog) to which the boy replied with much sympathy, "You don't have a house of your own!" (reported by Friedman, in Tewkesbury, 2006).

Housed in the basement of 12 Maresfield Gardens, the nursery school was attended by 8–13 children aged 3–5 years. In addition to normal children, the group included some children with special needs and some receiving or awaiting individual psychotherapy (Sandler, 1965). The nursery school provided intensive psychoanalytic cases for students training at the clinic. Initially the school offered a half-day programme, but in 1966 the Headstart Program in the USA stimulated the nursery to extend to a full-day programme that included disadvantaged families. Two consultants were assigned to the Nursery staff: Agi Bene and Anne-Marie Sandler, who were succeeded by Rose Edgcumbe and Peter Wilson.

Alice Colonna was amongst the first-year students who began observing the children. The student observers mingled with the children in the nursery school, adopting a neutral role (Wilson, 1980). Students and staff discussed their observations at weekly meetings. Observations in the nursery some-times drew on observations made in the War Nurseries and were combined with the assessment and psychoanalytic treatment of nursery children (Zaphiriou Woods & Gedulter-Trieman, 1998).

Manna Friedmann was initially daunted by the task of recoding obser-vations. She recalled Anna Freud's characteristically simple response:

> Make a note of anything you would feel inclined to tell a friend, either because it charmed you, or because it was funny and amused you, or it was irritating and angered you; make a note of anything which would confirm some psychoanalytic theory or which would contradict it; and

make a note of any behaviour which would seem to you precocious or the opposite.

(Friedmann, 1988, p. 280)

Parents first visiting the nursery showed pleasure, but also suspicion about the low cost of the extensive service provided. Staff explained that the Clinic was a training and research centre and that their children were needed to teach the students and workers about "normal" children. According to Manna Friedmann, "the word 'normal' was all-important and reassuring" (Friedmann, 1988, p. 285).

When Manna decided to retire after running the nursery for 21 years (1957–78), Anna Freud initially thought of closing the nursery. However, a young American, Nancy Brenner, succeeded Manna and "urged her (Anna Freud's) favourite project into renewed life" (Brenner, 1988; Young-Bruehl, 2008, p. 419). Nancy Brenner highlighted the somewhat unexpected advantages that recording observations brought for observer and child:

Originally, I believed that I was recording the observations primarily to have a report for students and colleagues. I soon realised that the importance of the observations was really for myself and the children. Recording observations helped me to get to know each child uniquely and intimately. They provided me with the material to think about and assess the child's personal strengths and needs and to reflect on my relationship to, and handling of each child. Non-nursery time used in this way was additional time given to the children, as its influence on the following day was always felt. It was as if the child and I had a private "visit" which enabled our ongoing relationship to deepen.

(Brenner, 1992, p. 89)

Nancy Brenner ran the nursery until 1990 when she was succeeded by Myriam Senez. Marie Zaphiriou Woods was the psychoanalytic consultant from 1986 to 1997. The nursery was closed in 1999.

The Well-baby clinic (1950s–97)

Established by Joyce Robertson in the 1950s, the Well-baby clinic aimed at helping and advising young mothers about how to handle their infant's physical and emotional needs. It provided a means for making long-term observations, beginning shortly after birth and, sometimes, continuing through nursery school. The focus was on preventative work. The staff tried to determine the extent to which guidance and support could relieve tensions arising between mother and infant, supporting mothers to cope with difficulties arising from the infant's sleeping, feeding and weaning and the repercussions of these bodily experiences on the infant's mind (Sandler,

1965). Over the years, staff included Ernst and Irene Freud, Nicky Model and Josefine Stross, the Consultant Paediatrician.

The parent-toddler groups (1950s–ongoing)

Joyce Robertson started the first parent-toddler groups at the Hampstead clinic in the 1950s. She realised that as the Well-baby clinic babies became active toddlers, their mothers were often at a loss as to how to understand and manage this new developmental stage. The once-weekly pre-nursery (toddler) group met in the basement of house 12 and used many of the Jackson Nursery toys brought from Vienna (Young-Bruehl, 2008). Anna Freud's initial idea was to provide two rooms: one for the mothers and a play room with teachers and toys for the children. The doors connecting the rooms were kept open to enable the toddlers to move freely. However, Manna Friedman noted, "the toddlers were not interested in our observational project and the attempt to implement it, turned into an unnatural and stressful situation" (Friedmann, 1988, p. 284).

The toddler group was later transferred to the small building that housed the nursery school for blind children (which became known as the toddler hut) at 21 Maresfield Gardens, under the leadership of Pauline Cohen and Barbara Grant. The group maintained close links to both the Well-baby clinic and the nursery school. Child Psychotherapy trainees observed what was originally called the "Mother–toddler observation group" as part of their training and discussed their observations in weekly seminars (Cohen & Grant, 1985).

Francis Salo and Marie Zaphiriou Woods succeeded Barbara Grant and Pauline Cohen in 1988. Marie started a new tradition of using Child Psychotherapy trainees as assistants. With the institution of the MSc in Psychoanalytic Developmental Psychology in 1993, the number of toddler groups increased from one to four to accommodate the greater number of observers. Marie Zaphiriou Woods became the Psychoanalytic Consultant to the service in 1999, and later its manager (2002–2008).

Funded by a grant from the Inman Trust, the "Footprints" group for visually impaired toddlers and their parents ran for two years (see chapter 7). In 2003, funding from the government's Sure Start initiative enabled a group to be established in a local council estate (see chapter 8). This group relocated to the local Children's Centre in March 2008. In 2007, additional Sure Start funding was secured for a parent-toddler group at a local hostel for homeless families (see chapter 9).

Currently two parent-toddler groups are based at the AFC. Besides providing an invaluable clinical service to toddlers and their parents, these groups continue to fulfil their aim of "Mother–toddler observation group" (Cohen & Grant, 1985), although nowadays, fathers also attend (see chapter 6). Students of the MSc in Psychoanalytic Developmental Psychology observe the toddlers and their parents over the course of one year. Toddler observers adopt a neutral stance: two students sit in the play room, while others sit in a booth, behind a one-way mirror. After the 1½-hour observation, students record a few sequences of interactions (on index cards) which are discussed in weekly seminars. No pretence is made of achieving objective observations. The students experience a range of feelings towards particular children and interactions that often change over the course of the year. These subjective feelings provide an important source of understanding and enrich their observations (see chapter 5). They may also contribute to students' self-awareness. The students' observations are a valuable addition to the leader and assistant's own observations and thinking. Students often cite the observation component of the course, and interplay of theory and observation, as the highlight of the MSc course. MSc graduates frequently become toddler group assistants and some become leaders, trained and supported by a team which has, over the years, developed considerable experience.

Ongoing audit, research and evaluation of the groups was introduced in 2003. Parents joining and leaving the AFC-based groups are invited to participate in a modification of the Parent Development Interview (Slade et al., 1994). In addition, a video camera installed in the toddler hut in 2005 enables valuable recordings of interactions to be made for use in teaching and research. New parents and toddlers joining the group are often wary of being observed. The toddler group leaders reassure them – as Manna Friedmann did – that the students are learning about "normal" toddler development and most toddlers and parents soon ignore the students and camera.

The parent-toddler service maintains close links to the Parent-Infant Project, the heir to the Well-baby clinic, created by Tessa Baradon in 1997. Once a month, the toddler group and Parent-Infant Project staff meet for in-depth discussions of individual cases. This forum enables the two services to plan for the smooth transition of referrals to the toddler groups.

Marie Zaphiriou Woods convened the first International Toddler Symposium in 2001 on the eve of the Anna Freud Centre International Scientific Colloquium on November. Held annually since then, with presentations from the AFC and a guest speaker, this forum attracts lively discussions and has become a highlight of the year. In 2007, the parent-toddler service at the AFC received the 2007 Award for Excellence from the Association of Child Psychoanalysis for its "outstanding work with parents and toddlers".

Conclusion

Sigmund Freud speculated on the value of direct observation of children, but it was Anna Freud who started longitudinal observations of babies and the direct observation of pre-oedipal children. Anna Freud came to value her "double approach" to gathering data. In combining the reconstructive and observational approaches, she pioneered in her development of the technique of child psychoanalysis. The importance of direct observation and a psychoanalytic theory of normal development remain central to the parent-toddler work.

Anna Freud's early work in the War Nurseries confirmed that the first years of a child's life are absolutely critical for all later physical, neuro-logical, mental and emotional development, and – as recent neuroscience has shown – for brain development (Schore, 1993; Young-Bruehl, 2008). Freudian insights into the importance of early childhood experiences have been refined and have gained acceptance from the public, as well as policy makers. The general public has become more able to accept and understand the significance of good parenting and provisioning, of secure and loving early relationships and the significance of the prevention of child mal-treatment in preventing a lifetime of pain and suffering. This understanding led to the Head Start programme in the USA, and the Sure Start and Family Nurse Partnership programmes in the UK. Rooted in a desire to observe and study pre-oedipal children to complement and confirm psycho-analytic insight and develop a theory of normal development, the current parent-toddler groups are predominantly motivated by the preventative power of early intervention.

Chapter 2

Normal toddler development: Excursions and returns

Marie Zaphiriou Woods

. . . . selfhood begins with a walking away
And love is proved in the letting go.
> (Cecil Day Lewis, 1962, "Walking Away" in *The Gate and Other Poems*)

In observing a child of two we can easily see the coexistence of excursions and return journeys that carry with them but little risk, and excursions and returns that are significant in that if they fail, they alter the child's whole life.
> (D. W. Winnicott, 1966, p. 136)

This chapter outlines the main features of the journey through toddlerhood. It shows how fundamental issues to do with attachment, autonomy, separateness, and intimacy (Stern, 1995), as well as affect regulation, aggression, sexuality, and the growth of the imagination, are negotiated within the evolving parent–toddler relationship. Anna Freud's definition of development (Freud, 1976) as involving a complex interplay between endowment, maturation, structuralisation, and the environment underpins our thinking. We understand structuralisation to include the building up of a representational world (Sandler & Rosenblatt, 1962) reflecting actual and fantasied experience rooted in the earliest interactions between parent and infant. We do not intend to offer a comprehensive theory of toddlerhood here (for this, the reader is referred to the many excellent books on the subject, including Bergman, 1999; Fraiberg, 1959; Furman, 1992; Lieberman, 1993; Mahler, Pine, & Bergman, 1975). Rather, we set out the premises underpinning our way of working with parents and toddlers in our groups. This way of working is then described in the next chapter.

Toddlerhood[2]

Toddlerhood begins when an infant takes his first faltering, but independent steps. This maturational achievement, occurring usually at around one year, ushers in a surge in the developmental advance towards "intrapsychic separateness and, eventually, individuation, identity and autonomy" (Blum, 2004, p. 542). This is a lifelong task which is never fully completed (Stern, 1995). During toddlerhood, this progressive thrust culminates in the toddler achieving inner images of his mother, and of himself in her absence (Freud, 1965; Mahler et al., 1975), that are integrated and stable enough to enable him to manage himself (his body, thoughts and feelings) without her constant availability or that of a mother substitute, in a nursery school for instance. This usually occurs at around 3.

Margaret Mahler's concept of separation-individuation remains a central organiser in our understanding of the complex developments that enable a young child to achieve this level of independence. Mahler's detailed observational study of mothers and children from 4 months to 36 months chronicles the intrapsychic processes on the way to libidinal object constancy and the growth of a sense of self. Like her, and unlike some of the attachment theorists (e.g. Lyons-Ruth, 1991), we see aggression and conflict (both internal and external) as a normal and necessary part of the toddler's struggle for autonomy and independence, contributing also to his growing awareness that other people have a separate existence and are not part of his subjective reality (Winnicott, 1971). We also expect to see periods of regression disrupting forward momentum (see Blos, 1967, chapter 5; Freud, 1965). In our view, the parent's sustained emotional availability in the face of the toddler's emotional storms and developmental shifts is of crucial importance. The way in which she understands and responds to them will shape her toddler's emerging representations of self and other, and will determine whether, for example, he experiences his moves towards autonomy and mastery as pleasurable or aggressive and hurtful (Mayes & Cohen, 1993).

While our approach is essentially psychoanalytic, we also draw on developmental research, attachment theory and neuroscience. In the last two decades, our expanding knowledge of brain development has enabled a deeper understanding of the underlying psychobiological mechanisms. A major conclusion of developmental neuroscience research is that the infant's brain is designed to be moulded by the environment it encounters (Thomas et al., 1997, p. 209) and that emotion operates as a central organising process within the brain (Seigal, 1999). The most sensitive period for brain growth and the time of optimal neuroplasticity are in the first two or three years of life (Balbernie, 2001). During this period, the child's emotional environment will shape the neurobiology that is the organic basis of the mind. To a lesser extent, experiences with people continue to sculpt the brain throughout the life cycle.

Outline of toddler development

Practising

The toddler period starts with what Mahler and colleagues (Mahler et al., 1975) called "practising proper". They observed that the achievement of upright locomotion ushered in a period of elation, "a love affair with the world" (Greenacre, 1957), during which the toddler joyfully explores the world around him, relishing his newfound motor capacities and his expanding universe. He is intensely curious, constantly on the go. Schore (1993) quotes a study which suggested that the practising toddler spends up to six hours a day on play activities. The newly walking toddler may be so focused on discovering and extending his physical capacities that, for a period, he is impervious to minor insults to his body such as knocks and falls, and even hunger and tiredness. He may accept less familiar adults in a way he would not have done a few months before and will not a few months later.

> Iris (15 months) had older parents with various physical problems. In particular her father, who was the main caregiver, was partially sighted and could only see within a very limited radius. When Iris came to my toddler group she was neither crawling nor walking; she would sit within her father's range of vision and play. After two visits, during which she carefully observed the other toddlers and me moving freely around the hut, she started to walk, reaching for my hand to steady herself. On one particularly exhausting afternoon, she insisted I repeatedly accompany her on a route she set, across the toddler hut, down the stairs to the garden, round the outside of the hut, upstairs and in again, until she could manage confidently without help.

Mahler and her associates observed that when toddlers start walking, they typically walk *away* from their mothers. However, they and subsequent researchers (Ainsworth, 1963; Ainsworth, Blehar, Waters, & Wall, 1978; Bowlby, 1969) agree that the young toddler's apparent freedom to range is predicated on the parents' continued physical and emotional availability and support; the parents are "the external secure base that anchors the child's comings and goings" (Lieberman, 1993, p. 3). Although Iris seemed single-minded in her determination to use me as a walking aid, she glanced at her father on each return to the toddler hut, checking perhaps that he was still there and sharing her pleasure. Another toddler might have sought physical contact as a way of "refuelling" or "recharging the batteries" (Mahler et al., 1975), while a third might have called out and pointed in a bid for a "joint attention" (Bretherton, 1992). Young toddlers often use vocalisation, noises and/or gestures to involve their parents and to indicate their wishes. This enables the new more "long distance relationship"

(Edgcumbe, 1981, p. 97) and the continuation of their magical belief that their actions, even their thoughts, bring about events (Fraiberg, 1959). At around age 1 many children begin to use words to name desirable objects ("mummy", "daddy", "doggie").

Iris may also have been glancing back at her father to check whether I was a safe person. The newly exploring toddler regularly looks back to the parent for this sort of "social referencing" (Emde, 1980). If she responds positively and with enthusiasm to such approaches he will resume his activities with renewed gusto. Tulkin and Kagan (1972) have shown that at 10 months, 90 per cent of maternal physical and verbal behaviours consist of affection, play and caregiving with only 5 per cent involving prohibitions. Running off, which evidences the practising toddler's elevated stimulus-seeking exploration and wish to escape from the merged relationship with mother, may become a favourite game, if it is followed by the reassurance of being scooped up, kissed and cuddled. The intensely positive affective exchanges that occur during practising strengthen the attachment process. Schore (1993) proposes that the affective, behavioural and cognitive aspects that are unique to this phase reflect a biologically timed period of sympathetic-dominant limbic hyperarousal, which develops earlier than the parasympathetic inhibitory processes, and that behavioural overexcitation is adaptive in the personal environment.

It seems that at every level, the parent's enjoyment of her toddler combined with her sensitive attunement to his exhilaration and excitement, strengthens his attachment and ability to self-regulate while also supporting his dawning sense of himself as an individual and active agent in the world. It also encourages his intellectual and creative activities, including his capacity for imagination, dreaming and play. In "Sum, I am" (Winnicott, 1968), Winnicott emphasised the mother's need to be reliably there to support the infant in discovering the world (objective reality) at a pace he can manage, while retaining some belief in his omnipotence (subjective reality). Winnicott (1966) describes "excursions and returns" (p. 135) that are more psychological than physical, as the child navigates the difficult transition from subjectivity to objectivity, the excitement of discovery alternating with the return to what is familiar. If he can sustain the illusion of mother's presence during her absence, aided perhaps by a transitional object, he encounters a world enriched by his creativity and self-realisation (Winnicott, 1971; Wright, 1991).

At a time when most mothers stayed at home to look after their children, Winnicott (1971) stressed the importance of continuity of care, and Bowlby (1988) the need for a secure base to which the toddler can return if worried or anxious. In their observational setting, Mahler et al. (1975) noted that if the mother is absent, even for a short period of time, the young toddler tends to become sober, "low keyed", turned inwards, perhaps trying to evoke an internal image of his mother to feel safe. He may halt his explorations until she returns. With more than half of mothers of young children working nowadays (Office for National Statistics, 2006), security may in some cases need to be provided by a sensitive and graduated handover to a carefully chosen substitute caregiver (grandparent, nanny, child minder or nursery worker) who can provide continuity. If she can recognise and respond to the toddler's continued need for love and protection while also supporting his quest for autonomy, he will remain adventurous. Towards the second half of the second year, however, there may be a return to seeking greater closeness.

Rapprochement

The toddler's busy explorations inevitably bring him up against experiences which challenge his illusion of magical control; an exciting-looking chair topples over when he climbs on it, and his beloved mother is sometimes busy and not available. Even more importantly, her wishes do not always coincide with his, and he realises increasingly that she is a distinct person with a mind of her own (Blum, 2004). This growing awareness of separateness and difference punctures the young toddler's prevailing mood of elation. He realises he is small, vulnerable and dependent. He experiences a "fierce and truly terrible" need for his mother (Winnicott, 1963b, p. 88), and at times also sadness, aloneness and loss. Terrified of losing his beloved parent, he may "shadow" her during the day, not letting her out of his sight. At night-time, sleep difficulties may occur as he struggles against relinquishing her and falling asleep. Peekaboo may become a favourite game, as the toddler actively attempts to master the painful experiences of separateness. Sigmund Freud's famous observation of the "fort-da" game (Freud, 1920) is of an 18 month old finding a creative solution to his mother's absence; he repeatedly makes a cotton reel disappear and then reappear.

Blum (2004) notes that "[t]he emergence of separateness . . . occurs in parallel with new levels of reciprocity and mutuality" (p. 543). Mahler et al. (1975) observed that, from around 15 months, the young toddler seeks "rapprochement", a renewed closeness with the parent as someone with whom to share discoveries and to play. Stern (1985) describes this in terms of the child's search for "inter-subjective union with another" (p. 20). The following is an example of typical rapprochement behaviour:

> Norman (21 months) catches sight of an older toddler systematically emptying the cupboard in the kitchen corner and placing "food" on a table. Norman takes the "pizza" and walks over to his seated mother, thrusting it at her with an emphatic noise. She thanks him and pretends to eat it. He goes back to get her some bread rolls, watching her while she pretends to eat them too. He continues to go back and forth across the toddler hut,

pausing briefly to play with the toy buggy or large car, but then returning to "feed" his mother. The game ends when he gets into the car and bids her "bye bye".

Norman and his mother seem to enjoy this interaction, which repeatedly affirms their separateness while also re-establishing closeness through Norman pretending to feed mother.

Bergman (1999, p. 158) suggests that sharing games like this one contribute to the rapprochement toddler's developing representations of self, other, and self with other. "Each time the toddler finds (mother) he brings along a new piece of the world outside, and each time he leaves her he takes with him a part of her. Increasingly this part is an image. . ." (Bergman, 1978, p. 158). Gradually, words replace gestures and vocal expressions as the toddler struggles both to express himself, and to communicate his wishes e.g. "look", "bickie". His vocabulary begins to expand (see Bates, O'Connell, & Shore, 1987; Fraiberg, 1959; Hobson, 2002), and he enjoys language-enhanced social exchanges, and giving as well as receiving pleasure. The parent helps the child organise his affective life into language (Bergman & Harpaz-Rotem, 2004), creating with him, over time, a narrative that will be woven into his increasingly complex representations of his self and the outside world.

Anality

During the second year of life, anality joins the stream of development, disrupting rapprochement, and powering further developments. There will probably have been some pleasurable anal and urethral sensations from birth, stimulated by defaecating and urinating, handling and cleaning, but at around 18 months, the toddler begins to take an active pleasure in soiling, wetting and messing, and perhaps also touching, smelling, and looking. Parents often report a sudden increase in provocative behaviour, such as deliberately shaking juice out of a beaker, or repeatedly tipping bath water on the floor. The toddler may become negativistic, saying "no" at every opportunity and resisting attempts to bathe and dress him. Both Furman (1992) and Fraiberg (1959) have pointed out that such behaviours serve the dual purpose of instinctual expression and the establishment of separateness; they are a "declaration of independence" (Fraiberg, 1959, p. 65). "To do just the opposite of what his mother wants strikes him as being the very essence of his individuality. It is as if he establishes his independence, his separateness from his mother, by being opposite" (p. 64).

With increasing awareness and control of his urethral and anal sphincters, the toddler discovers that his intense pleasure in passing urine and expelling faeces may be supplemented by the opposing pleasure of holding it all in. His attention may become focused on these particular parts of the body, and the associated contradictory impulses – forceful ejection as well as possessive withholding – become evident in his attitude to his loved ones and other "possessions". He may become intensely ambivalent, claiming someone or something as "mine", clinging possessively, and then rejecting hatefully. He may even try to deny separateness, coercing his parent(s) into following his will, and throwing tantrums when thwarted. At other times, he seems to enjoy thwarting and tormenting them, and others, for instance older siblings, and the family pet.

It has been argued (e.g. Tyson & Tyson, 1990, p. 56) that the toddler is not actually sadistic – more bent on acquisition and mastery – but observation of the gleam that accompanies the toddler's testing behaviour and the adult's counter-response, which can be equally hate-filled and cruel, suggests some sadism. It is often difficult for the parent to manage the feelings aroused by her toddler's instinctual expressions; "the seduction to partial or temporary regression" (Furman, 1992, p. 151) may touch on *her* unresolved issues to do with anality, sexuality and aggression. She may feel anxious, overwhelmed, disgusted, guilty and/or ashamed, disowning her impulses, and externalising them onto her toddler who she then reproves or rejects as messy or disgusting.

> It was Sally's second birthday, and her mother had brought an elaborate chocolate cake to celebrate. Joe, 21 months, became totally absorbed in eating his portion, slowly and sensually licking off the icing, crumbling the sponge, getting it all over his face and hands. His mother reproved him for making such a mess and tried repeatedly to clean his chocolate smeared face with baby wipes. All pleasure spoiled, Joe eventually left his cake and went off to play in another part of the hut.

One can only speculate that Joe's uninhibited enjoyment of messy eating aroused his fastidious mother's reaction formations against oral and anal pleasures. Toddlers of this age challenge adults' normal repression of infantile sexuality; they may be unashamedly sensual, dreamily exploring different parts of their face and body, how they look, how they feel, and what they produce: mucus and tears as well as faeces and urine (see Lieberman, 1992). At the same time, they are becoming increasingly aware of their selves and their bodies, able to recognise themselves in the mirror (at around 18 months) and may, at times, become shy and self-conscious as they realise they may be seen from outside as well as inside. Genital play may also occur and many toddlers become aware of sexual difference at about this time (see the section on gender below).

This is a turbulent time, as the toddler struggles with powerful impulses from within, and difficult realities without. "Surges of aggression and sexual excitation may combine and easily overwhelm his tenuous control" (Tyson & Tyson, 1990, p. 56). He wants to retain his omnipotence, to maintain the illusion that he can have it all (Lieberman, 1993), and struggles against his internal contradictions and the constraints of reality. He loves *and* hates passionately, he wants to be close *and* separate, to explore (e.g. go in the large car) *and* be protected (e.g. sit on his mother's lap). External conflicts are added to internal ones as the adults around him increasingly thwart him by setting limits, to keep him safe (e.g. he cannot play with the plug socket) and to socialise him – to help him learn to share, to take turns and not hit or hurt other children.

The rapprochement toddler's expectations of positive affirmation are repeatedly dashed as he receives more instructions, directions and prohibitions (on average, one prohibition every nine minutes, Power & Chapieski, 1986). He appears at times to be deflated and ashamed. According to Schore (1993), shame represents the rapid transition from high arousal (sympathetic dominance) to low arousal (parasympathetic dominance). The low mood seen in the late practising and rapprochement toddler reflects the maturation of the parasympathetic nervous system, responsible for inhibition and hypoarousal. Schore sees the socialisation experiences in the second year of life as instrumental to the final structural maturation of an adaptive cortical system that can self-regulate.

Again, the toddler's parents are the agents of these crucial developments. They need to be able to manage their own feelings in order to stand firm in the face of their toddler's ambivalence and contradictory behaviour, to accept his spontaneous gestures, and repair the relationship following the inevitable disputes and breakdown. Their resistance (opposition) to his attempts at omnipotent control and survival of the destructiveness which Winnicott (1969) saw as inherent in primitive love enable him to give full vent to his loving and hating feelings, promoting object constancy, i.e. the ability to hold on to an image of the loved person in the face of anger and frustration. It also helps him to learn to delay gratification, to tolerate frustration, and channel his anger.

The balance between limit-setting and permissiveness is a delicate one. While the toddler needs some conflict with authority to test and enrich his individuality, the parents' consistent loving availability helps the toddler to balance his aggression with his loving feelings, to avoid excessive splitting of the world into good and bad objects (Klein, 1935) and to develop concern (Winnicott, 1963) as he discovers that the mother he loves is the same person as the mother he hates. Put in classical terms (Anna Freud, 1965; Furman, 1992; Mahler et al., 1975) it promotes fusion of loving and aggressive impulses, and the transformation of aggression into the ordinary assertiveness which is necessary in relationships and activities. Alternatively formulated, the parent's containment (Bion, 1962), i.e. absorption and processing of the toddler's unmanageable feelings and anxieties, will, over time, be internalised by the toddler, and contribute to his capacity to regulate his own negative affective states.

Moving on from rapprochement

Towards the end of the second year, the toddler's increased command of communicative language, his ability to play symbolically, and his growing identification with his parents, help him with the difficult task of renouncing omnipotence and accepting separateness, a process which has been compared to mourning (see Bergman, 1999). He becomes able to move on from what Mahler et al. (1975) called the "rapprochement crisis", a term which is perhaps misleading for a normative phase of development, since it is suggestive of insecure attachment (see Blum, 2004; Gergely, 1997; Lyons-Ruth, 1991). While insecurity undoubtedly exacerbates the conflicts inherent in rapprochement, the following developments may help both securely and insecurely attached toddlers to find more comfortable and pleasurable ways of being both separate from and close to their parent(s), and less overwhelmed by feelings and impulses.

1. Language

By the end of the second year, there is "increasing linkage of words and inner experience" (Edgcumbe, 1981, p. 80). The toddler comes to be able to talk about his experiences and wishes, and to differentiate between feelings, e.g. that he is "sad" that daddy has gone away. He begins to use personal pronouns, referring to himself as "me" or "I" as in "Me do it" or "I want that" (Bergman, 1999; Hobson, 2002). His growing command of language both reflects and contributes to his growing ability to think, to be self-aware, and to communicate with others. It reflects the momentous move from concrete literal experience to the ability to represent it (Joyce, 2005), and, most importantly for the toddler and his parent, contributes to affect regulation and mastery of the drives as intense feelings are modulated and transformed in language (Blum, 2004; Katan, 1961; Weise, 1995).

Occupying, as it does, "a midway position between the infant's subjectivity and the mother's objectivity" (Stern, 1985, p. 172), language facilitates separation-individuation. During rapprochement, it becomes an important means of creating shared moments of togetherness and mutual understanding, while at the same time contributing to the discovery and recognition that others have separate minds with different thoughts and feelings (Fonagy & Target, 1996). This paves the way for negotiation, which is a feature of the third year of life (Lieberman, 1993).

However, as Stern (1985, p. 162) pointed out, language is a "double-edged sword"; it can lead to a split in the child's experience of self, away from the intensely passionate and personal towards the more abstract and interpersonal level. This split can perhaps be minimised by following the child's lead when introducing new words, and then going on to amplify and embellish his experience. Hobson (2002) emphasised that this was a form of

emotional sensitivity, and Phillips (1992) counselled nurturing "the necessary to and fro between the articulate and inarticulate self" (p. 36).

2. Pretend play

Throughout toddlerhood, the transitional objects and soft toys of infancy,
embodying both "me" and "not me" (Winnicott, 1971), may function to
bridge the distance between parent and child, especially at moments of upset
and transition, such as leave-takings and bedtimes. Moving toys (balls, cars,
aeroplanes) may be used to express the urge towards independent activity
but equally they provide the physical means for reconnecting, e.g. the big red
car may be "driven" right across the toddler hut, then turned round with
much grunting, in order to return to bump against mother's knees. Sensory
and manipulative play helps toddlers to learn how things work, but at the
same time expresses their instinctual preoccupations – their contradictory
tendencies, their curiosity about body openings and functions, and anal and
urethral interests in particular. Accordingly, toys may be filled and emptied,
opened and closed, built up and crashed down. Sand may be hoarded,
shaped and dumped, while water may be trickled, poured, and splashed.
Making a mess will be hugely enjoyed, but so may wiping up, drying and
cleaning, especially if encouraged by the mother's approval and enjoyment.

As separation proceeds, experience is increasingly represented at a
symbolic level that can be shared. The mother gives meaning to and
elaborates the toddler's play; together they pretend e.g. that the baby doll
needs a bath, the car needs petrol, and that the playdoh lumps are delicious
food to eat. Alternatively, parent and toddler may exchange roles, and
playfully enact emotionally loaded experiences to do with separation and
reunion, aggression and reparation (see chapter 4 and Bergman, 1999).
According to Bergman, "[p]layful interchanges, occurring in the context of
the mother–child relationship, provide the scaffolding for evolving representations of both self and other and self with other" (p. 148). Through
playing as well as talking, toddlers and parents can transform their relationship, communicating in a pleasurable way while also learning about
their essential separateness and difference. The parents' enjoyment of their
toddlers, their ability to reflect on their thoughts, feelings and wishes, and
to help them express themselves in language and play give the toddlers a
sense of satisfaction and agency. They begin to learn the difference between
fantasy and reality, and to understand that their parents can share that
difference (Fonagy & Target, 1996).

3. Identifications

Becoming like their beloved parents is a way for toddlers to hold on to
them internally, to cope with increased separation, while also learning new

skills and building their sense of identity. These identifications will be reflected in words, gestures, and/or typical 2-year-old play, such as dressing up, and pretending to cook, drive a car, or fix a toy. Toddlers may both literally and figuratively step into their mother's or father's shoes. In so doing they adopt another perspective; they may look at things, including themselves, from a different angle and so become more capable of thought (Hobson, 2002).

By the age of 2, these identifications include simple verbal commands and prohibitions, which toddlers can now both understand and internalise. They begin to be able to restrict their impulses in order to please their parents, and keep their love and approval. One little girl, who had found it difficult to manage the ending of the toddler group sessions, started coming to the group with a hat and bag just like her mother's. As soon as people began to tidy up in preparation for leaving, she announced "home time" in a loud voice, taking up her bag just as her mother took up hers.

Such identifications may function as superego precursors, enabling toddlers to comply with what is expected. They soften the blow of submitting to a more powerful authority and enable them to feel big and competent rather than painfully small and helpless. Clear consistent expectations that the toddler can meet and a tolerance of failure facilitate the development of a benign aim-giving superego.

Consolidating individuality and moving towards emotional object constancy

During the third year of life, the toddler ideally consolidates these earlier developments according to his individual temperament, his particular life experiences and especially his relationship with his caregivers. He builds up an increasingly complex, solid and discrete sense of himself and of the important people in his life. They will have inevitably been perceived as both good and bad, but if positive experiences have dominated, and the parents have been able to contain their own as well as their toddler's ambivalence, his hate-filled feelings will have been modified by his loving feelings and his image of himself and his parents will have become integrated into predominantly positive (lovable and loving) self and object representations. These need to be sufficiently robust to survive short absences or times of frustration and rage, and will then contribute to his ability to maintain self-esteem, to be alone and eventually to manage longer separations.

These developments are supported by the toddler's increasingly sophisticated language and play. As Blum has written, "[l]anguage and symbolic thought free the toddler from the immediate present, and permit trial action, judgement, and higher levels of learning, information processing, communication, and affect regulation" (Blum, 2004, p. 543). It becomes possible to converse with the toddler about what mummy or daddy might be doing while at work, what they might think, feel, say or do when they see each other again, what they did in the past, and what they may do in the future (go on a bus, visit grandma, read a book). The toddler may use toys to play out these various scenarios, or role play with an expanding cast of characters that may come to include bus drivers, postmen, and doctors. As Bergman (1999) points out, the ability to role play is predicated on a self that is sufficiently firmly established to put itself in the place of the other. It enables toddlers to express feelings and fantasies in ways that draw on their expanding experience of the world, which may then be integrated into their increasingly complex representations of self and object.

Ownership of the body

The toddler's body – the myriad exquisite sensations within it and emanating from it, its increasingly co-ordinated free movement – remains fundamental to the senior toddler's growing individuality and sense of self. Fraiberg (1959) wrote that the toddler values his body both as a source of pleasure and as a source of self-feelings; "the more conscious the child becomes of himself as a person, an 'I', the more he values this body which encloses and contains his personality" (p. 130). By the age of 2, most toddlers firmly inhabit their body. They use it to express feelings they have about themselves, and to gain the attention and admiration of the adults around them.

> Maria (2 years 4 months) climbed onto a chair and stretched her arms upwards, tilting her head up to the light and smiling. The toddler group leader put out a hand to steady her and said "what a big girl you are standing on the chair". Maria stood there for a few seconds and then clambered down, with the leader supporting her arm. She then moved to the next chair and carefully climbed on to this one. This time she did not stretch out her arms but stood straight and still on the chair. The leader said to another toddler, "Look Jessica, Maria is being a big girl standing on the chair". After a few seconds on this chair she climbed down and moved towards her mum. Maria's mum thought she was coming for a cuddle and put out her arms. Maria said "No!" and moved to an empty chair. Maria's mother said, "Are you going to climb on all the chairs?" as Maria climbed onto a third chair and stood with a proud look on her face.

Maria is about to become a big sister. In this observation, she seems to revel in the toddler group leader's recognition of her "big girl" self, expressed physically by her climbing on chairs. She proudly conveys her status as a person with a mind of her own, which she will defend with determination and aggression if necessary. Her mother accepts this grace-fully, though perhaps a bit regretfully.

Typically, the older toddler's increasing awareness of and investment in his body brings with it the determination to own and control it: "I do it myself". The parent who, for over two years, has been almost totally responsible for the care and protection of her child's body has to manage a graduated handover in accordance with the toddler's growing wish and ability to manage independently. Failure to do so can result in bitter battles for ownership and control over essential bodily functions such as feeding, sleeping, and toileting, which may spread to other areas such as dressing and bathing or showering. The 2-year-old's tantrums may express a range of feelings about not being in control, and about displeasing or disappointing his parent(s): they include frustration and rage, but also anxiety and shame as the adults around him expect more from him, and he fears not managing to fulfil their expectations and not retaining their love or his own self-regard based on his gradual internalisation of their standards.

Toilet training

To achieve bowel and bladder control, the toddler needs to have matured sufficiently to notice when he is about to urinate or defaecate, and to be able to postpone the urge to wet or soil until he can get himself to a potty or toilet. He also needs to have a sufficiently positive relationship with his parents to wish to please them, and to identify with their expectations that he become clean and dry. This will include identifying with their disgust, subtly conveyed, about body waste products. The age at which toddlers are ready to do all these things varies enormously, but it helps if they have sufficient language to understand what is required of them and to clearly indicate their own wishes.

Some toddlers show that they are ready to be toilet trained by developing an interest in ordering and organising their toys. On the other hand, their excited (erotic and aggressive) feelings and fantasies about their body products may complicate matters. It is quite common for 2 year olds to view their faeces as a part of their body or selves, from which they do not wish to be separated, or precious gifts (even a baby or penis) which it is in their power to give or withhold. They may also be experienced as destructive weapons which may be more safely kept inside or forcefully ejected. Toddlers' anxiety and curiosity about what is going on inside their own and their mother's bodies may be compounded if they have observed a pregnancy. And their sexual theories about how babies are made (perhaps mummy's tummy got so big through eating a lot) may need to be understood in order to reassure them that it is safe to perform ordinary bodily functions.

Sean (2 years 3 months) was a boisterous little boy who loved Thomas the Tank Engine, trains and tunnels. Toilet training began smoothly, but he became upset and frightened about defaecating when his mother, who was heavily pregnant, was due to have her baby. It emerged that she had told him that babies come out of your "bottom". When it was clarified that babies came out of a different place from poos, and that he was making a poo not a baby, he stopped straining to withhold his faeces but remained anxious when he sensed them coming. His mother was encouraged to compare his faeces to a train that needed to come out of a tunnel. Sean and mother then developed a game in which green lights signalled the arrival of a poo, and red lights its stopping. He came to be able to use the potty again, and both were delighted and proud of his growing mastery.

This shared game enabled Sean to overcome his anxieties and to feel more in control of his body and what came out of it. It demonstrates Lieberman's point that "toilet training is the epitome of partnership through give-and-take, withholding, and letting go" (Lieberman, 1993, p. 155).

The toddler's achievement of control over what goes in and out of his body has a useful developmental function in contributing to his increasing awareness of body boundaries, of inside and outside, and of "you" and "me", i.e. to the building up of separate representations of self and other. Furman (1992) writes "mastery of self care more than any other single development makes the toddler feel he is a person, a somebody" (p. 116). Furman has described the "shared steps" that mother and child need to go through on the way to bodily mastery as (1) doing for, (2) doing with, (3) standing by to admire, and (4) doing for oneself (p. 119). The parents need to be able to judge when their toddler is ready to take the next step, to communicate their expectations clearly (including accurate naming of body parts), and to tolerate the occasional accident or setback as part of the ordinary to-and-fro of development. If all goes well, the toddler, in identification with his mother, gradually takes over his self-care, regarding dressing, bathing, sleeping and eating as well as toileting, and takes pride and pleasure in gaining control over his body functions. Furman sees these hard-won achievements as underlying the ability to learn and to work.

Gender identity

The senior toddler's high investment in his body brings with it acute concerns about bodily integrity and completeness (Fraiberg, 1959; Furman, 1992). Following Greenacre (1953), Furman stresses the fragility of the 2 year old's body image, comparing the toddler's feelings about his newly owned body with an adult's feelings about a brand new dress or car. The toddler may become extremely anxious about the slightest "hurt" or sign of physical imperfection, and may need careful explanations and reassurance.

This extreme sensitivity means that observations of sexual difference may have a huge impact. A number of observers (Fraiberg, 1959; Galenson &

Roiphe, 1971, 1974; Mahler et al., 1975) have noted that girls react to the observation that they do not have a penis with a sense of narcissistic injury, while boys may become fearful that since girls do not have a penis, they could lose theirs. The attitude of *both* parents to their toddler's gender, and their feelings about their own and each other's bodies and sexuality will affect how their girl or boy toddler integrates their perception of sexual difference into their self-representation. Careful naming of sexual parts can help toddlers to build up a clearer idea of their sexual bodies, but will be another way in which the parents' more conflictual feelings about their own bodies and gender may be transmitted.

Research by de Marneffe (1997) suggests that most 2 to 3 year olds have a clear recognition of their own external genitalia (I have a vagina or I have a penis) and gender (I am a girl or I am a boy), but remain confused for some time as to how the two relate. Children of this age often believe that they can change their gender by changing their activities or clothing, i.e. they lack gender constancy, or that they could become a boy or girl over time, i.e. they also lack gender stability (Money & Erhardt, 1972). However, it has been observed that they tend to play with dolls with the same genitals as themselves (de Marneffe, 1997), and with other toddlers of the same sex (Coates, 1997). Their identifications with the latter may enhance their sense of being a boy or girl.

Senior toddlers' feelings and fantasies about their gender are profoundly affected by their relationship with their parents. A little girl who feels dissatisfied and angry with her mother may experience her lack of a penis as an additional cause for grievance. Her resulting hostility towards her mother may interfere with her idealising her and identifying with her femininity. Her father will have an important role in rescuing her from an angry enmeshed struggle with her mother, and fostering, through his pleasure and enjoyment of her as a girl, a positive investment in her feminine body (Tyson & Tyson, 1990).

The father also has a crucial role in supporting the boy toddler's need to consolidate his sense of self as separate and different from mother. By offering himself as a positive model of identification, he enables the little boy to disidentify with mother, his primary object, and to stabilise his sense of himself as a boy with a penis to be proud of. In the following observation, a father stepped in to help his son who was painfully jealous and envious of his two older sisters who, apparently equally envious of him, flaunted their pretty dresses and other feminine adornments:

Harry (aged 2) wanted to wear bows and slides like his sisters. He became miserable and whiny, clinging to his exhausted mother and refusing to engage with the toys, staff or other children in the toddler group. On one occasion he insisted and was brought to the toddler group with tights under his shorts. We encouraged his busy but playful father to make special time for Harry. He bought him a toy tool box like his own, and they went around the house together fixing things. On one occasion, he used Harry's green plastic hammer to put up a picture. On another, they both came to the toddler group wearing bow ties. Harry became much more active and happy, evidently identifying with his father's exuberant masculinity, and stopped demanding his sisters' things.

Starting nursery school

By 2½ to 3 years, most toddlers are ready to take advantage of a good nursery school experience. Winnicott (1957) pointed out that nursery school can be a relief from the passions at home, while also bringing home the reality that mother has a life of her own, and belongs to someone else. Painful feelings of jealousy and exclusion may therefore be added to the "triad of feelings" (sadness, fear and anger) which R. Furman (Furman & Katan, 1969) describes as consequent to starting nursery school. If the toddler is to manage these without becoming overwhelmed, he needs to have reached sufficient object constancy to be able to hold on to a positive inner image of his mother in her absence. This, combined with his ability to express himself effectively in both words and play, will help to regulate some of the intense affects aroused by the school experience. Writing about children's readiness for nursery school, Anna Freud (1965) pointed out that the young child also needs to have reached some independence in managing his bodily needs (eating, toileting, and keeping safe), and to have moved on from experiencing his peers as a threat, to beginning to play alongside them and even enjoying them as playmates in their own right. He is then in a position to take full advantage of the opportunities for new relationships and play and learning experiences that attendance at nursery can offer.

The two toddlers in the following vignette are ready for nursery school, in fact one has started part-time.

> Emily (2 years 6 months) and Ahmed (2 years 7 months) are standing side by side at the sink helping the toddler group leader wash up after snack. Ahmed announces "I'm washing up", cleaning a cup with a brush. He then says "I done that", and follows the leader's instructions to give the cup to Emily for rinsing. She takes it and pours water from one cup to another. He continues to wash up, humming to himself, and repeating "I done it" in a sing song voice as he passes cups and plates to Emily, who holds them under the trickling tap. She asks for more water, "I want cold water", and then a brush. The play is absorbed and harmonious, presided over by the toddler group leader who is drying the cups and plates that Emily passes on to her. Ahmed makes to leave but then holds his brush under the tap saying "I'm washing my brush now". The toddler group leader thanks him for lovely helping. He pulls off his apron enunciating clearly "I done it by myself". He

walks over to his mother and tells her "I washed up, mummy". Emily continues on her own, scouring plates and cups, turning the tap.

Both Emily and Ahmed convey a strong sense of themselves, separate from their mothers who are talking in another part of the room. They are engaged in parallel play which is also co-ordinated and co-operative, helping the toddler group leader in a shared task. They understand and follow instructions. They can express their thoughts and wishes clearly and in the first person. Ahmed expresses pride in his autonomy and competence: "I done that, I done it by myself". Both children convey a quiet satisfaction about getting things clean. Emily, who was recently toilet trained, particularly enjoys regulating the flow of water.

If nursery school is to be a "breathing-space for personal development" (Winnicott, 1957, p. 16), the transition needs to be carefully managed. The principle of introducing the world in small doses (to paraphrase Winnicott, 1949) can be usefully applied if it is understood that starting nursery will evoke previous separation experiences in both the child and the parent (see Wittenberg, 2001). In practical terms, this means careful preparation, perhaps even a home visit by the nursery teacher, followed by visits to the nursery with mother (or father), exploring it in her presence, and then managing without her for developmentally appropriate amounts of time (Belsky, 2001). Such carefully managed "excursions and returns" should enable the toddler and soon-to-be nursery school child to feel sufficiently confident in his own autonomous functioning to embark on the new journey which is school life.

The toddler's parents

This description of toddlerhood demonstrates the crucial importance of the parents' flexible and sensitive responsiveness and availability in the face of the toddler's ever-changing developmental needs; his mother has to be there to be left (Furman, 1982), to mirror and share in his experience, absorbing, transforming, and giving it back in her physical care, words and play. She has to manage and contain his anality – his excited aggressivity and messing, his contrariness, his provocativeness, his attempts to control and thwart her, his contradictory wishes which cannot be satisfied, and his tantrums when overwhelmed with frustration, rage or anxiety. She has to empathise and deal with his sensuality, his exhibitionism, his curiosity about his own and others' bodies, and the related fantasies and anxieties. Gradually, she has to let him take over ownership of his body and its care, while at the same time bearing in mind his dependence and vulnerability, and continued need for her love and protection. This means moving on from experiencing him as part of herself to perceiving him as a unique individual, separate and different from herself. It will include preparing carefully for change, allowing other relationships (with father and other adults, and children), perhaps even giving him a little push towards independence (see Mahler et al., 1975), and then tolerating periods of regression as well as rejection. It involves respecting his growing autonomy, while also communicating realistic expectations, setting appropriate limits, and being a positive model for identification.

These are very challenging tasks, which can become overwhelming if there are external stressful circumstances, e.g. work, financial or housing problems, disturbance or illness in the family, or other young children to look after. Parents who are socially isolated or very young and making their own, second, attempt at separation-individuation (Blos, 1967) may find looking after a toddler particularly difficult, if they lack opportunities for respite and cannot engage in autonomous activities of their own. Most parents in the UK nowadays, out of choice or financial necessity, return to work, leaving the care of their child to a relative, child minder, nanny, or day nursery.

Whatever the arrangement reached, most parents spending time with their 1 or 2 year old will encounter conflict, not just in their relationship with their toddler, but also within themselves. For instance, their close identification with their toddler may put them in touch with regressive (needy, erotic, aggressive) feelings which make them uncomfortable. And their toddler's drive to separate may revive earlier unresolved losses. They may find themselves struggling with a range of negative feelings, from mild disappointment and exasperation to helpless rage, hatred, even despair. It will be easier to contain these feelings and recover from the inevitable battles of will, misattunements and misunderstandings, if parents have realistic expectations regarding themselves and their toddler, and the benign support of family and friends (see Stern, 1995).

Fraiberg (1980) pointed out that disturbances in the infant–parent relationship arise when the baby comes to "represent figures within the parental past, or an aspect of the parental self that is repudiated or negated" (p. 61). Faced with typical toddler behaviours such as the urge to independence, to control, to succumb to a huge tantrum, a beleaguered parent may come to associate her toddler with a neglectful partner, more successful sibling, or mentally ill parent, and feel reproachful, angry or frightened. Seeing in him the negative attributes she rejects in herself, e.g. aggressivity or dependence, she may become "nonattuned" (Stern, 1985), like the unreflecting mirror referred to by Searles (1963) and Winnicott (1967); in this way "damage is done to the child who becomes walled off from his own emotional self by a similarly rigid and impervious wall" (Wright, 1991, p. 6). Alternatively, he becomes a convenient receptacle for her externalisations and projections, and she directs towards him her unconscious self-disgust and hatred. This impacts on the toddler's ability to individuate, since self and object remain insufficiently differentiated in the toddler's mind. His self-representation is loaded with unwanted aspects of the parent, while other areas of his own experience, such as his autonomous strivings or vulnerability and need, may remain split off and inaccessible. He may develop a false self (Stern, 1985; Winnicott, 1960a), denying whole aspects of his true feelings and needs, in order to remain connected to his parent. Alternatively, parent and toddler may become enmeshed in a sado-masochistic mode of relating, each externalising unwanted aspects of themselves on to the other (see Novick & Novick, 2005). Whatever the outcome, the toddler will have difficulties developing a true or coherent self-representation, and his chances of doing so in the future are much reduced if it does not feel safe to explore his parent's mind (see Fonagy, Gergely, Jurist, & Target, 2002). Research shows that he is unlikely to develop a good capacity for self-reflection (Fonagy & Target, 1997) or a secure attachment (Main & Weston, 1981), and this will in turn militate against the process of separation and individuation. Blum (2004) explores the implications of such developments for adult mental health, linking secure attachment with resilience and mastery of later trauma, and insecure attachment with developmental disorder, borderline personality, impaired object relations and chronic depression with suicidal tendencies.

Fathers may promote their toddlers' development in various ways. Research shows that attachment styles can be different for each parent (e.g. Steele, Steele, & Fonagy, 1996). Mothers and fathers can function as a "third object" helping the child to evolve second-order representations of the specific attachment to the other (Winnicott, 1949). To the extent that the father is experienced as different from mother and other than self (Wright, 1991), he contributes in crucial ways to the toddler's separation and individuation, "drawing him from the regressive undertow of the maternal symbiosis" (Wright, 1991, p. 114). He may be an important playmate and limit setter, promoting differentiation, the modulation of aggression and the establishment of gender identity. As a third in relation to the mother–toddler dyad, he introduces a different perspective for thinking and reflecting. He may support the mother in managing the demands of parenting a toddler, e.g. helping her wean him or return him to his bed at night. And the couple may provide a model of loving mutuality that the toddler may internalise, while also beginning to recognise that he is excluded from their adult relationship, and so beginning to find his place in the generational order.

Chapter 3

A psychoanalytic developmental approach to running a parent-toddler group

Marie Zaphiriou Woods

Introduction

This chapter describes the Anna Freud Centre's approach to running parent-toddler groups, at the Centre itself, and in two outreach settings (chapters 8 and 9 will describe the outreach groups in greater detail). We set out the aims of the groups and show how the structure of the service at the Anna Freud Centre, the group setting, and individual interventions within the groups are all designed to promote the development of the toddlers attending the groups with their parents. The Appendix outlines the service.

The groups

The groups that meet at the Anna Freud Centre are small, with a consistent membership of parents who are committed to bringing their toddlers regularly for at least a year. Some toddlers stay for two years, and parents may attend for longer, if younger siblings join and continue. Parents are encouraged to bring their toddlers back to visit the group in the term after they leave to go to nursery.

The groups provide a space where, to paraphrase Winnicott (1966), steady experiences in relationships enable toddlers to enjoy the enrichment that comes from discovery of their internal and external worlds, and to practise the excursions and returns that both support attachment and enable separation (see previous chapter). The consistency of the setting enables much learning and development to take place spontaneously as group members interact, talking, playing, building new (lateral as well as vertical) relationships (Mitchell, 2003), and discovering alternative ways of seeing and doing things. The room is light and spacious, and is well stocked with attractive, age-appropriate toys and activities. The staff are warmly welcoming. They move freely among the parents and the toddlers, observing and reflecting inwardly, and intervening when necessary, as this chapter will illustrate. They aim to maintain an "internal analytic setting" (Parsons, 2007) to make sense of the unconscious communications and intense transference and countertransference feelings that inevitably arise. However, group members are not seen as patients and interpretations are rarely made.

The over-arching aim of the groups is to promote the toddlers' development. This includes enhancing attunement and attachment between the parents and toddlers, with a view to strengthening their relationship, and facilitating separation and individuation, so that toddlers can manage the next step towards growing independence, which is a half or whole day at nursery/school. Understanding the developmental needs of toddlers and parents, and the powerful feelings engendered by the toddlers' attempts to assert and define their emerging selves, are essential aspects of the work, informing interventions in the group.

Writing about mothers and infants, Stern (1995) pointed out that their external and internal worlds are so interconnected that both their interactions and their representations of both themselves and each other will be affected by a successful therapeutic action, regardless of the point of intervention or "port of entry". In the parent-toddler groups, the "port of entry" may be the group as a whole, or the behaviours, feelings, or thoughts of individual parents and/or toddlers. Interventions with an individual parent or toddler will not only affect their dyadic partner, but also the rest of the group.

Since attachment and separation are likewise interrelated during the toddler period, interventions will often have an impact on both, even though the primary focus may be one or the other. The groups can be conceptualised as supplying both a maternal and a paternal function to parents and toddlers alike, that is, on the one hand holding, nurturing and mirroring, but on the other hand also offering a different perspective, representing reality, supporting differentiation and containing and modulating ambivalence. They provide a "mental environment" that can contribute to the establishment of a reflective self (Fonagy, Steele, Moran, Steele, & Higgitt, 1991a). These functions can be internalised by young children and their parents at a time when they are particularly open to and in need of positive input. They then constitute a sound basis for the negotiation of future developmental hurdles (Zaphiriou Woods, 2000).

The external structure: Providing a reflective space for staff

The leader and assistant are responsible for the day-to-day running of their groups (including setting up, providing the mid-session snack, and overseeing tidying up). By being seen to think and work together for the good of the group, the two of them provide a model of co-operative partnership that the parents and toddlers may internalise. Inevitably, however, they also attract powerful (grand)parental transferences, which may be intensely ambivalent and hard to manage. They meet together after each group to share their observations and experiences, and may bring them to the weekly team meeting, which is a forum for the discussion of the groups as a whole, and of their individual members. This meeting can help them to understand and process the intense transference and countertransference feelings aroused by the groups and limit acting out.

> Following her first visit, which was much enjoyed by her toddler, a young depressed single mother missed several subsequent meetings, sending contradictory messages, including one to the effect that she "did not like the group and would not return". Irritated, the toddler group leader was tempted to respond with an ultimatum, conveying retaliatory rejection. Discussion within the team helped the group leader to a more sympathetic understanding of this mother's anxious testing, and enabled a more welcoming response, which modelled tolerance and containment of her toddler-like ambivalence and provocation, and facilitated her return.

Sometimes the toddler group staff may need ongoing support to manage what can feel like a parent's relentless projections and externalisations:

> Mrs D consistently presented herself as a model wife and mother with a perfect marriage and lucrative work assignments. She engendered feelings of envy and inadequacy in the other mothers, who avoided her. She also repeatedly undermined the toddler group leader, competing with her to be the expert, and contradicting and even ridiculing her interventions. Although Mrs D did sometimes engage and play with her toddler, this was inconsistent; he sometimes looked physically neglected and suffered a series of minor accidents. The toddler group staff described feeling paralysed in the presence of this mother, unable to intervene effectively or to move to protect the child.
>
> In team meetings, the toddler group leader admitted to dreading this mother's arrival ahd to feeling tempted to show Mrs D her (very impressive) curriculum vitae. She acknowledged the anger and anxiety that this mother aroused in her. The team hypothesised that Mrs D was externalising her own feelings of inadequacy on to the toddler group leader and the other mothers, and decided to discuss her regularly within the team. This containment enabled the leader to tolerate and survive Mrs D's humiliating attacks, sometimes recognising them, and even gently teasing her ("you are so experienced, I had better watch out for my job"), but not retaliating.
>
> After nearly a year, Mrs D began to reveal her own feelings of inadequacy: she talked about the fights with her husband, which she compared to her violent relationship with her father. She admitted that she was afraid of repeating the violence with her children, with whom she found herself becoming very angry, to the point that she had hurt one of them that morning.

These powerful intergenerational feelings had to be borne by the group before Mrs D herself was able to own and work on them so as not to repeat her own traumatic early experiences with her children. With time it became possible to address Mrs D's "ghosts" (Fraiberg, Adelson, & Shapiro, 1975), within the group. With some parents, this is too difficult and they may be offered individual sessions with the psychoanalytic consultant (see Chloe below). Meeting without their toddler, while still benefiting from the ongoing containment of the group, parents are often able to become aware of the unresolved issues that may be interfering with their parenting in just one or two individual sessions. When these issues are part of a wider problem, parents may be referred for individual, couple or family therapy.

The group setting: Fostering attachment and managing separation

"The provision of a predictable planned environment is a fundamental backdrop to the survival and health of a psychotherapeutic mother and baby group" (James, 2005, p. 128). By meeting in the same place and at the same time each week, and preparing carefully for anticipated changes (holiday breaks, changes to the room, arrivals and departures), the parent-toddler groups provide a model for the sort of secure base that parents need to provide for their own toddlers. Parents are encouraged to attend regularly, and continuity and cohesion are fostered by remembering what is going on in the lives of group members and making links between sessions ("oh, you liked that toy last time") and between group members ("Jane was looking for you last week"). Cards are sent during the long summer break, and developmental milestones and birthdays are noticed and celebrated. "Being remembered models the positive value of connection and relatedness. This may be crucial for traumatised mothers who have suffered cultural dislocation" (Woodhead & James, 2007, p. 123). In their discussion of outreach groups for parents and infants, Woodhead and James (ibid.) stress the importance of respecting the need to "drop out" as well as to "drop in". I would add that the feelings of rejection and uncertainty engendered in the staff by the toddler mothers' irregular attendance can be a way in to addressing their feelings about their toddlers' phase-appropriate ambivalence and moves away.

Fostering the parents' sense of attachment and belonging to the group, of "being in it together" (James, 2005), enables them to talk more openly about their toddlers' difficult behaviours (negativism, clinging, hitting, snatching, tantrums, etc.), their own ambivalence, and the associated shame and guilt. They can draw comfort from observing or hearing that other toddlers and parents feel and behave similarly. The staff convey interest, respect and empathy. They take care not to judge the parents, and not to present themselves as better parents. They may draw attention to their own fallibility and regressive tendencies.

> After trying unsuccessfully to persuade the toddlers to share the food at snack time, the toddler group leader expressed her exasperation for the group. She spoke humorously about it being impossible to get things right all the time, adding "it is amazing how you sometimes end up feeling and behaving like a two year old yourself".

The staff actively encourage parents to learn from one another, reframing problems in shared terms so that they know they are "not the only one" (James, 2005, p. 135). They may bring together two parents who they know have struggled with similar issues or take advantage of snack time to introduce a sensitive topic (e.g. weaning, sleeping in the parental bed, mess or leaving to go to nursery). Often, a parent who has been avoiding an issue is able to think about it with the empathic support of the group. The ensuing discussion, in which the parents may be more confronting than the staff, may empower her to find a solution that suits her and her toddler, and to feel more competent, and less harshly self-critical. The staff may then elicit and empathise with her feelings of sadness and loss as her toddler separates.

The growing attachment to the group means that separations from the group are intensely experienced and become a means of exploring this core toddler, and human, issue.

> One toddler group leader worked hard over the better part of a year to help her group, which included a disproportionate number of parents with disrupted and dislocated histories, to recognise the value of regular attendance. She then had to cancel a week for another professional commitment. Even though this break was carefully planned and discussed, the group reacted with chaotic disorganisation. The three parents and toddlers who came to the meeting immediately after her absence made a huge mess and broke some of the toys, while two more phoned in during the session to announce triumphantly that they had other things to do.
>
> When the whole group returned the following week, it was possible to show them that the break had led to a range of reactions, from explosions of "messy" feelings (rage and destructiveness) to defensive withdrawal and turning passive into active. These could then be used to help the parents to understand their toddlers' needs for a secure base and their reactions when their wishes for continuity and control were thwarted.

Since separation is in fact a weekly event in every toddler group (every session must end), it is usually possible to address these feelings in more manageable doses within the group, by preparing carefully for tidying up time, verbalising the toddlers' feelings about stopping, and reassuring them that they and the toys will be there the following week. Tantrums are inevitable, however, with more compliant toddlers sometimes "getting permission" from the more vociferous ones to express their protest directly. If toddlers are anxious or hesitant about entering the toddler hut after such a scene or after an absence, this behaviour may be linked to their upset or to having been away, and feeling unsure about whether everything will still be the same.

The ways in which the staff manage the toddlers' reactions to the beginnings and endings of the group can be a useful model for parents as they strive to understand and deal with their toddlers' (as well as their own) intense reactions to difficult transitions. And these ways of managing are in turn internalised by the toddlers:

> After leaving the toddler hut at the end of a session, Omar (2 years 3 months) ran back to tell the assistant: "I forgot to say 'see you next week'".

Individual interventions

These may range from direct intervention with an individual toddler to listening to a parent with a view to enhancing her emotional awareness and availability to her toddler.

Facilitating creative play and playfulness (see also chapter 4)

"Play provides a haven for exploration of internal and external reality, so long as the child's sense of reality or imagination is not challenged in too literal a way" (Joyce, 2005, p. 75). Toddlers develop pretend play partly as a means of recapturing their early sense of union with their mothers, while paradoxically it affords them an opportunity to learn more about their separateness, the difference between their own and others' minds, and between fantasy and reality (see chapter 4). The toddler group staff encourage parents to share their toddlers' play, and communicate with them on a symbolic representational level. The toddlers may then use this new medium to express excited risky feelings and fantasies in an enjoyable and safe way, and to master age-appropriate anxieties to do with aggression and loss, separation and merging. They may also play out frightening external events, such as falling out of their buggy, or daddy going to hospital.

Sometimes parental difficulties intrude; *their* anxieties about excitement and mess, separation and loss, their projected aggression, and their need to inhibit and control may prevent them playing with their children. The staff may then join in or even initiate play with the toddler, supplying ideas and materials, and playfully amplifying their actions and affective communications.

> Farrah (2 years) hated sharing and was quick to push and hit at other children. During an especially fraught group, the toddler group leader led her, cross and frowning, to the musical instruments. Sitting with her, she banged loudly on the drum, trying to match her mood. She repeated "I'm very cross, I'm very, very cross". Farrah began to join in with her words and took over banging the drum. Her fury gradually subsided, and she smiled for the first time in the group. In subsequent groups, she returned to the drum whenever she felt cross, bringing it to the leader, or just marching around the room with it. She then introduced the game to other toddlers, showing awareness of their anger, and encouraging them to drum noisily with her. They began to initiate angry drumming even when Farrah was absent.

The toddler group leader's empathic playfulness enabled Farrah to express her anger in a more symbolic way, to begin to relate empathically to the other toddlers, and even to help them to express their angry feelings playfully.

The toddler group staff also help toddlers to construct pretend narratives, for instance using the toy cars or doll's house to play out visits to grandma, going shopping, or bed-time scenarios.

> When an older toddler repeatedly removed the baby doll from the family of dolls, the leader played along, adding that it was hard having to share mummy with his baby sister. She told his mother, who had been shocked by his sudden outbursts of aggression, that he was showing her how he felt about his baby sister at times. When he then threw the baby doll onto the doll's house roof, mother was able to laugh. The anxiety and anger between them was diffused, and the toddler went on to play at being an angry biting crocodile.

The staff work to model pleasurable, playful ways of being together for both toddlers and their parents. They may draw in a parent who is inhibited or depressed, or draw out a toddler from an over-enmeshed relationship. Such interventions both strengthen the attachment relationship and promote separation and individuation, as toddler and parent discover, through playing together or apart, that they have different minds (Fonagy & Target, 2007).

The toddler staff may also facilitate play between the toddlers, e.g. by encouraging them to "cook" side by side in the toy kitchen, or to play hide and seek (see chapter 8). Through this play, the toddlers are helped to discover each other as companions and playmates, and this helps to prepare the way for peer relationships in nursery and beyond.

Verbalising the toddlers' feelings and wishes

In her classic paper on verbalisation in early childhood, Anny Katan (1961) wrote, "If the child does not learn to name feelings, a situation may arise in which there develops a discrepancy between the strength and complexity of his feelings on the one hand, and his modes of expression on the other" (p. 186). Verbalising a toddler's feelings and wishes enables him to begin to delay action, to communicate his experience, and to distinguish between fantasy and reality (Furman, 1978; Weise, 1995).

The toddler group staff often verbalise what they perceive as the toddlers' feelings and wishes, supplying words to identify and legitimise the toddlers' experience. Finding himself accurately reflected in another's mind helps the toddler to feel less overwhelmed, out of control and alone.

The staff may speak directly *to* the child:

> Stefan (1 year 9 months) threw a huge tantrum when another toddler would not relinquish the car he wanted. The toddler group assistant tried to help him calm down, saying how cross he felt, and suggesting that his mother hold him. He continued to be distraught, pushing her away, and eventually the leader came over and spoke to him. Noticing that his expression had become sad, she said that he seemed sad now, adding that he had been feeling cross, but now he felt sad. He calmed down immediately, and was able to move away from the car and play with the other toys.

The leader's correct naming of Stefan's affects enabled him to regulate his emotional state and play with something else. Such interventions help toddlers to build up coherent representations of their internal states (Fonagy et al., 1991a). They contribute to the development of a robust sense of self and of agency. Over time, the toddlers are helped to make the transition from actions to words, and from words to thoughts (Furman, 1978).

Sometimes staff speak *for* or *about* the child's feelings or wishes to the parent. This may be the most effective way of raising parents' awareness of their toddler's state and enlisting a contingent response from them:

> Seeing a toddler flinch when her mother roared loudly, holding the toy tiger too close to her face, the toddler group leader said "You are frightening me, mummy. Please put the animal away".

> Noticing another toddler slide up cautiously behind his mother after he had been upset, the leader said on his behalf "I think he needs a cuddle".

Such interventions aim to promote effective communication by the toddlers and sensitive responsiveness from the parents. Helping parents to tune in or "feel with" (Furman, 1992) their toddlers strengthens attachments. Since the mirroring is not exact and is "marked", that is, slightly exaggerated and at the same time tinged with a contrasting affect, differentiation is also furthered, both for the toddler, and for the parent who is helped to recognise that her toddler's experience is different from hers (Fonagy & Target, 2007).

Managing aggression and setting limits

The toddlers' aggression manifests itself in the groups in various ways, ranging from ordinary testing and negativism to biting, hitting, and angry tantrums. Some parents are able to anticipate and deal with these behaviours appropriately and firmly, but some, no doubt because of their own conflicts about activity and aggression (Hoffman, 2003), become either frightened and helpless, or overcontrolling, rejecting and/or punishing. The toddler may be left to feel equally helpless, and may learn to fear that aggression is indeed all-powerful, causing loss or terrifying retaliation. If aggression cannot be expressed safely, it may not be possible for the toddler to learn to harness it to help define and consolidate his sense of self, or to use in constructive or creative activities. The toddler may become defiant or overly compliant.

The toddler group staff support parents in thinking about and helping their toddlers with their aggressive feelings and behaviours. Sometimes, however, they may need to act in an immediate way, to protect the toddler(s), and to reassure all members of the group that aggression can be safely contained.

One new mother expressed her fear of her toddler's tantrums; she said she thought that he had ADHD (attention deficit hyperactivity disorder) and that he would become uncontrollable in adolescence.

> At the end of their first group session, Ian (2 years) wanted to play with a toy in the shed. His mother reiterated that it was time to go. Ian started to cry and threw himself repeatedly against the closed shed door. His mother watched helplessly, and Ian eventually lost his balance, falling backwards where he would have hit his head on the concrete, had not the toddler group leader caught and held him. She spoke soothingly to him, reassuring him that the toys would be waiting for him when he returned next week. He turned to her, sobbing into her neck, and eventually calmed down. She then handed him to his mother, who continued to hold him.

Here, the toddler group leader needed to act to prevent Ian from hurting himself. In comforting him, she demonstrated to both toddler and mother that Ian's rage and frustration could be contained, challenging his mother's view of him as an uncontrollable adolescent, and offering an alternative perspective – that he was small and helpless, and in need of holding.

Sometimes the staff need to act to prevent the toddlers from hurting one another. One mother brought her little daughter to the toddler group because of her aggressive behaviour towards other children. She thought that Chloe

(1 year 3 months) was "copying" her older brother, who had behavioural difficulties, and seemed resigned that Chloe too would shame her.

> On her first visit, Chloe immediately and violently knocked another child flying. She repeated this behaviour on subsequent visits, watching all the while for her mother's reaction. Mother, who had recently separated from Chloe's father, appeared exhausted and defeated, helpless to do anything. Sensing her brittleness, the staff felt equally helpless, and the other parents avoided her. Following a discussion in the team meeting, they referred her to me.
>
> During our individual meeting, Chloe's mother was able to recognise that some of Chloe's aggressive behaviour might be linked to sad and angry feelings about her father's departure. She was intrigued by my suggestion that putting Chloe's feelings into words might reduce her need to act them out. She acknowledged her own paralysing anger, and agreed to let the toddler staff help her learn to manage Chloe's behaviour. With her permission, they shadowed Chloe, anticipating her aggressive attacks and physically restraining her when necessary. They verbalised Chloe's feelings and wishes: "I don't want to share that toy", or "I want mummy to come and play with me".
>
> After a few weeks, Chloe's mother was able to take over this role, and to play with Chloe, following her lead. Chloe responded by becoming calmer and more focused in her play. Though Chloe would still occasionally become aggressive when her mother was distracted, her mother was now able to intervene appropriately.

The toddler group staff may also intervene to prevent fights over toys and to promote turn-taking and sharing. They may verbalise the toddlers' frustration at having to wait, and their pride and pleasure when they manage to be patient or kind. When successful, these interventions can help to build a toddler's capacity for affect regulation, impulse control, socialisation, and the building up of a benign superego. The staff play a paternal role in the groups, coming between enmeshed mother–toddler dyads and helping to modulate aggressive drives and fantasies (Herzog, 1982).

Supporting toddlers' moves towards independence and autonomy

The toddlers' progression along the developmental line towards body independence (A. Freud, 1965) is noticed and celebrated in the groups, as, for instance, they join the other children at the snack table, eat and drink independently, take off and put on their coats, and begin to use the potty or toilet. These progressive moves contribute to the toddlers' increasing sense of competence and mastery and prepare the way for their independent functioning at nursery.

Most parents feel pride and pleasure, and indeed relief, as their toddlers begin to take ownership of their bodies, their functioning and care. However, some need support to enable them to "stand by to admire" (Furman, 1992, p. 119), and to gradually let go, especially when their toddler's progressive moves stir up painful feelings of loss (Furman, 1994).

In the following example, the toddler group leader responded physically and verbally to a practising toddler's explorations, encouraging her growing physical competence and self-reliance. This was her third visit to the toddler group.

> Fatima (1 year 4 months) showed an interest in the trampoline. Her mother helped her climb on it, then off and on again, gently bouncing her. The toddler group leader spoke to both of them, providing a lively commentary for their activities. She drew mother's attention to Fatima's widening interest in toys. As she was speaking, Fatima struggled to get off the trampoline by herself. Her mother stepped forward, but the leader gently restrained her, suggesting they see if she could manage alone. She did, smiling with delight. The leader remarked on her pleasure in mastering this new skill. Fatima proceeded to practise it, getting on and off the trampoline a number of times. When the leader moved away, mother invited Fatima to breastfeed, and avoided the leader for the rest of the group.

Fatima's mother was a political refugee with a traumatic history of rejection and loss by her original family. Although Fatima was ready to use the toddler group leader's intervention, her mother was not; she clearly communicated her continuing need for Fatima's dependence and closeness. It took many more months for her to build a trusting relationship with the toddler group staff and to allow Fatima more independence.

Another mother, with a different history of loss, was more able to tolerate a verbal intervention by the leader, because of their shared experience and joint understanding, built up over a year of attendance, that she had difficulty with previous milestones.

> James' mother, who had had a previous stillbirth, had delayed weaning and giving James his first haircut. She often expressed intense sadness at his "growing up". When she decided to toilet train him, when he was 2½, she told the toddler group leader that he was resisting. The latter pointed out that he had gone to the toilet when he had wet his nappy and then held up his legs for a nappy change. She suggested that mother might be resisting. Mother recognised this immediately, bringing more signs of his readiness, and began to train him that week. The following week, James showed great pride in managing his zip on his own, saying "I can do it".

Some parents lack confidence in their parenting, and ask the staff for specific advice at each new stage about how exactly they should wean, toilet train, or get their toddler out of their bed. The staff are wary of presenting themselves as experts, and reinforcing parents' sense of inadequacy. They try to join with them in finding solutions, perhaps supplying some ideas and guidance, but encouraging them to pick up on their toddler's cues and work out what is best for them. They may then support them in their decision, for instance to say "no" to their toddler's continued demands for breast-feeding. In supporting the parents' independence and autonomy, they perhaps enable them to do the same for their toddlers.

Feeding back observations and understanding behaviours

Parents are encouraged to observe their toddlers' behaviours and to think about what might be going on in their minds in order to enhance their emotional awareness of their toddlers, and to enable them to understand and respond to them in their own right. The immediacy of the observations may enable them to see characteristics or developments in their toddler that they may have overlooked, because of their own preoccupations and conflicts.

> One very young single mother arrived in the toddler group complaining that Abiola (1 year 9 months) was selfish and did not share, even with her. When, three months later, the toddler group leader drew her attention to Abiola sharing a game with another toddler, mother was able to state proudly "Abiola is a very friendly child". She sat down with both children and mediated their play. Two weeks later, she joined Abiola in giving out crayons to the group. She observed to the leader "she has started to share now".

Abiola's mother's comment suggested that she had taken in explanations by the toddler group staff that it would take time and support from her for Abiola to begin to overcome her age-appropriate possessiveness and lack of concern for others. Realising that Abiola's behaviour was not purely a reflection of her poor mothering enabled her to become less rejecting, and more emotionally available, although it also became apparent that her own very deprived and abusive background made it difficult for her to stay in touch with Abiola's needs.

The staff try to help parents take into account their toddler's age-appropriate emotional, cognitive and physical capacities so that they can better tolerate both their dependency and attachment needs, and their urge to separate and individuate. This may mean modifying unrealistic expectations and normalising behaviours which parents find bewildering or unacceptable. To quote Hoffman (2003) many parents "believe that good parenting involves the elimination of aggression, conflict or ambivalent feelings" (p. 1220). Their toddler's contradictory behaviour, aggressive outbursts and/or regressive shifts may make them feel anxious ("is it normal?"), guilty ("have I damaged him?") and/or condemning ("he's bad"). Putting such behaviours in a developmental context or linking them to external events may reduce parental anxiety, freeing them to be more in touch with their toddler's feelings and fears.

> One father was relieved when it was explained that his toddler's sudden refusal to go down the slide he had previously adored was linked to his new awareness of the dangers of heights and separation from his mother.

> A mother was able to be more sympathetic about her toddler's aggressive clinging when she was helped to understand that while their recent visit to her home country had been important for her, it had been overwhelming for her toddler, who had been flooded with experiences of unfamiliar people, sights, and sounds.

However, an experienced older mother was unable to accept the leader's normalising of her little son's wilful, exploratory behaviour until this was reinforced by the support of the whole group.

> Mother regularly complained that Robert (1 year) had become "naughty and difficult", trying to control him and comparing him unfavourably with her two older daughters. When Robert, aged 14 months, refused to get into his buggy after a shopping expedition, mother arrived at the group enraged and close to tears. Although she was too humiliated and upset to take in the leader's explanations, she nevertheless listened when the leader drew in another mother to talk about *her* difficulties with *her* toddler. When more mothers joined in, vying with one another to describe angry scenes around feeding, sleeping, and shopping, Robert's mother visibly calmed down, feeling reassured that she was not alone.

The staff model reflectiveness, and encourage parents to think about the meaning of their toddlers' behaviour, in order to help them avoid the temptation of blaming and rejecting their toddlers for behaviour that they find hard to understand. This may enable them to see their child as "developing and separate" as well as "dependent and connected" (Green, 2000, p. 28). Reflective function is enhanced and with it the likelihood of a secure attachment (Fonagy, Steele, & Steele, 1991; Slade, Grienenberger, Bernbach, Levy, & Locker, 2005).

Recognising and containing the parents' experience

E. Furman (1994) has stressed "mothers' deep appreciation of an under-standing containing person" (p. 160), and Stern (1995) has written about mothers' special need to be validated, supported, and appreciated by a maternal figure, adding that if a mother is "held" in this way, her "maternal functions are liberated or discovered and facilitated" (p. 188).

The toddler group staff offer a supportive relationship to each parent, holding in mind their individual needs, and offering them time in each session to communicate their current state of mind. They listen atten-tively and sympathetically, so that the parent feels heard, understood and accepted. This process may help parents to process potentially overwhelming feelings and experiences without having to cut themselves off from their toddlers or externalise and project onto them, condemning, rejecting and trying to control them (see chapter 10). Put in attachment terms, if they have expectations of being criticised, punished and abandoned that are disconfirmed, they may learn ways of relating characterised by mutuality and caring, rather than anger and fear (Lieberman & Pawl, 1993). The "good grandmother transference" (Stern, 1995) which develops may enable them to become more accepting of their own and therefore their toddlers' dependency needs, and means that they are less likely to feel envious of the good care their toddlers are receiving. The attention paid to their own feelings may also help them to differentiate better between their own and their toddlers' needs and feelings (see chapter 6).

> Once the positive relationship has developed, parents might be more willing to have their view or handling of their toddler challenged. They might even tolerate tentative links with present or past relationships. For example, when a mother recalled being bullied by her older brother, the leader said "now I can see why you are so worried about Tommy (2 years 8 months) being too rough with Owen (8 months)".

Such links are aimed at freeing the parent's relationship with her toddler from impingements by other unresolved relationships, and enabling her to become more attuned.

Writing about similar parent–child groups, Hoffman (2004) highlights the role played by both the transferential bond to the staff and the bonds mothers make with one another in enabling new mothers to address their anxieties. It seems likely that parents and toddlers select what they need for their development from the various "therapeutic possibilities" (A. Freud, 1965) provided by the "supportive matrix" (Stern, 1995, p. 177) of the parent-toddler groups, and that is analogous to the process that Anna Freud (1965) described of child patients taking what they need from the more classical child analytic setting.

Chapter 4

The role of play[3]

Jenny Stoker

One of the main aims of our toddler groups is to encourage a playful relationship between parents and their children. This chapter will look at the role of play – its form and content – in toddler development. It will also look at the struggles that toddlers and their parents have with play and will describe how we try to facilitate play in our toddler groups.

The process of play: its role in development

The words play and playing are difficult to define. We use them in different contexts: to describe the pretend world of make-believe with its infinite possibilities, or structured activities like board or computer games. We talk of playing games of tennis or football. Playing can be serious or hilarious or anything in between. As Michael Parsons (1999) showed, play is characterised by a sense that what goes on when it is taking place is different from what goes on outside it: play takes place within a frame. When we play a game we have rules and expectations or ways of behaving and understanding our situation that are not the same as ordinary life. This is as true for example in the pretend play of a toddler as it is for the games played by professional footballers.

Even very young babies seem to have the capacity to create a frame within which there is a shared knowledge that what is going on is different from what might go on ordinarily. For example, when a baby happily joins in a game of peek-a-boo with a parent, he appears to know that what is going on is different from ordinary experiences which would normally be upsetting. It is as if both mother and baby know that the experience of appearing and disappearing in the game is not real. This and the shared awareness of expectations being confounded turn it into a game.

As Anna Freud (1965) pointed out, play starts with the body: the baby's and his mother's. She described how play begins with the libidinal activity of the baby's investment in his own body – his auto-erotic pleasures, involving the mouth, the fingers, and the skin – and in his mother's body, normally during feeding. These playful explorations of the body very soon develop into more structured "games" between parents and their baby such as peek-a-boo or tickling. Anna Freud described a developmental line of play, which she thought moved through phases; through attachment to' transitional objects and cuddly toys to play materials which allow children to gratify and sublimate their instinctual urges while at the same time serving their developing search for knowledge.

Klein (1930) saw the presence of anxiety and its acceptance and transformation through the elaboration of phantasies as central to the origins of play. Klein's account implies the need for a mother who can stand the child's anxiety, helping him to tolerate and modify it, and thereby making safe his aggressive feelings.

Winnicott (1971) wrote about the link between the physical, objective, and the emotional, subjective experiences in play. He argued that play was at the heart of creativity, and that it originated in the earliest days of life: by providing the baby with a feed at the moment he wants it, the mother gives the baby the illusion that he has *created* the feed. The experience of having his wish being satisfied reinforces his belief that the environment is responsive to his wishes. This early experience of omnipotence over his environment lays the foundation for his later development of a capacity to deal creatively with frustrations and absences. For Winnicott, the mother's subsequent gradual frustration of her baby's needs as he becomes older and she becomes less available is crucial in spurring on his development. This incremental intrusion of reality is beneficial to the child.

Winnicott described how a baby characteristically responds to his mother's decreasingly adaptive behaviour by creating for himself a transitional object, typically a security blanket. For the baby, the blanket becomes a proto-symbol of his mother's breast, body and ability to comfort as he attempts to recreate them in her absence. Thus, he finds a way to recreate the feeling her presence gives him in her absence. The blanket becomes a subjective object – it is no longer the blanket of the external world but has become a subjective creation of the baby, although of course it still exists simultaneously in the outside world. The blanket provides the right degree of softness and texture for the baby to establish a medium through which to access the pattern of feelings associated with his mother's presence. This moment of creativity in a baby's life arises from his sense of lack, and an external form is found which is imbued with personal meaning to recreate that missing experience (Wright, 1991).

Winnicott envisioned the process of creativity and play as taking place in a particular kind of space. This "transitional space" forms as a kind of interface between the world of thoughts, feelings, and fantasies on the one hand; and the outer world, where meanings are fixed and cannot be changed, on the other. In the transitional space an interchange is made possible between the inner and outer world – external objects can be endowed with a personal meaning by the subject. The experience of transitional space allows us to feel that the world can be transformed and moulded in line with our wishes. This is the realm of creativity and illusion.

According to Winnicott, a child's ability to inhabit transitional space varies according to the child's experience of his mother, particularly his experiences of separation from her. She has to remain reliable, but she must gradually become less and less adaptive and under his sway, to give him the opportunity to develop and sustain the illusion of her presence through his use of a transitional object in her absences. A consequence of this capacity is that it allows further independence from the mother.

This creative capacity is related both to the search for unity with the mother and to acceptance of her otherness. Unlike Anna Freud, Winnicott thought that the development of the capacity to play was not related to the satisfaction of instinctual needs. He thought instinctual demands could pose a threat to the establishment of a transitional space. If a baby is left alone, or is left hungry for too long, then the illusion engendered by the transitional object cannot be sustained. Similarly, if we are too anxious or preoccupied it is not possible for us to play or to be creative. We tend either to become preoccupied with the inner world or to become manically active in the outer world and the necessary relaxed intermingling between the two cannot take place.

Recent research in child development has provided empirical support for Winnicott's theories (Gergely & Watson, 1996). This research confirms that the experience of similar but not identical mirroring ("nearly, but clearly not the same"), occurring in "motherese" and during playful interactions, is important in the development of babies' sense of their own and others' identity. Parental mirroring helps babies to begin to establish that the other is similar but not identical to them; that the other is another. Gergely and Watson (1996) emphasise that the congruence in the imitation or mirroring between parent and child must not be perfect. It must be distinguishable from the parents' own realistic emotional expression (Gergely and Watson describe this characteristic of parental mirroring as "markedness"). It must not be too real. Nor however must it be too different. Either may have pathological consequences.

These researchers have linked their work to psychoanalytic theories (Bion, 1962; Kernberg, 1984; Mahler et al., 1975; Stern, 1985; Winnicott, 1967) which stress the role of the mother in providing an environment that reads, modulates, echoes and reflects back the emotional state of the infant. All this work shares the view that normal development requires both moments that offer an experience of fusion of boundaries between subject and object and experiences of separation.

Gergely and Watson (1996) see the necessary "markedness" that should characterise mirroring between parents and babies as the forerunner of the typical exaggeration and decoupling of affect that occurs in pretend play.

The process of play and the toddler

As the developing child becomes more mobile in toddlerhood, both playing and language become mediums through which he can continue to feel himself to be connected to his parents, despite his increased mobility. As in babyhood, preconditions for the toddler to be able to play are attunement with mother, but also frustration of this attunement at times. In pretend play, the toddler uses his primary omnipotence to shape the world according to his desire. As in the creation of a transitional object, playing out and symbolising his experiences of being with his parents enables him to continue to feel linked to them in their absence. A consequence of learning to play is greater independence. Knowing he can create subjective objects in his world allows the toddler to be more separate.

The following vignette from one of our toddler groups illustrates the role of play as both an outcome of and a catalyst for separation from mother:

> Alex's (2 years 3 months) mother had talked about her worries that he was too clingy. Alex investigated the medical kit, while his mother sat passively on a chair beside him, her newborn baby in a car seat on her other side. With some encouragement mother held out a doll to Alex and asked him if he thought the doll needed to have her heart listened to through the toy stethoscope. Alex nodded solemnly, and with the stethoscope in his ears, he held it against the doll's chest. Still solemn, he gave the doll some "medicine". They talked about whether she was feeling better. Then Alex put a bandage on the doll's hand. Meanwhile, Alex's baby sister had started crying. Mother fed her. Afterwards Alex turned to them and started to listen to his sister's chest through the stethoscope. He smiled, and the mother asked if the sister also needed "medicine". With a knowing look on his face, Alex smiled again in response, and then gave his sister some medicine. They talked some more about whether she was better. Alex then got in the push along car and moved to play at the toy garage on his own.

Here we can see the creation of a transitional space in which Alex cares for the pretend sick doll. When mother then has to feed her baby she is no longer so available to him. In that gap, Alex, with assistance from her, creates his own subjective world, in which the doll and medical kit are given personal meaning. In his pretence we glimpse his internal world of fantasies; perhaps he identifies with his mother in looking after his baby sister, perhaps he is expressing a wish to be cared for by his mother, perhaps both. Together they master some of his feelings about mother's caring. Mother does not challenge his scenario but rather extends it. By pretending with her, he can feel united with her. This experience of shared pretend then allows him to separate more easily into creating his own pretence at the garage.

Writing about the development of reflective function in children, Fonagy and Target (1996, 2007) have discussed the intersubjective quality of play. Very young children believe that their own and other people's thoughts accurately mirror the external world. They are unable to distinguish between fantasy and reality. Thoughts and feelings are therefore potentially very frightening. However, through pretend play with the participation of a benign adult, a young child begins to learn that there is a distinction between their thoughts, feelings and fantasies and the external world. As the adult and the child play together, the child begins to recognise that their shared pretend play is a representation of reality. He gradually learns that reality does not exactly mirror his feelings and fantasies. He comes to share the adult's knowledge that what they are playing at is not real. Imaginative play then becomes safe, as well as being a shared experience, although, as with older children and adults, there may be moments (especially at times of high emotional arousal) where the capacity to distinguish fantasy and reality is temporarily lost.

Another observation of Alex's play on a different day demonstrates this:

> Alex was hurt by another toddler. He cried and clung to his mother, and was still inconsolable after 10 minutes. Alex's baby sister was woken up by his crying, and she began crying as well. Mother and Alex, both distraught, went out into the garden. Alex insisted that his mother stayed with him to help him on the slide. Despite her awareness of her baby's distress mother was unable to separate from Alex. Eventually, after the toddler group leader suggested that she read to Alex while she fed the baby, they came inside. With some difficulty, Alex's mother started feeding his younger sister, while Alex fetched the fire engine book to read with her. Together they read about the fireman and his engine, and how they put out fires and rescued people. After talking about the book with his mother, Alex began to play with the toy fire engine and the firemen, who had yellow hats, just like the ones in the book. He found a large yellow fire helmet and tried it on. Finally Alex began to smile and moved away from his mother.

One could speculate that in the first part of this observation, mother and Alex were each paralysed by their conflict over their loving and hating feelings for each other. Alex, initially angry with his sister, transferred his fury on to his mother for not protecting him, and mother, while identifying with Alex's hurt, was also angry with Alex for being so clingy that she was not free to feed her baby. Their hostility to each other may have felt so overwhelming that they were afraid that if they parted they would be lost from each other forever. For those brief moments, what was true in their internal worlds was also true in the external world.

Later, we can see in the content of the imaginary play how Alex mastered his intense fiery feelings about his mother and his sister, as well as his wish for rescue from these feelings. In the form of his play, in his pretend world, we can see how he was discovering that his internal experience, his destructive rage at his mother, did not have to be externally true. Through reading about dangers and threats to life and playing with staff and his mother, Alex came to understand that others were familiar with the sorts of feelings he was having and that these feelings were based in the mind, in fantasy, rather than in reality. He learned that there was a world of feelings, both in his mind and in others' minds, that was different from action. Even his mother, in common with most of us at times of crisis, was soothed by the book and the play that reminded her that our internal fantasied world is so similar and yet so importantly different from the world we inhabit.

In Kleinian terms, one might say that Alex's mother, with a little support, was able to contain his aggressive feelings, and that this enabled Alex to move on to symbolise them in his play about fires and firemen.

Content of play

The vignettes above show that it is not only the process of play that is important in development. The content of Alex's play was also important in helping him to deal with specific internal emotional experiences.

Children explore the external world in the content of their play, finding out like little scientists how things work. They also explore their internal worlds of feelings and fantasies and use play to overcome painful affects as well as to experience pleasurable ones. Toddlers have to learn to inhibit their instinctual urges so as not to risk losing their parents' love. For example, they have to learn to deal with the sudden eruption of their unpredictable destructive feelings towards those they also love and depend on. Playing provides an intermediate arena where the content of such painful conflicts can be explored.

Observing his grandson playing with a cotton reel by throwing it over the edge of his cot and then pulling it back up, Freud (1920) inferred that children's play offers them an opportunity to master uncomfortable feelings. They take pleasure from doing to someone or something else (in this case, casting away the cotton reel) what has been done to them (in this case, separation from his mother), turning a passive experience into an active one. Like Freud's grandson, toddlers often re-enact their experiences of separation in their play:

> Ali's (2 years 8 months) mother had been away for 3 days for the first time. She said Ali had been very angry with her. He hammered toy animals with great gusto. He and a staff member developed a game where he exuberantly hit down the animals and she stood them up again. He laughed, saying "Again" repeatedly. Later he made some of the animals captive, hiding them and checking on them periodically. He, his mother and the staff member

laughed together and the initial intensity of the bashing of the animals was dissipated.

Here, Ali was able to transform an experience where he had had to accept the loss of his mother passively by creating a play scenario in which he could actively express his anger. He could do to the animals what he felt had been done to him (made to feel hurt, captive and hidden). He elaborated and mastered the upsetting events he had suffered, deriving joy from creating a scenario in which his angry wishes were not so overwhelming that they would actually send his mother away for ever. Importantly, as in Alex's play above, Ali's mother and the toddler leader accepted and encouraged his game, allowing him to feel that his emotions could be shared and tolerated when they were expressed in this way.

Toddlers also often use play to deal with traumatic experiences, as in the following case:

Fred (2 years 9 months) had witnessed a car accident, and during one session he talked about it. He drove the toy car in the garden. When it stopped he said it had crashed or was stuck and he asked the toddler group leader to bring tools to fix it. He played this game repeatedly for several weeks.

Repetition is an important ingredient in all these vignettes, as it was in Freud's grandson's game and in much of toddlers' play. Each repetition of the experience of mastery of painful feelings seems to increase the delight. Each repetition, it seems, proves to the toddler anew that he does not have to remain the victim of his suffering. Repetition seems to reinforce the toddler's capacity to make a difficult experience manageable, in part through the creation of fantasy worlds that are distinct from the less controllable realm of reality.

Children may use play to express unacceptable feelings as well as to master overwhelming experiences:

Sasha (2 years 10 months) was a polite, placatory child. She was tired after a morning at nursery and had not wanted to change out of her school clothes. She played with the toy wild animals and mother asked her what the tiger ate. Sasha hesitated and then said "you". Mother laughed. Sasha went on "He hates you". Mother wondered aloud whether she was saying "ate" or "hate" and Sasha repeated "He hates you". Mother wondered what she could do to make the tiger like her again, and they resumed talking about all the animals.

Here we can speculate that Sasha defended herself against owning her destructive feelings for her mother (whom she loved and on whom she depended) by attributing those feelings to the tiger. Her mother helped her by encouraging the play and trying to find a resolution from within the game.

Difficulties with playing

Most parents find it difficult to play with their toddlers at times, but some parents find it impossible to develop a playful relationship. There may be a number of reasons for this, but a useful starting point is Winnicott's warning that too intense preoccupation with our own unconscious instinctual demands will interfere with the capacity to find the transitional space in which to play.

Such preoccupation in the adult may take the shape of an unconscious fear of a loss of the dependent baby. The parent's fear of separation prevents the development of an "as if" space: the loss has to be denied and often prevented.

> Isabella (2 years 8 months) could not engage in pretend play. She put herself rather than the dolls in the doll's cot. She moved in a desultory fashion round the room, picking up dollshouse figures and toy animals, but never developing play with them. Mother sat solemnly at a distance watching her. When encouraged by staff to join Isabella at the dollshouse, she would arrive just as Isabella had moved on.

Isabella's mother was from a traumatised and deprived background. It is likely that she never experienced any playfulness herself. She was single and isolated and had struggled with mental illness. She seemed invested in keeping Isabella dependent like a baby, continuing to breastfeed her and to share a bed with her. At the same time, she may have felt guilty about her wishes for Isabella's dependence. This conflict led her to attempt to provide some means of playing with Isabella, but as above, she could not find a way to make it last and she would then remove herself. She found it impossible to create an as-if world of illusion with her and so inadvertently deprived Isabella of a safe and manageable way to separate. As a consequence, Isabella and her mother remained locked in a deeply ambivalent relationship where there seemed to be little distinction between fantasy and reality.

Other parents may be struggling with strong feelings which they project onto their child:

> On arrival at the toddler group, father said they had had a terrible night with Richard (2 years). He had been awake for much of the night. Father said he himself felt exhausted, and he looked very tense as he took off their coats.
> Later Richard wandered across the hut with a toy broom in his hands, waving it vaguely around in the air, while his father trailed behind him. The

staff member wondered aloud if Richard was wanting to do some "cleaning". Father interjected that at home Richard loved playing with the hoover, but he continued to hover anxiously over Richard, saying he was worried that Richard would use the broom to hit someone. After a short time he took the broom away from Richard.

Father's projection of his own anger on to Richard stopped him from helping Richard play. Preoccupied with his own instinctual urges, he saw only aggression in Richard's activity, seeing his behaviour as threatening rather than playful, and was unable to encourage the creation of a transitional space.

Many parents have a tendency to become didactic in their play with their child, teaching them instead of following their lead. In these cases, the child's necessary omnipotence in creating the game is challenged by the parent and the child is unable to create his own subjective space. It is as if the child has become a possession of the parent and cannot be allowed to play on his own terms. Some parents find that the particular characteristics of their child's toddlerhood, with its preoccupation with issues of control and the body, evoke a defensiveness in themselves just when the relationship requires more of a capacity for playful regression. Other parents find the visceral directness of children's play inhibiting. Toddlers' play with their bodies, their messiness, and their sensuousness can prove problematic for parents who control their own messy feelings with obsessional traits. Such parents can find it hard to join in their children's glee at splashing water, smearing playdoh or toppling towers of bricks noisily. Jealousy of a partner's relationship with the toddler can also inhibit play. A father may feel shut out of the closeness between his partner and their child. His resentful feelings about this may make him avoid having any fun with his child.

One father's resentment at being the main carer of his child seemed to permeate his play with his son:

> John (2 years 9 months) put the toy dolls into beds. He whispered that they were going to sleep and we should be quiet. Father said he should put a blanket under the dolls as it would be more comfortable for them. He insisted on this, showing John how to do it. John replied firmly that he did not want to, but father continued to insist that otherwise the bed would be too hard and "You don't like sleeping in a hard bed". John pushed his father's hand away and put his own hands around the beds to avoid his father's intrusion. Father added, "I don't like sleeping in a hard bed", but did not persist. By then John's interest had diminished and he had moved on to something else.

Perhaps out of rivalry or jealousy of John's freedom, John's father wanted him to play the game his way. This wish for control might also have come from a concern that the child was not learning at a pace or in the way his parent would have liked.

Supporting playfulness in the toddler groups

It is important that staff in the toddler groups are not competitive with or undermining of parents in their relationships with their child. A parent who plays with her child because she has been made to feel guilty will not be playful. Nor will a parent who has been made to feel inferior to the staff. If the staff become didactic themselves they risk depriving the parent–toddler relationship of the potential for creativity. The ultimate aim must be for the parent and toddler to enjoy their play together.

This aim is pursued in a number of ways. Sometimes staff will work to support the mother or father emotionally to help them to modulate the intensity of their feelings, so that their child can be released from inter-ference based on parental projections (as in the cases of Alex, Richard and John above) to play on their own terms. Here, the group functions in a parental role for the individual parents, offering an experience of feeling safe and cared for. In the case of John's father (described above), staff spent many weeks talking to the father about his difficulties with his wife, as well as gently speaking on John's behalf, helping father to think about what might be going on in John's mind and to see that John had a valid point of view that was different from his.

Sometimes, the more inhibited parents benefit simply from being given permission to have fun and make a mess with their children. They will watch as staff or other mothers in the group gleefully encourage children to splash, make delighted "wheee" noises as the car runs along the ground, or joyfully bash pegs with a hammer. Staff will gently encourage them to join in and their newly found pleasure is then reinforced by their children's and the game takes off. Supported by the staff and enabled to feel less anxious, overwhelmed and defensive, they come to be able to identify with their child's needs for their involvement on their child's terms, and allow them-selves to become more childlike in their play.

Although staff do not teach the parents how to be with their child, many parents find it helpful to think with staff about what may be going on in their child's mind during this particular phase of development. Thinking together with staff about, for example, their child's apparently aggressive play, and learning that this is a normal phase, that it does not necessarily mean that their child will grow up to be a bully, and that there are accept-able ways in which it can be sublimated, can help a parent feel less persecuted by their child. Not taking the aggression so personally will free the parent up to help the child find alternative playful ways of expressing his aggression. Similarly, parents often find it helpful to understand that their child has to learn to share their toys; that it is normal for toddlers to be self-centred and possessive. Knowing this, parents feel less shame about their child's behaviour and can be more playful and less fierce in controlling it.

Conclusion

The ability to play and be creative is central to our development throughout our lives. Playfulness occurs in the gap between our own individual subjective worlds and the external objective world. In this arena, we make the objective world what we want it to be. We create our own personal narratives, we explore and we experiment. In realms as diverse as theatre, painting, music or poker games, we create our own hypotheses that we choose or not to share. Through the illusions we create in our play, we can safely experiment with our primitive instinctual urges, whether libidinal or destructive. We can safely try out different forms of relationships and we do not need to feel threatened because this world of illusion and experiment is not externally true. In the realm of play we learn to mediate between our internal world of feelings and fantasies and the external world of action and behaviours. The content of play allows us to experiment and the process of play reminds us it is an experiment: it reinforces the distinction between fantasy and reality.

In this chapter, we have seen that playing starts at birth and is crucial in early development. Play contributes to the establishment of a sense of identity and to the differentiation of the self from the other. Play starts with the body. Play is an outcome of and a catalyst for the increasing separation between mother and child, especially during the toddler phase. Toddlers use the content of play to master painful affects, to explore their internal worlds, to experiment with identifications and to express unacceptable feelings.

A critically important function of our toddler groups is to be the catalyst for a playful relationship between parent and child. For most parents this is not easy all the time, and it can seem impossible for some, yet the rewards of a few moments of shared pleasurable play between a parent and a child are great. Both parent and child can benefit from playful metaphors that remind them that their internal fantasy worlds are similar to and yet importantly different from the world they inhabit. This awareness reinforces their relationship and, in turn, facilitates further playfulness. In the feedback we have received from parents after they have left the groups, it is significant that they report that the single most important aspect of their experience in the groups was watching and sharing their children's pleasurable play in the group.

Chapter 5

Normally difficult and difficult normality: A toddler observation paper

Anna Plagerson

The progress from the symbiotic oneness of child and mother to that of separateness from her is marked by the formation of internal regulatory capacities which are assisted and promoted by maturational – especially motor, perceptual, verbal and cognitive – advances. This process is at best a pendular one. . . . Regressive and progressive movements alternate in shorter or longer intervals, easily giving the casual observer of the child a lopsided maturational impression. *Only observation over a period of time enables us to judge the behaviours of the average toddler . . . as to its normal or deviant nature.*

(Peter Blos, 1967, pp. 163–4) (my italics)

This quotation highlights the essence of my experience of observing a mother and toddler fortnightly at a toddler group at the Anna Freud Centre. This nine-month observation revealed the challenging and complicated journey they made from when this toddler (whom I shall call Amy) was 2 years 3 months to just before her third birthday.

My observation of Amy and her mother proved harder than I had anticipated. My difficulty began to make sense to me, as I came to understand more about the place of aggression in normal toddler development. I realised that I had chosen to observe this particular dyad because they seemed to present an idealised image of mother and daughter. In Amy and her mother (whom I call Ms B), I saw an opportunity to observe a "good enough" experience. Ms B seemed to represent the "good enough mother" (Winnicott, 1945): attuned, sensitive, empathic and engaged. Ms B took her cues from Amy's interest, and then elaborated them. She was inviting and reflective rather than being intrusive or didactic.

The following observation provides an example of this "good enough mothering":

> Amy went to the book corner followed by her mother. Amy began to choose books and clearly recognised some. She pointed to one book and said, "peep–oh". Her mother smiled proudly, saying "that's right". Amy sat

close to her mother waiting for her to read. Amy's mother read the whole book, and drew Amy's attention to something of interest in each picture. Amy responded to these prompts, but otherwise sat quietly and listened. Amy was actively engaged throughout the long process and both were fully absorbed with each other. (2 years 3 months)

This comfortable intimacy and ease of exchange drew me into observing Amy and Ms B. It became much more difficult to observe them when their relationship became troubled and when Amy became increasingly quiet and withdrawn, sometimes rejecting her mother quite cruelly.

Ms B and Amy had to cope with difficult external realities that impacted on their relationship; they moved house, stayed with close relatives and suffered a bereavement. Furthermore, Amy was affected by her mother's clearly stated wish for a new baby, although this wish was not fulfilled during this observation. The positive contribution of Amy's father probably provided a counterbalance to these stressful experiences. This chapter will examine Amy's development chronologically, alongside my own experience of observing this mother and toddler. I hope to show how complicated (and perhaps unwise) it is to attempt to assess normality or possible pathology in a period of such drastic change in physical and cognitive maturation, internal representations and environmental realities.

Setting the scene

Amy was the only child of Ms B and Mr B, a professional couple in their early thirties. Ms B gave up her highly-skilled job to become Amy's main carer. She was an attractive, intelligent, calm woman, who dressed sensibly in jeans and dark T-shirts and sweaters. She made no attempt to appear overly feminine, in contrast with Amy, who was often dressed in pretty dresses and "girly", though practical shoes. I often felt that Amy looked a little uncomfortable in these clothes. Her slight physical awkwardness, sober hairstyle and serious face presented something of a contradiction to these cheery outfits. I frequently observed Amy and her mother intensely engaged in reading a book together.

Contradictory impulses

Having been through the "love affair with the world" (Greenacre, 1957), the toddler becomes increasingly aware of her mother's separateness. This increases her need for her mother's attention, which the child gains by sharing her discoveries about the world with her. It is a time of contradictions; the child's increasing independence is counterbalanced by increased vulnerability and demandingness. The toddler wishes to be close to the mother, yet also rejects mother in order to be independent. Amy showed these contradictory tendencies at 2 years 4 months.

> The toddler leader and Ms B talked and played with dough. Amy went to stand behind the cooker. She looked at the tray with plastic fruit and vegetables. She picked up a piece, named it, "sweetcorn" and pretended to taste it. Her actions were calm and considered. She repeated this with the other "foods", saying their names very softly. She picked up the melon and said "mmm melon" and repeated this in a louder voice. She said it louder and louder, but neither the toddler leader nor Ms B looked up. She put down the melon, and returned to her mother. She picked up a green dough ball that her mother had made and said "green ball". Ms B immediately responded to this, and Amy joined her at the table. (2 years 4 months)

Amy showed a desire and capacity for independent activity; she left her mother, and became very engaged in exploring and naming the world. However, she also wanted to share this with her mother, and when she did not receive the attention she desired, she returned to her mother to get what she wanted. Amy knew that her mother would respond if she verbalised her mother's activity. This observation seemed to offer a clue to Amy's good verbal development; in this educated and articulate family, speaking and vocabulary were probably highly prized and Amy's linguistic skills were a direct result of her learning how best to attract mother's attention and capture her interest.

The mother's response to the toddler's ambivalence is crucial at this stage. As Mahler and colleagues have written, "One cannot emphasise too strongly the importance of the optimal emotional availability of the mother . . . it is the mother's love of the toddler and the acceptance of his ambivalence that enable the toddler to cathect his self representation with neutralized energy" (Mahler et al., 1975, p. 77).

Ms B tried hard to remain emotionally available to Amy. However, I observed how hard it can be, for Ms B as for any mother, when faced with the contradictory neediness and wish for independence of their toddler. The above observation showed Ms B's flexibility in allowing Amy to wander off and welcoming her when she returned.

In the following observation Ms B had perhaps a first experience of not being needed by her daughter. One of the functions of the toddler group is to help the toddler to form relationships with other adults and children, and so aid the separation-individuation process (Zaphiriou Woods, 2000).

> Amy instantaneously accepted the toddler assistant's invitation and walked off to play, without glancing at her mother. Ms B started chatting to another mother without looking at Amy. After the conversation ended, Ms B went to find Amy engrossed in her play with the toddler assistant. Ms B stopped

> slightly awkwardly and folded her arms as though at a loss about what to do.
> She did not look rejected, but rather mildly amused. She started to play with
> another child whilst returning to her previous conversation. (2 years 4
> months)

Ms B's flexibility allowed the moment of separation; she did not interfere or impose herself on her daughter's play. She appeared to deal with this experience of a gap, or an absence of role, by engaging another child.

Amy became increasingly curious and independent. This was at times perhaps felt by her mother as rejecting. Even a "good enough" mother such as Ms B may show signs that this is a difficult and painful period for the mother, as well as for the toddler. The following observation, made four months later, showed a change in both mother and daughter's reactions.

> Amy went towards the table saying "I want to do a drawing". Ms B said "you
> want to do a drawing sweetie", and started to get out paper and crayons.
> Meanwhile Amy noticed the watering cans, and got them off the shelf. She
> walked across the room, paying no attention to Ms B who sat at the table
> ready to draw. Ms B watched this looking a little deflated and rejected. Amy
> walked, then jumped noisily across the floor. She went to the books and sat
> squashed in a corner looking at a book. Ms B watched her and put the paper
> and crayons away. She called across the room to Amy "Shall I read that to
> you?" but Amy did not respond, and again Ms B sat alone at the table
> looking somewhat sad and dejected. (2 years 8 months)

This observation demonstrated a shift in their relationship. Ms B's usual sensitivity in following Amy's interest did not produce the expected response from Amy. Considering that reading together was one of their favourite activities, Amy's rejection of her mother's offer was very significant. Amy's determined movement away and noisy jumping seemed aggressive and even provocative. Ms B appeared to understand Amy's behaviour as having this meaning, and seemed to feel the rejection.

As Furman (1992) explains, aggression towards the mother often takes the form of negativism. She describes a child who was not physically aggressive but often hurt her mother's feelings by disregarding her suggestions for activities or doing the opposite. At the same time, this child also rejected interactions from the toddler group workers. What at first appeared to be a loyalty conflict turned out to be a conflict around intense anger towards her mother. Furman's example resonated deeply with Amy's behaviour in the above observation. During this period, she often also declined the toddler leader and assistant's overtures. I wondered what Amy was so angry about, and what she was punishing her mother for. Both Mahler (Mahler et al., 1975) and Furman (1992) suggest that aggression towards the mother is a necessary and appropriate reaction to fear of loss of the mother's love. It is an essential part of the move towards separation and individuation. It can combine with, and be compounded by, the toddler's resentment over toilet training, which the toddler experiences as an impingement. The observation below occurred six weeks later and suggested that by this point in time, toilet training had been going on for a while.

> Amy seemed even more distant from Ms B than last week. She sat alone in the book corner, looking at a book with her back to the room. She made almost no eye contact with Ms B, as if blocking her out. She cried when it was time to go home, claiming that she did not want to go to granny's house. Ms B told the toddler leader that they were "making no headway" with toilet training. (2 years 9 months)

Amy's anger and exclusion of her mother seemed linked to her "making no headway" with toilet training. It gave me an impression of a struggle for power or control, with Amy resisting complying with her mother's wishes.

Furman (1994) suggests that the toddler's increasing separateness can cause great emotional hardship for a mother. Her child's growing independence means that she has to perceive her child as a separate object and no longer as a self-object. The mother loses the child as a part of herself and has to adjust to loving her as a separate person. Furman examines why this shift in investment is so hard for the mother, and the defences that mothers may use to defend against this narcissistic loss. She suggests that "The mother of the young child tends not to experience conscious anxiety; instead she turns the tables by leaving her child first, bodily or mentally, and unconsciously puts him in the situation of experiencing the overwhelming anxiety" (Furman, 1994, p. 154). I began to wonder if Ms B was using the idea of having a new baby as a defence against the loss that she felt as Amy moved away. Amy's tantrums, her solitary play, and her increasingly controlling and aggressive behaviour (described below) suggested that her unconscious experience of this wish produced "overwhelming anxiety".

The idea of a new baby

Six months into the observation (when Amy was 2 years 9 months old) Ms B told another mother that she was trying to conceive. Ms B had given up her identity as a professional woman, in order to become a mother to Amy. Amy was now behaving as if she no longer needed her mother. Into this gap came the idea of a new baby who would need Ms B totally. This new baby in Ms B's mind affected Amy, who then unconsciously had to deal with her loving and hating, needing and resenting her mother. I surmise that as soon as she achieved a new level of autonomy, her mother's wish for a new baby was felt as a rejection, which then led her to reject her mother further.

During this period of the observation, I observed Amy and her mother getting caught in a vicious circle of rejection, leading each one to move away from the other. This was difficult to experience as an observer. I found it hard to stay focused on Amy; I wanted to observe other children and resisted writing up these painful observations of Amy, perhaps as a defence against the feelings they stirred in me. On reflection, I wondered whether my feelings might have paralleled Ms B's experience. My wish to have a less painful experience of observing, by focusing on other "easier" children, might well have paralleled her wish to turn to a new baby, and so have a less painful experience of parenting (Wilson, 1980).

I think that Amy immediately demonstrated an awareness of mother's wish for another baby.

> Amy stood at the edge of the Duplo table. Close by, Ms B talked to another mum about trying to conceive a new baby. Amy was engrossed in her play, carefully putting Duplo figures in and out of different beds. Each time she gently covered them with a blanket. One figure was put in the bath and covered with a blanket. Ms B watched another child doing "frog jumps", and called to Amy to do frog jumps too. Ms B squatted on the floor in a frog position, trying to encourage Amy to join her. Amy continued with her play, barely looking in Ms B's direction. Then Amy bent her knees and did a tiny jump. Ms B commented on this with enthusiasm, but Amy continued to focus on the Duplo figures. (2 years 9 months)

I believe that Amy's play with the dolls represented her attempt at understanding the family dynamic, her place in the oedipal triangle, and perhaps her early theories on sexual reproduction: what Sigmund Freud (1905) called her "epistemophilic instinct". We could see the figures getting in and out of bed as her parents, and perhaps understand her play as a representation of a seen or imagined primal scene. The figure in the bath might represent Amy, excluded from the parental couple, and therefore isolated. The gentleness with which she covered them made me wonder if this was a defence against the aggression she felt about her exclusion and the possibility of being replaced. This play was so intensely absorbing and important that she would not be distracted from it, and only made a small attempt to "do frog jumps".

My sense of Amy in this particular toddler group meeting was that she felt disturbed and unsettled by the thoughts and fantasies that her play seemed to convey. Her play became more focused when she acted out both her interest and aggression towards the idea of a new baby, as can be seen below:

> Amy moved from the kitchen, picked up a train and gave it to the father of another child. She looked at Ms B talking to the toddler leader, then at a

child jumping on trampoline, and returned to the kitchen. She watched another child "cooking", suddenly ran back to the baby doll and then to the books. She didn't seem able to settle anywhere. She scanned the bookshelf, then looked in the cot. She started to bang the cot against the wall, holding it with both hands. She picked up a baby bottle, shook it, and started to feed a baby doll. She picked up two other bottles, and fed the doll using all three bottles. Each bottle was used for a two-second feed. She then had four bottles and then five, all lined up in a row on the floor. She seemed isolated, preoccupied and solitary in her play. (2 years 9 months)

Here I suggest Amy showed her aggressive wishes – banging the cot and shaking the "baby" – and that these were then manically defended against by feeding it with multiple bottles.

Another observation, later that day, suggested that Amy became overwhelmed by her own feelings of aggression and possessiveness, when thinking about the imagined new baby.

Amy sat on the beanbag "reading" a book to herself. Ms B sat nearby. Freddy and his mother came to Ms B, and as they started to talk, Freddy leant on Ms B's lap. Amy looked up, saw Freddy, and then kicked at his feet with her leg. She said, "No no no no no". Freddy's mother talked to Freddy, but he leant on Ms B again. Amy started to kick him more and again screamed, "No no no no no no". She looked very distressed, and remained so, even when Freddy was taken away by his mother. Ms B stroked Amy's head, and she calmed down. Amy then resumed reading. (2 years 9 months)

Ms B was able to contain and withstand Amy's aggressive outburst, and played a much-needed role in channelling and neutralising Amy's aggression. I thought that the aggression directed at the other toddler could be understood as a displacement of her original anger at her mother.

Relationship to father

Amy's father only appeared once in the toddler group, but provided Amy, and, I surmise, Ms B, with enough stability, support, and loving to enable them to survive these difficult times. The following observation occurred when Amy attended the group with her father.

Amy played alone on the floor with the dollhouse. She carefully placed the figures around the table. She seemed to be creating a family. She also placed some of the figures in bed. She was absorbed in this play for about five minutes. She then looked up to see where her father was. He sat on the carpet talking to the toddler assistant. Amy got up from the floor and walked around the edge of the room until she reached her father. He stretched out his arms saying, "hello sweetie". Amy smiled and fell into his arms, lying across his legs on her stomach, then curled up, like a baby between his legs and in his arms. (2 years 9 months)

This suggests that Amy and her father had an intimate and reliable relationship. Just like Ms B in an earlier observation, Mr B was available to Amy as soon she approached him, and he welcomed her warmly. Apparently pleased and reassured by this response, Amy fell into his arms and perhaps regressed happily to an earlier, less complicated because less ambivalent infantile experience. Both Mahler et al. (1975) and Furman (1992) suggest that the worst of a toddler's aggression is directed at the mother because she is the most important love object. Amy may have experienced her relationship with her father as less problematic.

The observation of Amy with her father occurred when Amy was still working out her ambivalence to her mother and reacting to the idea of a new baby. It may also be that as her father worked full-time, he was less involved in the complications of toilet training, and so received less of Amy's ambivalent feelings.

Lacan (1964) suggests the father acts as the third who comes between the mother and child to lessen their intense relationship and create a space in which the child can begin to separate and disidentify. I imagine that Mr B was able to function as a support to Ms B, to help her manage Amy's ambivalence and rejections, and so lessen any narcissistic threats. Mr B's presence and support may also have accounted for Ms B's general calm and self-assurance. She rarely mentioned him in the toddler groups, unlike other mothers who let off steam about their partners. In this family, it is important to acknowledge that there was a father, a third, and that therefore Amy and Ms B were not an isolated dyad.

Aggression

Having observed several examples of Amy's aggression, towards her mother, the doll and another child, I became curious about the development and experience of aggression for a toddler. I examined Amy's aggression in more detail.

I observed that Amy's aggression was at first controlled and defended against. When Amy was about 2 years 3 months, I noticed that she became very upset at a roaring sound made by the toddler leader who played with a boisterous boy. Following Furman (1992), I speculate that the roar itself represented her own growing internal experience of, and fear of, her own aggression. Furman (1992) suggests that at this early stage there is still some difficulty in differentiating self from other, and so anyone's anger could be one's own. The toddler worries that aggression could get out of control, and hurt others, or oneself. This fear of aggression stems from the toddler's weak ego that is unable to defend against the raw force of the toddler's own aggression and the real or imagined damage it could do. Furman proposes that some toddlers protect themselves and their mothers from mutual aggression by "giving it to . . . objects which they then feared" (Furman, 1992, p. 190). This is perhaps another reason why hearing others roar was so frightening for Amy.

By contrast, at 2 years 10 months, the idea of roaring was much less threatening and Amy was able to enjoy the excitement, and share this with another child:

> Ms B pushed Amy on a swing. Simon was being pushed by his mother in the other swing. The two mums chatted together. Simon started to laugh excitedly as he went higher. Amy was watching him and started to laugh. Soon both children were roaring with laughter, as they swung high in the air. Their mums smiled, and laughed too. Ms B said to Amy, "Are you a laughing lion?" Amy laughed and shouted at Simon gleefully, "you're a laughing lion, you're a laughing lion". Her whole body moved as she laughed. (2 years 10 months)

While observing, I was touched by how much freer Amy's movements and expressions had become. This suggested that her aggression had been neutralised, and could be released as excited laughter. Ms B's struggle to contain and tolerate Amy's aggression had succeeded, and drive fusion had started to occur, making these difficult feelings more tolerable. Ms B had survived Amy's fury and aggressive attacks, and so Amy was less concerned that her anger could destroy. I surmise that Amy had learnt that roaring can be fun, and because she no longer needed to fiercely defend against her own aggression, she was freer to explore other exciting feelings.

The story of toddler development is, however, rarely straightforward or simply progressive. As Blos (1967) highlighted, development is pendular, and unfortunately for Amy and her mother, external circumstances caused an understandable regressive movement at this point in Amy's development. Ms B's father, with whom they had been staying while moving house, died suddenly and unexpectedly. Ms B showed considerable sensitivity to Amy's needs by deciding to bring her to the toddler group. She told the toddler leader that she thought it would help Amy's stability. However this visit was only a day after the funeral, and both Ms B and Amy were (unsurprisingly) quiet and withdrawn. They retreated to their old and familiar reading in the book corner.

Amy's subsequent behaviour in the toddler group returned to its previous aggressive and controlling form. This can be seen in the following observation, made one month after their bereavement.

Amy hurt herself by falling outside and cried loudly. She allowed Ms B to kiss better, but not put a plaster on her scratched elbow and knee. She calmed down and went to play in a quiet corner. The toddler leader approached her and offered her some fruit. Amy screamed and pushed her and the fruit away. At the end of the meeting Ms B said to the toddler leader, "there is too much going on and Amy is feeling it". Amy became very upset when it was time to go home, pushing Ms B away. (2 years 11 months)

This sequence was painful for me to observe, as there was so much raw emotion close to the surface. I felt distressed on Ms B's behalf when Amy became angry and pushed her away at the end of the group. Here, I suggest, we can see how devastating the death had been for both Amy and her mother. Ms B's brief communication to the toddler leader suggested she must also be grieving. Her phrase "too much going on" is understated, considering that they had been staying with Ms B's father at the time of his death and were intimately faced with his loss. In reaction perhaps to Ms B's lowered emotional availability and resilience, Amy appeared to have been consumed again by her own difficult feelings, and was less able to use Ms B for comfort or emotional regulation than she had been a month earlier.

Concluding remarks

In the final week of my observation Amy was almost 3 years old.

At the end of the group Amy said to Ms B, "I don't want to go home, I don't want to go home". When Ms B didn't respond to this Amy shouted the same words at her. Then, suddenly her mood changed and Amy said, "Then going to the shops", and she walked outside to the pram without Ms B. Amy waited patiently by the pram, while Ms B gathered their belongings and said goodbye. Amy helped Ms B to push the buggy out of the gate, clearly not intending to sit in it. (Almost 3 years old)

Watching this gave me a sense of Amy's new-found independence and separateness. She knew she had to leave, and was able to avert the power struggle she knew she must lose. She found a face-saving compromise of deciding to go shopping. It was striking to watch her walking out of the toddler hut alone, and there was something remarkably grown up about her waiting by the buggy so calmly. My last sighting of Amy had symbolic resonance; she left not seated in the buggy, but walking side by side with her mother. This left me with the sense that there were two separate people in this relationship; they were no longer in a state of "symbiotic oneness" (Blos, 1967, p. 163).

Bergman (& Harpaz-Rotem, 2004) highlights that however emotionally available the mother is, the toddler's growing awareness of separateness and aloneness is painful. She writes, "A representational crisis was taking place that was not entirely contingent on the mother's behaviour or even her emotional availability. . . Both mother and toddler seemed to experience the loss of an earlier way of being together." Furthermore, she explains that the toddler's experience of depressive moods led to temper tantrums, and that loss and anger are understandable reactions to the toddler's growing awareness that "the mother could no longer be present in ways that were good enough: she could not repair the loss of the new awareness of separateness" (Bergman & Harpaz-Rotem, 2004, p. 558).

Bergman's words enabled me to imagine more of Amy's internal world at this time and therefore helped explain the intensity and ferocity of her behaviour. Indeed, I titled this chapter, "Normally difficult, and difficult normality", because throughout this observation I found myself wanting to watch a "good enough" toddler experience. However, watching how difficult it actually became, and noticing how hard this was to observe, I wonder if some of my anxiety about the health of their relationship was a reflection of emotions felt by Ms B, who might also have experienced Amy's increasing aggression, and rejection, with concern.

Had I observed this dyad for a shorter period of time, I would perhaps have reached different conclusions about the prognosis of their relationship. However, observing Amy and Ms B, over a nine-month period, and seeing how they survived and managed various crises gives me, I believe (and as Blos suggests), a more balanced overview. Furthermore, my reading of psychoanalytic theory of the toddler period reassured me that I was not witnessing anything more than normal difficulty in this mother–toddler relationship, despite their environment adding more pressure to an already stressful time. I therefore finished this observation with a strong belief that Amy and her mother survived – more than adequately – their time of difficult normality.

Chapter 6

Being seen to be able: The relationship between a partially sighted father and his daughters born with floppy baby syndrome[4]

Inge-Martine Pretorius and Julie Wallace

This chapter describes our work with two sisters and their father, who attended the Anna Freud Centre's parent-toddler groups over a period of 4½ years. Louise and Mary had congenital hypotonia (floppy baby syndrome), and their father, their main caregiver, was partially sighted.

The chapter considers the sisters' development, bearing in mind that a toddler's self-image, which is intimately related to her body-image, is the core on which her sense of identity is built (Greenacre, 1958), and that a child born with a congenital physical disability faces particular challenges in developing a positive self-image. Research has shown that, besides factors like the degree of pathology and the prognosis, the parents' attitude towards the child's disability is crucially important (Castelnuovo-Tedesco, 1981; Luiser, 1980). We observed that this father's own disability enabled him to be particularly empathic and attuned, and this facilitated the establishment of a sound self-image in his daughters. Father and daughters used the containing environment of the toddler groups to facilitate this process. Father and Louise attended IMP's group when Louise was aged 17–38 months, and father later attended JW's group with Mary, when she was aged 11–30 months.

Family background

Both mother and father had pursued professional careers until Louise's birth. Father, who suffered from a progressively degenerative eye disorder, became Louise's main carer when she was 5 months old and mother returned to full-time work. Louise and Mary were both born with benign congenital chronic hypotonia (floppy baby syndrome), a non-progressive weakness of the muscles (Berkow & Fletcher, 2002). Infants born with this syndrome have poor muscle tone and poor head control but, aided by physiotherapy, develop normally. Mary – born when Louise was 28 months old – had a milder form of the condition.

Louise and her father (IMP)

A very attractive and lively little girl, Louise babbled engagingly when she joined the group at 17 months. She was able to propel herself rapidly around the room by shuffling on her bottom and made her needs known through vocalisation and pointing. She occasionally shrieked loudly, perhaps frustrated by her restricted movement. Father revealed his attitude towards Louise's hypotonia on the day they joined the group.

> He said "Louise will walk when she's ready. There's no sense in pushing children – they do things in their own time". When a parent commented on her "bum shuffling" he said "Think of all the money I'm saving on shoes!" (17 months)

Father perhaps anticipated that others might think differently about Louise; that they might be impatient and try to push her. His words evidenced his optimism about her future development and concern that we share that optimism. He and mother seemed able to adjust their expectations of Louise, thus lessening the grief, shame and disappointment they might experience when she was not able to crawl or walk at the ages other children typically did (Wikler in Lamb & Billings, 1997).

Father's experience of his own very different and progressive disability perhaps made it easier for him to accept and feel confident about Louise's surmountable disability. It also seemed to make him more sensitive to other people's potential attitudes, and to Louise's experience – her enforced passivity and resulting potential frustrations. For instance, he showed awareness that her visual field was limited when sitting on the floor, and sometimes lifted her to see what the standing toddlers were doing on the table. He reported that Louise knew exactly what she wanted from an early age and started pointing for it at 6 months, adding that she was strong-willed like her mother. He seemed to perceive her as able and indeed, in this area, she was advanced. Pointing, to indicate the focus of attention, typically emerges at 9 months (Bates, 1990; Bates et al., 1987; Edgcumbe, 1981).

Louise's language development was also advanced. Father reported that she started talking at 1 year and by the time she joined our group (at 17 months), she was able to express her needs, feelings and frustrations. His habit of describing their actions as they played together, or verbalising affects, for instance, when a child cried in the group, probably facilitated Louise's capacity to understand and talk about emotions (Brown & Dunn, 1991). She once told me "it's pandemonium at home", showing her sophisticated vocabulary. However, unlike many children learning to talk, she did not create childish words; her speech was more imitative. When she was excited, she spoke very fast, becoming incomprehensible to almost everyone apart from her father. She also flapped her arms when she was excited or upset. Due to her poor control of the rest of her body, flapping her arms seemed to be her only means of discharging physical energy. The accelerated development of Louise's ego and theory of mind (as evidenced by her precocious pointing and verbal skills) was perhaps a compensation for her motor restriction (A. Freud, 1952).

Over time, father's willingness to share his own experiences and his empathy towards other parents established him as a core member of the group. He often sought me out to discuss an aspect of Louise's development, and showed appreciation of our conversations. He seemed to use me and the group to enhance his confidence in his parenting and to deal more effectively with his own frustrations, for instance at finding reading – a pastime he loved – increasingly tiring and difficult.

Empathy

At the time when she joined the group, Louise also began regular physiotherapy which improved her muscle control. Her shrieking disappeared soon thereafter. In the group, father and daughter showed an unusual awareness of each other.

> Father seated Louise on the floor and rolled some coloured balls to her. She named their colours as she caught them. Having gathered all the balls, she rolled them back to her father. A few balls rolled under the trampoline, out of father's sight. Louise called out their colours while pointing to them, "yellow, there, there". (21 months)

From an early age, Louise seemed to be aware of her father's poor sight. Unable to fetch the balls herself, she helped father to find them. In turn, father was sensitive to her attempts to control her body.

> Father pulled Louise around the garden on the wooden train. When she began to get off, father moved to help her. She said, "no, Daddy, Louise do it by herself," and father replied "you want to get off alone, okay then!" Louise hesitated and then leaned forwards and placed her hands on the grass. With considerable effort, she dragged her bottom to the ground. Father smiled proudly at her achievement. Later in the afternoon, Louise shuffled out of her father's sight. As he approached to find her, she said, "no Daddy". Father replied, "Daddy has to keep an eye on you once in a while," and moved away. (23 months)

Louise was becoming assertive and seemed determined to gain a sense of agency. Although she was unable to pull or push herself away as father approached, she told him verbally to go away. He allowed her space for trial and error, and this made it possible for her to feel that her father saw her as able. Having refrained from intervening unnecessarily when Louise pulled herself off the locomotive, he recounted his annoyance at being led across a street by a well-intentioned person who had not consulted him. His experiences of having his autonomy interfered with enabled him to be particularly respectful of Louise's attempts at independent mastery. Louise, in turn, showed an unusual understanding of and empathy for others as well.

> Louise looked at Alice's birthday balloons. She asked her father to tie one to her wrist, saying, "Louise walk with balloon". Father explained that they belonged to Alice, who would be sad if they were taken. Louise looked at the balloons for a few moments and then said, "Alice's balloons, Alice's balloons," and moved away. (26 months)

To act empathically, the child must be able both to imagine the self as an object who can be experienced by the other and to imagine the objectified other's subjective state (Stern, 1985). Despite her prolonged period of dependence, Louise seemed to have a clear understanding that others had independent feelings and thoughts. Father's careful explanations, combined perhaps with her awareness of her own vulnerability, may have contributed to this.

The need for movement

Louise's play seemed to be driven by her need for movement, rather than curiosity. She loved pushing cars or the little pushbike to and fro. These toys seemed to afford her a sense of control, mastery and activity that she did not yet feel in her body. She enjoyed rolling balls to her father or other adults, and preferred playing away from other children. Although she was a delightful little girl, I did not find it easy to play with her. She tolerated parallel play, but tended to become controlling and rapidly turned away from my attempts at interactive play with her.

At 22 months Louise began to pull herself to a standing position. One month later, she was able to walk from the garden gate to the toddler hut for the first time, holding her father's hand. It was difficult to discern whose face radiated more pride! The other parents (and students) celebrated her achievement. Louise was given her first pair of proper shoes for her second birthday.

Father commented that since learning to walk, Louise had become more physically affectionate, occasionally walking to him for a hug. It seems that when she could not physically move away from father, she did not seek proximity. However, once she was able to move away, she returned for regular emotional refuelling; behaviour typical of the "early practicing phase" (normally about 7–10 months) (Mahler, Pine & Bergman, 1975).

At two years old, Louise showed the exhilaration that is typical of a toddler in the "practicing proper subphase" (about 10–18 months). Her delight and pride in her newfound mobility was captivating. She preferred active play outdoors, irrespective of the weather! A favourite activity of Louise's at this time was to push a doll in a pushchair around the toddler hut. The pushchair afforded her some support as she practised walking and running. Perhaps, in this game, Louise identified with the passive doll and was turning passive into active in her play (A. Freud, 1936). Louise began to wear pretty hairclips decorated with butterflies or flowers and basked in our admiring comments, showing a growing pride in her feminine body and appearance.

Double frustration

Mary was born when Louise was 28 months old. Very soon thereafter, Louise started throwing dramatic tantrums that left her father feeling helpless.

> Struggling to get her leg over the pushbike saddle, Louise suddenly fell onto the grass. She started crying loudly, and refused the assistant's offer to help her up. Louise lay immobile on the grass, remaining where she had fallen, and becoming increasingly uncontained and upset. I approached, empathised and encouraged her to let me help her up, but she continued to refuse any assistance. Father came and picked her up, but she did not calm down. She remained very agitated, crying, flapping her arms and talking about falling on the grass. I stood with father while Louise oscillated between accepting and resisting comfort, fighting in her father's arms. His soothing talk and his offers to play with her and to help her back onto the pushbike did not calm her down. After about 10 minutes, he said he would put her down and when she had calmed down, he would play with her. She lay down on the grass and continued crying loudly. Eventually, father again offered to help her onto the bike, and this time she accepted. (30 months)

There was a theatrical quality to Louise's refusal of help and choosing to continue to lie in the position in which she fell. The intensity of her distress probably reflected her upset at her sister's birth, which was compounded by the further narcissistic blow of losing control over her body and falling. Rages and temper tantrums have been observed in children when the restraint imposed due to illness or a physical condition is lifted (A. Freud, 1952). During this period, Louise often refused father's comfort and became angry with him, leaving him feeling distressed and helpless.

Although Louise was showing the exhilaration of the "practicing proper subphase", she was not impervious to the knocks and falls typically observed in children in this period. She entered this phase much later than most children and her advanced cognitive skills and high expectations of herself may have made it especially difficult for her to accept her lagging physical mastery.

The emergence of Louise's dramatic tantrums coincided with our impression that father's sight had deteriorated. We made some changes to the hut – like painting white lines on the stairs – and started engaging Louise more actively in play in an attempt to promote her sense of agency and develop her emotional language.

Father started bringing Mary to the toddler group when she was 3 weeks old. Some months later, Louise started attending a nursery school in the mornings. Helped by her mother, she settled in well, but after a few weeks, father reported a distressing incident.

> Father reported that Louise had had some aggressive outbursts at school; she had thrown some chairs over and pinned a little girl to the ground. Father seemed overwhelmed and wondered whether he had contributed to this. He said that Louise hated having a dirty nappy, but that she hated having her nappy changed even more. He was concerned that his need to "pin her down" sometimes to change it had contributed to her behaviour. (34 months)

He went on to say that he was aware that he did not handle his daughters as patiently or gently as a woman might. This surprised us, since we perceived him as a gentle and caring father, and we wondered whether he was alluding to some latent anger at his own disability. Father's poor sight might have prolonged the nappy-changing process, which Louise then experienced as impinging. Her tantrums may have expressed a double frustration – both her own and her father's. Father also thought that Louise was aware that her peers were toilet trained and we discussed the possibility that her shame about still wearing nappies might also be fuelling her aggressive outbursts.

Physical disability has the capacity to stimulate the imagination and fantasy (Castelnuovo-Tedesco, 1981), but this did not seem to occur in Louise. Her rather concrete and repetitive play could be conceptualised as an ego defence of mastery and control, resulting from her early experiences of lack of control over her body (A. Freud, 1936; Sandler & Freud, 1985). Louise often left the realm of illusion abruptly. For instance, once, when her father playfully encouraged her to eat a banana, telling her, "it wants to be eaten," Louise replied, "bananas don't want to be eaten. Bananas don't want anything daddy!"

At 2 years 11 months, Louise still referred to herself by her first name. Most toddlers begin to use the personal pronoun "I" at 15–18 months (Bates, 1990; Edgcumbe, 1981). It seems that Louise's slow development of a sense of agency with respect to her body complicated and delayed her integration of different versions of "I" and "me" in the development of her self-concept.

Toilet mastery

Louise's play remained very active, as if she was catching up for lost time. She gradually began to allow my assistant and me into her games and showed signs of creating order in her play, suggesting a readiness for toilet training. This began before her third birthday. The following observation was made on her third birthday, when father had brought a cake to celebrate.

> Father said that Louise was being toilet trained and had had a number of accidents. After an accident at school, the teacher apparently called her "ignorant and a baby who should still wear nappies". Louise was ashamed and her father was furious. He said he had asked the mother to speak to the teacher, as he would have "exploded with anger". Father said that Louise wore nappies a few more days after that incident, and then she declared she was "a big girl now" and would no longer wear nappies. She had had very few accidents since making that decision.
>
> As everyone prepared to leave, Louise called for the potty, which her father produced swiftly. Louise used the potty and carried it proudly to show me – spilling much of the contents in her excitement! We emptied it together and praised her achievement. She flapped her arms and seemed absolutely thrilled (as were all the onlookers). (3 years)

The teacher's humiliating words seemed to have incited Louise to achieve toilet mastery (Furman, 1992). Father's fury at the teacher's insensitivity was perhaps heightened by his identification with his disabled daughter. He asked mother to speak to the school, fearing he would be unable to contain his anger.

Just as Louise had become more physically affectionate after she had learned to walk, so she started to show more vulnerability and sought more comforting, after she had reached this further milestone. Her enhanced sense of self and mastery seemed to lessen her narcissistic vulnerability, and this enabled her to seek comfort in an age-appropriate manner.

> While playing with the aeroplane, Louise tripped and cried loudly. Since her father was holding Mary, I went to her instead. Louise lifted her arms to be picked up and clung tightly to my body as I carried her to her father. Holding Louise on my lap, I sat next to the father as he held Mary. Louise said a few incoherent words between her sobs. She remained on my lap a long time,

> while father and I spoke to her softly. Once she calmed, she enjoyed choosing a colourful Elastoplast for her bleeding knee. (3 years 2 months)

When she left the toddler group at the end of that term, Louise had become a capable, confident and active little girl, aged 3 years 2 months.

Mary and her father (JW)

When I first met Mary, aged 11 months, she was a rather small child, with blonde hair and a serious expression. She sat in her buggy and listened as her father explained her condition in a very matter-of-fact way, saying that it just meant that her development would be slightly delayed. His tone was positive and accepting; he had been through it all with Louise, and everything was now fine. He explained his own condition in the same manner, omitting to say that this would also be fine. He did not want the rest of the group to know about his poor sight, saying that he would tell them in his own time.

I never met mother, who worked in a demanding profession. The effect of mother's absence could sometimes be observed in Mary's play and behaviour, and I experienced it in that I became a parental transference figure on whom both Mary and her father depended for support.

Father's deteriorating eye condition made his caring role more difficult, but his anxiety and frustration about it also made him especially sensitive to Mary's difficulties.

> When I noticed how much Mary was kicking her legs, he told me with feeling in his voice, of her frustration at not being able to crawl. (11 months)

Castelnuovo-Tedesco (1981, p. 145) notes that when psychopathology is linked with physical defect, it is often of the narcissistic variety, while some disabled individuals are "surprisingly unimpaired psychologically". Father's wounded feelings about his degenerative condition sometimes compounded his frustration about Mary's.

> Father brought a cake to celebrate Mary's first birthday. We played together with the "Duplo" house. Mary smiled at me and began to hand me the contents of the house. She struggled to retrieve parts of the toy. Father commented on the amount of energy she invested in her attempts to become more mobile, which rarely showed satisfactory results.
>
> When we shared out her birthday cake at snack time, another child stole Mary's piece of cake. Mary protested loudly, and father, who had not seen the other child's stealthy move, became quite angry with Mary for

protesting. I intervened and father admitted that he had not seen what had happened. He used this as an opportunity to explain to the parents about his eyesight. (1 year)

Reflecting on this incident, I could not decide whether father was feeling angry about the limitations imposed by his own disability or more concerned about the restrictions that Mary was experiencing. Momentarily, he had been unable to protect her from an external "threat". The strength of his reaction was unusual, and I understood it as a breakthrough of an impulse he more usually defended against expressing.

Mary was a very verbal child who used a number of recognisable words from about 14 months. As with Louise, this aspect of her development was accelerated as a way of compensating for delays in other areas. Many incidents demonstrated father's ability to understand Mary's feeling states, needs and wishes, and his patient willingness to help her express herself verbally and physically. Members of the group warmed to him as a "good father".

> Mary and her father went to play with cars, away from the noise and the rest of the children. She struggled to pull herself into a car, so father placed her inside. He said, "Look at this", while pushing the car's horn, "Can you do it? Look!" Mary tried to copy her father's action, but her fingers were too little and weak to make the horn beep. He responded to this by showing her the palm of his hand and then the palm of her hand, saying, "Do it like this". She managed to make the horn beep successfully, which made both of them smile. He responded, "That's it! Well done!" and he kissed her. (13 months)

During this interaction, their attention was focused entirely on each other. Mary's father responded to his daughter's needs effectively and both their expressions and movements were in tune with each other.

The preoccupation with movement

Like Louise, Mary was preoccupied with mobility; her play revealed a fantasy world in which the characters who were introduced were often riding on animals or driving cars. Similarly, she chose story books about transport and movement, which I felt expressed her wish to become more mobile.

In the following observation, Mary plays with the Toddler Leader while checking back to father.

> Father offered to wash up after snack time. I helped him initially to show him where to put the things and then went to play with Mary. Her

> increasing mobility was noticeable; she propelled herself around the floor on her bottom, using one arm to push herself along. She pointed to a toy vehicle. I identified the one she wanted and she moved towards me to claim it with a look of delight on her face. She played at moving it back and forth. When she managed to send it some distance, she shrieked with joy. Occasionally she turned to look at her father, to reassure herself of his presence, and then she repeated the sequence of play with another car. (14 months)

Watching her peers also stimulated forward movement. Greenacre (1958, p. 612), in her paper, "Early physical determinants in the development of the sense of identity" wrote, "The reinforcement of the sense of the own body by the constant association with others of predominantly similar appearance is apparent throughout life". I often observed how Mary would stop her activity to watch the other children toddling, and would then show an expression of excitement and an urge to move. Sometimes she flapped her arms excitedly or moved towards a toy that expressed her wish to become more independent. At other times, watching other children moving freely made her cry tears of frustration.

Double frustration

Father and daughter's difficulties sometimes compounded each other.

> As soon as she arrived, Mary became very busy. She crawled quickly to the double-decker bus, pushing and driving it. Then she moved toward another corner of the room to push a pram with a doll sitting in it. Later she crawled to the trampoline and pointed at a basket of balls, moaning. Her father followed her and asked, "What do you want?" Mary answered "Na, na, na" and threw a ball onto the trampoline. It rolled off and into a corner. When father could not find the ball, Mary's pitch increased. He said, "I cannot find it". Mary moaned some more and then, hearing the sound of a drum, crawled off to investigate. (16 months)

On this occasion, an interesting sound distracted Mary from the frustration that neither she nor her father were able to find what she wanted. On another occasion, her frustration escalated. Mary pointed to an object and father struggled to see what she wanted. Although he was very patient, picking up a number of different balls, the one she had lost had rolled out of his line of vision. While Mary flapped her arms and pointed with increasing frustration, I found myself feeling the frustration for them both, and verbalised this for them.

Both Klein (1946) and Winnicott (1960a) discuss the importance of the environment on the child's development, and emphasise that if the environment fails to adapt, the child's developing sense of self is lost and can be regained only by withdrawal and isolation. Defining disability as an environmental impingement, Thomas and McGinnis (1991) observed that the individual could adjust naturally to this impingement if a good enough (treatment) environment could be provided. Thomas and Garske (1995) apply Winnicott's (1960a) ideas to individuals with congenital disabilities. They emphasise the risk that a false self may develop if a child has to comply with an environment that impinges. While Mary's condition meant that she was at particular risk of developing a false self, because of the influence of her particular environment, I could not detect the presence of such a defence. An observation made after father had recovered from an eye operation, and was enjoying being able to read for short periods of time, supports this view.

> Mary shuffled on her bottom towards the bookshelves. Father followed and sat down on the beanbag in the corner, saying, "Good, you'd like me to read a story, I can sit down then". Mary sat below the bookshelves waving her arms and banging her legs. He interpreted this as her wanting a particular book, which he lifted. Mary increased her arm and leg movements, shaking her head, and saying, "Na, na" to indicate it was not the book she wanted. He picked out another and got a similar response. Father said, "Would you like me to read you Spot?" He lifted it and received the same negative response. He then lifted Mary to her feet saying, "I'll stand you up so you can get the one you want". She chose a train book with wheels attached, which father offered to read. Again, this was not what she wanted. Mary took the book from him and pushed it along the carpet. She smiled and father smiled in response. He said, "Ah! That's what you wanted to do". (17 months)

Neither party settled for a false solution, persevering until Mary had achieved what she wanted.

A few weeks later, I received a message from father in which he explained that they would be absent for a few weeks, as he had to have an operation. On their return, he was philosophical about his health problems, transferring his concern to Mary, who he had been unable to pick up for a few weeks. Her mobility had improved noticeably. Father held her arms while she made stepping movements.

Father's hospitalisation left me feeling concerned about this family's multiple experiences of disability and vulnerability. In the absence of Mary's mother, at times I became a maternal figure for father and daughter, while at other times, I occupied a paternal role, preventing father and daughter from becoming enmeshed.

> At snack time, father encouraged Mary to join the others at the table. She was not tempted by the fruit, but grabbed all the biscuits. Father explained

that she could not have them all, but she became increasingly upset. He moved them out of her grasp and she became rigid with fury. She cried so loudly that he carried her away from the table. I joined them and spoke soothingly to Mary about how upset she was. Father said she was "out of sorts" and wondered whether she was teething. I wondered aloud whether anything might help. At that point, the Toddler Group assistant brought out the musical instruments to play with another child. She encouraged Mary to join them. Mary did so, and her usual good humour returned. I said to father that he looked tired and he said he was; his wife had been away on business for some days, the girls missed her and the weather was awful. Louise was off school and Mary was throwing tantrums. He said he looked forward to his wife's return and appreciated the break provided by the group. (19 months)

The group provided space for father to express his disgruntled feelings, and both father and daughter had the opportunity to draw on the resources of people outside their relationship.

Achieving physical independence

At 20 months, Mary showed signs of attempting to walk and father helped her to toddle by holding her hands. He was clearly delighted with her progress and told me how independent she was becoming.

Mary seemed miserable when she arrived, but once father took her out of her buggy, she became more animated and made for her favourite toy. He told me that she was beginning to stand up and pull herself along by holding onto the furniture. He added that her speech was developing well, enabling her to make herself understood better. Mary demonstrated her independence by bottom shuffling off to join the children playing outside the hut. When we went to join her, she had momentarily disappeared behind the far side of the hut. She was sitting down, sweeping the plants. She smiled widely and shuffled back towards her father. (20 months)

Around this time, her tantrums increased. They seemed to be triggered when she could not make herself understood, or when she was about to leave. As other children were also finding it hard to leave the group at that time, I initially thought she was exhibiting separation behaviour similar to them. However I began to notice that she arrived in an agitated state and left in the same state. I wondered if her agitated behaviour was linked to the additional restriction of having to arrive and leave in her buggy, while the other children were able to walk.

Writing about the effect of invasive medical procedures on children in hospital, Anna Freud (1952) notes the observations made by Thesi Bergman, of children on an orthopaedic ward. Bergman described the defence mechanisms children employed to manage the restraints imposed on their mobility, and also the tantrums which appeared when the restraint was partially removed, or replaced in an unexpected way. Mary's recently acquired mobility, which was still less than the other children she observed, perhaps made the additional restraint imposed by the buggy feel unbearable.

> Mary watched another child pushing a toy buggy and shuffled over to get one. She pointed to the handles. I asked if she wanted to hold on and push. She said, "Yes" and I held her upright as she pushed the buggy, delighting in the activity. Father joined us and commented on how much stronger her muscles had become. Mary even managed to take a few steps unaided. When she wanted to go outside, father took over, explaining that it was tiring on the back muscles of the person supporting her. (20 months)

This seemed to be an occasion when the parent both wants to encourage a child's development, and is also adjusting to the behaviour of a less dependent toddler. On another occasion father told me that Mary's increased mobility put an additional strain on him, as he could no longer always manage to "keep an eye on her".

When Mary and her father returned after the summer break, I was delighted to see Mary walking unaided and exploring her favourite toys from a new perspective. The joy on her face as she looked down at the balls cascading down the chute was infectious. Sadly, father's eyesight appeared to have deteriorated further, and he spoke of his wish to keep Mary at home for as long as possible, emphasising that she would be his last child, and he wanted to see as much of her as he could.

Conclusion

Both Louise and Mary experienced considerable frustration as a consequence of their delayed motor development, and this was at times exacerbated by their father's visual impairment. However, congenital disorders are not experienced as a loss in the way that disabilities with a later onset are (Castelnuovo-Tedesco, 1981), and the girls' condition had a good prognosis. With support, father was able to keep this in mind, while at the same time using the experience of his own disability to be in touch with both their frustrations and their pressing need for autonomy and movement. Louise's inherent determination helped her to overcome her disability. She became a confident little girl, albeit with some unevenness in the development of her sense of self and ability to regulate affect (she still flapped her arms when excited or distressed). Mary, too, showed an attitude of quiet determination as she learnt to manage the frustrations imposed on her by her condition. She struggled to separate from a father who, perhaps because of the progression of his disability, appeared at times reluctant to allow this. At this time he leant more on the group and on the leader in particular, and their support helped to enable the separation process to take place. Ultimately, the parental (father, mother and group) attitude of acceptance and optimism, together with their empathy and sensitivity, enabled both girls to feel seen to be able, an experience that was essential to their development.

Part II

Adaptations and applications of the Anna Freud Centre approach

Chapter 7

Difference and disability: Experiences in a specialist toddler group

Jenny Stoker

"It's disturbing!" Mary's (2 years 11 months) comments about Harry's (2 years 10 months) incomprehensible mutterings were made with the uninhibited frankness that becomes increasingly rare beyond toddlerhood. She mostly dismissed Harry as a baby, but at times she had a striking capacity to articulate uncomfortable feelings on behalf of the group.

This chapter concerns the "Footprints" parent-toddler group at the Anna Freud Centre (AFC). More sheltered than other parent-toddler groups at the AFC, this group ran for two years and took referrals of children with special needs and developmental delay. As well as describing the background to the group and some of the work done within the group, this chapter will explore some of the uncomfortable feelings that Mary referred to, demonstrating how they were evoked in the group and how they affected its development.

Background

"Footprints" was initially set up as a group for toddlers with visual impairment and their parents, funded by a grant from the Inman Trust.[5] It aimed to answer a clinical need. The relationship between a parent and a child with visual impairment is known to be at risk (Fraiberg, 1977) and difficulties often arise towards the end of the first year. The absence of sight means that the normal patterns of relating between the baby and his carers, such as mutual gazing, joint attention seeking and social referencing, have been compromised (Fraiberg, 1977; Sandler & Hobson, 2001; Wills, 1965, 1979a, 1979b, 1981). Related professionals were unambiguously enthusiastic about the plan to start the group. The group was also expected to provide an opportunity to study the role of vision in a child's early development, continuing the tradition of work on visual impairment carried out in the Centre's former nursery for blind children (Wills, 1965).

Based on the AFC parent-toddler group model, the group was to have eight parent-toddler pairs, a leader and an assistant, as well as a visual impairment teacher to provide specialist expertise.[6] The group was to meet regularly for 1½ hours per week of free play and a structured snack time.

Development of the group

In the event, despite enthusiasm from the professionals involved with the target group, there were very few referrals. We will return to this later in the chapter, but at the time it seemed that medical advances meant there were fewer children with simple visual impairment than in the past. Not unusually, two of the children who had already started the group had other problems of developmental delay. Other professionals also reported that it was often safer and easier for parents whose children had a diverse range of difficulties to come together, as painful comparisons were not quite so easy to make. We decided to widen our criteria to toddlers with eye disorders and other special needs.

The group became a group for toddlers with special needs and their parents. "Special needs", "disabilities", "developmental delay" and similar terms were ambiguous in an important way. For these toddlers, even if they had a firm diagnosis, there was much that was unknown about their condition and how it would affect them in particular, which made the ambiguity necessary. Most of our parents had to live with uncertainty about the extent of the damage in their children, for example, uncertainty about whether their handicap was mental, physical, or both.

So, at about 1 year old, when the children joined the group, neither the staff nor their parents knew how much their children had in common with each other. The criteria were that they were atypical, and had been so from their earliest days. Difference from the norm defined the group's constitution. It described the parents' struggles and it also described the process of the group itself. Mary's comment, quoted above, shows that the disturbance evoked by difference was something with which these children were also already struggling. It was hoped that the common ground of the experience of difference from the norm would enable the parents and the toddlers to get more of a glimpse of ordinary, rather than atypical, emotional development and, in doing so, focus less on the impairment which was inevitably so often centre stage.

The main aim of "Footprints" was to help parents and their toddlers deal with the emotional impact of difference in the shape of constitutional impairment and to try to mitigate the risk of development of psychological difficulties which could compound the original problem. Many authors have highlighted the risk of secondary emotional problems in children with disabilities. Selma Fraiberg's (1977) pioneering work drew attention to the obstacles to establishing satisfactory attachment relationships between parents and their blind children. Valerie Sinason (1992) identified "secondary handicap" in children with learning difficulties. She thought of it as a defensive behavioural pattern where secondary exaggerations hide the pain of the primary disability. A number of papers from the Anna Freud Centre, as well as from the Tavistock Clinic, have focused on the interrelationship between congenital disorders or chronic sickness and emotional development in the child (Burlingham, 1979; Moran & Berger, 1980; Sandler & Hobson, 2001; Simpson & Miller, 2004).

The toddlers

The following portraits of three of the toddlers who came to the group are intended to give a flavour of the diversity of their special needs and the nature of the work with the children and their parents.

Mary

Mary was almost 2 years old when she joined the group. Bright and articulate, Mary had a disorder of the retina. Her eyes flickered and she had a poor sense of depth of vision. She was an active child, but took a long time to learn to negotiate stairs, the slide, and the swings. When they learned of her condition when she was only a few months old, her parents were worried that she would not be able to see at all.

On their first visit, mother asked staff if Mary looked normal, as she was worried that she would be picked on by other children when she started school. Mary's parents made good use of the group and contributed to it. They found issues in common with the parents of more obviously impaired children. They raised the issue of sibling jealousy of the child for whom there was so much concern and anxiety. They shared their worries about the future: their uncertainty about how much the disorder would affect Mary's day-to-day functioning, and their worries about how much they should tell others about her condition.

Her parents struggled with Mary's controlling behaviour, which would have been normal in a child a year younger, but was troubling with nursery school on the horizon. The staff helped them to think about how best to deal with it.

> Mary was reluctant to come in the door: she fussed about her shoes being dirty. The staff reassured her that she could wipe them on the door mat. Father said she was being extremely wilful and contrary at the moment. He mentioned that she no longer used nappies. She had had a few accidents, but had been dry the whole day at nursery the previous week. The toddler leader remarked that Mary was struggling to understand control: if she was expected to control her body why not other things she did? She said that the strain could be hard for children and they often regressed and became upset when they did not get their way. (2 years 6 months)

By the time Mary left the group it was hard to distinguish her from any other child her age, despite the visual impairment.

Adam

An only child, Adam had retinopathy of prematurity: a detached retina in one eye which meant that he could not see with it. He had some vision in the other eye, although there was uncertainty about how much. When he joined the group at 15 months, he was barely able to sit up and did not eat solid food. Mother had also been told that he was profoundly deaf and should wear hearing aids. Highly stressed at this stage, she struggled, like many parents of very young children with similar impairments, to get him to wear his glasses and hearing aids.

> Sitting propped up on the carpet, Adam seemed alert and watchful. He was wearing both of his hearing aids and his glasses. He seemed to tolerate them a little longer this time, especially if he could be persuaded to hold a toy in each hand, before he pulled them off. When his mother walked away from him, his gaze seemed to follow her.
>
> Mother appeared preoccupied and unable to focus on Adam for any length of time. She talked poignantly about how she had to rely on her medical relatives to help her understand Adam's health problems. They were more realistic about Adam than her immediate family who denied there was anything wrong. She found she had to persuade them, as well as herself, how badly the premature delivery had affected him. (15 months)

We listened sympathetically to mother's experience and played with Adam, encouraging mother to join in. They attended for a few weeks, but then did not return until several months later, by which time they had made much progress. Adam's alert curiosity was feeding the development of his fine and gross motor skills. Mother was immensely proud of his achievements and was taking more pleasure in him.

> On arrival, they settled on the carpet. Mother said that he could see quite well with one eye. He was hearing low register sounds. The doctors had removed his hearing aids. She still struggled to make him wear his glasses. He was crawling and almost walking, and was very active with a good appetite. He remained tiny, but was remarkably dextrous. Sitting on mother's lap, he climbed up her body for closer contact. After a while, he settled down to explore the instrument basket, picking up the toys in turn and examining them carefully with his right eye, before discarding them with great abandon.
>
> Later he cruised round the kitchen cupboards and staggered a few steps alone towards his mother. He moved towards the door, but then stopped

and bent down repeatedly to feel the texture of the mat under his feet, with his hands. He scampered across the room pushing a trolley, slightly out of control, but keeping up with it. (1 year 9 months)

Harry

Harry attended the group for the longest period of any of the children and is described here in more detail. His rare and complex condition caused global developmental delay and some visual impairment. Prognosis is particularly difficult with the disorder he had, because it is hard to tell how badly the child is affected. It can cause autistic-like features.

When he joined the group at 20 months, Harry was barely sitting up and it was hard to know how much he could see. He did not vocalise at all but blew raspberries, and groaned rather miserably when unhappy. His parents were not sure that he recognised them or that they were in any way special to him. He lay or sat propped up, responding to lights and to sounds, enjoying music. If he managed to do something like take a rattle in one hand, it was considered a major achievement.

> Harry picked up the tambourine and maraca. He stretched for them as if he could see them. He enjoyed banging the wooden stick on the drum. Later, he lay on his tummy kicking his feet on the floor, as if to make the musical toy that was sensitive to movement, play its tune.
>
> Father said that they had moved from complete preoccupation with his diagnosis, to becoming more accepting of the uncertainty about his future. Father knelt down and leant over Harry. He played with him and tickled his tummy affectionately. Harry seemed to enjoy it. Father lifted him up and gave him a hug. Harry melted into his chest and snuggled against him happily. It was touching and in striking contrast to father's concern that Harry might not really know him as special.
>
> At snack time, father sat beside him and stretched his arm around Harry to ensure he didn't topple over. Harry grasped the beaker of juice. Father put some little pieces of kiwi fruit into Harry's mouth, explaining that he had difficulty chewing food. Harry sucked at the tablecloth, but managed to drink well. (1 year 8 months)

During these early weeks, staff members took turns with whoever brought him – mother, father or nanny – to interact and play with Harry. They tried to stimulate him, but also just let him be and encouraged affection between him and his parents. As with many of the families who came to the group, it seemed important to counter the constant search for progress that the parents and professionals tended to focus on. They talked with Harry's parents about the importance of thinking about his emotional development, to counter the constant emphasis on his physical and medical problems. They reinforced the family's need for normal time, when the parents did not have to work so hard at Harry's physiotherapy. They discussed the strain of not knowing what the future held, the guilt and sense of responsibility for his disability, the differences in his parents' responses to the situation, and concerns about the impact of Harry's problems on their older children. The staff members also spoke with the parents about their feelings when they saw children who were developing normally and their wish to be in touch with families with similar problems.

> Mother mentioned her concern about Harry's lack of progress. She liked to plan and she found it difficult to be so uncertain about when and whether he would be able to walk, and what school would be best for him. While we talked he picked up the shakers, favouring the yellow one. Mother played a teasing game with him, hiding it and offering him the blue one. She tried to get him to give her one. He did not do so, but he seemed to enjoy the sound of his mother's voice and playful involvement by smiling as she moved the little instruments around. He fell over a little later and grizzled, lying on the floor. Mother cheered him up by leaning over him affectionately and stroking his face with her hair. He smiled and seemed to enjoy her tickling. She also played a game asking him where his nose was and touching it. She was like a mother with a 6-month-old, and it was moving to see Harry respond so delightedly. Later, for the first time ever, he fell asleep on her lap.
>
> She talked about how it was hard to get the balance right between stimulation and over-stimulation. They wanted Harry to learn to take the initiative. At weekends they tried not to do so much for him and give him a more ordinary life. (1 year 9 months)

As time passed his parents' feelings about children with more minor problems than Harry joining the group were addressed. This was clearly painful for them, but they were philosophical about it, realising that everyone made comparisons and that despite many differences, they also had things in common.

It was easy to get drawn into the search for progress and at times this was appropriate – for example, it seemed important to talk with the parents about the staff's impression that Harry identified them as special, and to point out how his cries of delight in anticipation of bath time or of misery at nappy changing time were signs that he had a memory and an awareness of a world outside himself.

It was difficult to know how much Harry could see. His eyes diverged and moved around a lot, making it hard to tell if he was looking at anything at all. He did seem to stare and be troubled by the lights and he could reach for toys that were held close. There was a breakthrough soon after he joined the group, when he was given some wooden puzzle teddy bear faces that depicted different emotions.

> He leant closer to look at them and became fascinated by the "surprised" face. He stared at it and giggled, apparently searching it out and turning it back the right way up if it was turned upside down. (1 year 9 months)

The toddler group leader occasionally met Harry's parents on their own, at their request, to talk about their relationship with their oldest child who had become possessive of mother. They also discussed whether it would be appropriate for Harry to start nursery at that stage, and his parents decided against it.

Harry made great strides – literally – in his second year at the group. Intensive physiotherapy meant he could spend much of the group standing at and cruising along a table or counter. He could walk if he was supported with one hand. This increased mobility enabled him to turn towards the other children, and he began to express an interest in their activities. He seemed to be purposeful in his movements. With grommets in his ears he could hear better and he began to vocalise a little. When his parents complained about his tantrums, they were helped to see them as a positive development, showing that he had a will of his own; perhaps he had even picked up that others had wills of their own too, which had to be countered, in a way that was very typical of normal toddler development.

> Father talked of having had a difficult week. He and his wife had gone away for a short break, leaving Harry with relatives. The relatives had called them, because they were worried that Harry was very ill. His parents had a nightmare journey home and took him to hospital. The doctors found nothing wrong and the parents felt very confused. The toddler leader wondered if Harry had missed them and was upset about being left with people he did not know. Father thought he might miss his nanny but not them. He agreed that Harry had started to communicate: he now held his arms out to be picked up. (2 years 7 months)

Harry continued to make progress, to his mother's delight:

> Harry suddenly grasped a bit of orange and put it in his mouth. He then stood up on his own and sat back on his chair. Mother sang a song in excitement, "Bravo, Harry, bravo. . ." Harry stood up again. Later, mother took him to the kitchen where he played with the phones and then with a bucket, turning it around and exploring it. (3 years 2 months)

For any other child, mother's response would seem manic and overexcited but Harry was achieving much in terms of his own abilities and it is likely that she was relieved to see signs of his progress. For children like Harry who seem so unfocused on the outside world, one has to be exaggerated in one's activities in order to get a response.

Different group: Different aims

We will now return to those uncomfortable feelings that Mary spoke about, quoted at the start of this chapter, by examining the ways that the group developed and changed from its original aims.

Firstly, referrals were very slow. Although this improved slightly once the criteria were widened, it was nevertheless impossible to find eight parent-child couples to attend regularly. One reason was probably that, even though cab fares and parking were paid, there were not many toddlers with special needs within striking distance of the AFC. Of those who did live close by, many were "appointmented out". Furthermore it seemed that it was difficult for parents who were just coming to terms with a diagnosis, to come to a group which would either confirm the diagnosis ("I cannot face being included in a group of children like that – my child's disability cannot be so bad") or worry them, because their child's disability was worse by comparison with the others in the group and they could not bear to be with others who were better off than them. It seemed possible that parents who were struggling to come to terms with their predicament might be worried that their precarious defences might be vulnerable in a group setting, particularly when that group was about emotional functioning rather than anything concrete like physiotherapy or speech therapy.

The staff came to wonder whether their experience of having given birth to a baby (i.e. the group itself) that few seemed to want was related to and resonated with the parents' feelings of having given birth to a baby that was not wanted. Like the parents, their high hopes for their "baby" were followed by disappointment. In their frustrated wish to provide they were perhaps picking up on the parents' frustration at the unresponsiveness of their child.

Secondly, some parents' attendance was very intermittent, and the group functioned much more as a drop-in service. This made it difficult to build up the sense of continuity and trust experienced in the other AFC parent-toddler groups. Again, these families had very real time pressures on them. However, it was as if the staff's exposure to their unpredictable attendance and difficulty in maintaining continuity was a reflection of the degree to which the parents felt an absence of predictability and continuity in their child's development. Perhaps in response to feeling cast out from normal expectable patterns of child development the parents were casting the staff out, and testing them to see how much they wanted them.

Thirdly, friends and other members of the family often attended with the toddlers. It was as if parents needed additional support when they came to the group, bolstering their defences in this way and somehow protecting themselves from the staff and other members of the group.

A further difference was our awareness of a sense of competition between professionals. This might partly be to do with the low level of referrals, and competing provision for these toddlers. However, working alongside other professionals, we became aware of the strength of pressure to make reparation that motivated many of those who do wonderful work in this field. Niedecken (2003) writes about the unconscious grandiosity of professionals who try to protect the learning disabled from society's death wishes. But she also movingly describes the consequences: how she and her colleagues would be utterly committed to helping the children they worked with, only for their own omnipotence to be tested at some point, which then led to overwhelming feelings of helplessness, and anxiety. Ashamed and feeling like failures, they would break off the relationship. It seemed there was a risk of division, mistrust, disillusion and desertion among the staff that might undermine the provision.

A final difference in our group was our difficulty with engaging mothers. Fathers and nannies in the main brought the children and, apart from one, mothers were noticeable by their absence. At the start we noticed that our insistence on parental involvement meant that we excluded many referrals – it seemed many of the mothers returned to work, having arranged child care. They found that their developmentally delayed child showed no sign of separation anxiety and settled easily with strangers. The toddlers who did come tended to have fathers who had more flexible work, which gave them time to accompany their children to the group. In other cases, the mother started, but then found competing demands from work or training, which meant that a nanny then brought the child. These seem like very real issues, but it also led us to wonder about the frailty of the maternal defences, which perhaps made it hard for mothers to attend a group which focused on emotional wellbeing.

One hypothesis could be that mothers in particular felt overwhelmingly responsible for their child's impairment. They also felt tremendously anxious about what the future held and struggled with a sense of isolation with the problem. One mother talked with enormous feeling of the unfairness of their predicament and of the constant pressure to implement the various therapeutic techniques her physiotherapist and speech therapist required of her and her son, in order to maximise his potential for development. Of course, there is often a real need for physical intervention to help move these youngsters forward, but it was as if these mothers lived with guilt for the past damage and the anticipation of guilt for present damage if they were not superhuman in their reparative work. It was as if, unconsciously, they felt that they had given birth to a monster (Niedecken, 2003) and they were compelled to rid themselves of that role with the pressure they put themselves under. And all this when they were having to deal with the trauma of coming to terms with the diagnosis and having to mourn the loss of the perfect baby repeatedly, in their daily contact with their impaired child. It was hardly surprising that the mothers tended to be more preoccupied and more limited in their capacity to give to their child than the other caregivers, and that we found them difficult to engage.

Many questions remain. Toddlerhood normally arouses ambivalence in parents, but do parents of impaired children have more intensely ambivalent feelings about their toddlers? How can we find the evidence? Does the degree or kind of disability make a difference? Did coming to the group have any impact on the conflict experienced by the parents?

Research

In order to move towards answering some of these questions, a research focus was built into the group from the start. At the beginning and the end of their child's time in the group all the parents attended a semi-structured interview[7] that attempted to capture their experience of parenting. This tried to establish both whether they had particular difficulties in being reflective about their child's emotional experience and also to find out if their reflective capacity changed at all during the period they brought their child to the group.

Ethan Schilling, an MSc student (2005–2006), analysed four of the parents' responses to the initial research interview. He concluded that there was some evidence that parents found it "difficult to think about feelings within relationships in a reliably highly reflective way . . . and most responses (especially concerning the children's feelings) were not elaborated or convincing enough to be judged to reach a level of definite or ordinary reflective functioning". Underlying this, he identified themes that seemed to reflect a deep ambivalence towards the children: perceptions on the part of the parents that the relationship with their child was difficult for much of the time with very little reciprocal interaction, that it was time consuming and demanding, evoked much anxiety for the future, but also that it brought moments of joyful interaction. This was a very small sample, and as yet there has not been a control group study, but the findings do seem to confirm some of our overall general impressions.

Conclusion

Finally, returning to Mary's disturbed feelings, she was nearly 3 when she made the remark quoted, and issues of control were paramount. If she was struggling to control her own unconscious destructive wishes and impulses, it is perhaps not surprising that she found Harry's behaviour so disturbing.

But how are adults affected?

The fundamental reason for the differences between Footprints and the other AFC groups is that disability in babies and young children evokes powerful and disturbing feelings in everyone. Faced with the damage in the child, about which nothing can be done, it is as if adults are reminded of their own frailty and mortality. Despite their best intentions, at an unconscious level the child may represent a threat to creative vitality and potency. Without being consciously aware of it, there may lie deep within everyone a fear of becoming a failure like them, a fear of being contaminated by them, a fear of their dependency, and a fear of their potential lack of control. With the exposure to the loss of predictability and to their possible unruly impulsive behaviour comes anxiety that the atypical child may become an embodiment of unconscious unacceptable drives. Such feelings, of course, are often evoked in parents by ordinary toddler development – issues of control are typical of this phase – but what is different in relationships with these children is both the intensity of the internal conflict and the fear that it will continue in the future. With these impaired toddlers we fear that as they grow, we will be faced with what we have learned to control. Unconscious and unacceptable wishes risk eruption and it is this that upsets our equilibrium, pushing us into defensive positions of omnipotent reparation or feelings of failure and helplessness.

Chapter 8

Running a toddler group on a council housing estate: Invisibility, intrusion, dislocation and the importance of boundaries[8]

Lesley Bennett

This chapter describes running a toddler group on a large housing estate.[9] Psychoanalytic ideas and understanding are used to think about this particular context and its impact upon individuals and the group. We examine the role and function of parent organisations in helping make sense of issues that can arise between groups competing for and sharing scarce resources. Our experience of running this group shows that careful management of boundaries is as necessary for the healthy life and survival of a group as it is for the healthy development of the toddler. In thinking about the nature of this community toddler group, we will consider the vision that appeared to define the way that this particular estate was originally conceived by its planners. Issues of dislocation, invisibility, and intrusion, which reverberate within this community and have impacted upon both individuals and the group, will be illustrated with vignettes and observations. The importance of maintaining but communicating across boundaries will be highlighted.

The birth of the group

In 2003, the Anna Freud Centre (AFC) secured funding from Sure Start to run an outreach parent-toddler group in the community. The aim was to provide for parents and toddlers who might find it difficult to come to the AFC or local Sure Start Children's Centre. This aim of engaging vulnerable hard-to-reach families was jointly held by both organisations.

The funding was to provide toys, a leader and an assistant to run the group along the therapeutic lines of those run within the AFC, where regularity, continuity and maintaining reflective thinking within a protected space are seen as important. Members could attend on a "drop-in" basis, in keeping with the Sure Start model, but were encouraged to come regularly. Sure Start identified a venue on the estate and provided the Council responsible for maintaining the estate with funding for its refurbishment. In exchange, Sure Start was allowed to use the building to run several groups, though no formal contractual agreement was recorded. When the AFC toddler group began to use the hall for one afternoon each week, the building also became the venue for other new groups, including a youth group, a group for breastfeeding mothers and a second toddler group.

Brief history of the estate

The estate was designed in 1969 and building went ahead despite vehement opposition from local residents. The architect attempted to preserve urban living by applying the principles of terraced housing to the high-density requirements of the Council. A further consideration in its design aimed to limit sound from the trains that run its length. Rows of terraced apartments aligned in parallel with the track were arranged along the boundary to block noise from reaching the interior of the estate. Likened by some to "two large centipedes crawling into the distance", its dramatic tiered construction, while not to everyone's taste, was subsequently acknowledged with the granting of Grade II listing.

Maintenance of the estate has declined over the years and it now seems that only families with little choice available to them are moved there. Many of them struggle with poverty, social isolation and immigrant or refugee status, having fled from various war-torn areas around the world.

While the original aim was to insulate the inside of the estate from unwanted noise, it has come to feel as if there is an impermeable wall which prevents exchange with the outside environment. This impenetrable barrier serves to isolate the residents and impedes effective connections with the wider community. Families say that their mail is not delivered because postmen cannot find their apartments, and several visitors to the toddler group lost their way and failed to arrive.

Boundaries

Boundaries are important for toddlers to develop as healthy and separate autonomous individuals, and also for groups, organisations and communities to thrive and function. The concept of the organism, described by Vega Zagier Roberts (1994), is a helpful framework within which to think about community-based work with groups.

According to Roberts, essential to the healthy existence of an organism is "an external boundary, membrane or skin which serves to separate what is inside from what is outside" (p. 28). She suggests that "boundaries need to be solid enough to prevent leakage and to protect the organism from disintegrating, but also permeable enough to allow the flow of materials in both directions". If the boundary is impermeable then the organism becomes a closed system and will gradually perish. With this notion of exchange comes the important function of regulation, so that only certain materials enter and leave. Consequently, the boundary needs to be managed so that the task of the organism can be carried out.

Roberts stresses that in complex organisms where a number of open systems perform specialised functions, their activities need to be co-ordinated to serve the needs of the organism. Management systems are usually developed to provide this co-ordinating function. In times of stress or of crisis, the activities of some subsystems may need to be prioritised over others.

Psychoanalytic ideas can be creative in trying to make sense of and deal with issues that can arise. Like individuals, groups and organisations can develop defences against difficult emotions that are too threatening or painful to acknowledge. Such emotions can arise from conflicts between groups, especially when they are in competition, like rival toddlers, for scarce resources.

> Several weeks after the AFC toddler group was set up, the breastfeeding mothers' group arranged to meet earlier on the same day. Its inauguration cut across three toddler group sessions, which had to be cancelled at short notice. Initially, the breastfeeding mothers' group departed promptly, although the staff often remained in the hall to chat. Their manager also ran the other toddler group, which lost members after a while. After speaking with the AFC leader, whose group was well attended, the manager changed the other group's time to the afternoon only to find that its numbers still did not pick up. Concurrently, the AFC toddler group began to find that the hall was not vacated before their arrival. When they raised the difficulties this created, this was met with some hostility. The other staff advised their mothers that they were "in the way" of the AFC group. Soon after, they moved from the hall into a Health Centre, with the consequent "drying up" of numbers of mothers transferring from them to the AFC toddler group.

The group

The AFC toddler group continued to meet in this venue for four years. An initial core group was formed from several of the original parents who felt ownership of the group, one of them even offering to clean the hall when maintenance declined. Over time, other members joined and there continued to be a small core of regular attendees, despite many ongoing difficulties that were sometimes experienced as attacks.

Provision of a safe, protected space for parents and their toddlers was important, so that the ordinary mess and aggression associated with the emerging mind of the toddler could be tolerated, managed and experienced as ordinary rather than persecutory. Space for reflection became a significant function of staff supervision provided at the AFC, so that attacks on the group could be managed and survived.

The following diary of selected events illustrates some of the challenges of running this group, how these were thought about and managed, and how they have come to be understood within the context of the estate and its history and the lived experiences, both past and present, of the residents. Their traumatic experiences of dislocation, invisibility, and intrusion were experienced by the group, and indeed the staff. Difficulties which arose between groups and also at the interface with the community highlighted the need for effective management of the boundaries and clear, thoughtful communication.

At this point, I would like to describe something of the immediate surroundings and difficulties with access for our parents and toddlers to give some sense of the effort, both physical and psychological, that was needed to attend the group. The reader may feel that I am focusing too heavily on describing the external situation rather than what happened "inside", and I would say here that it is often difficult to reflect upon the internal world without first thinking about those external features that can be "defined", in order to create a sense of a safe space within which to think and function.

The hall provided a spacious area for play. The room was surrounded on two sides by windows that, because elevated, gave a broad vista of the estate for the person inside looking out. However, from the outside, the hall was virtually invisible to the passer-by. It was raised up on a plinth behind a wall, reached by steps that presented difficulty for parents with pushchairs and toddlers. When the hall was empty the windows were covered by sliding metal shutters to prevent vandalism. Running floor to ceiling, they were operated electronically and were visible confirmation of the dangers that existed on the estate, seeming to represent the barriers residents faced in trying to take ownership of their neighbourhood and function together as a community.

Little was known about the families when they joined the group. Their backgrounds emerged only gradually as trust developed. Families were not referred, but heard about the group through word of mouth and said that they came to meet others and for their children to play. Around 30 families attended during the four years the group met in this venue. Some managed to attend regularly, while others came spasmodically. The group, which was originally intended to comprise around eight families, varied in size, rising to 13 families and children at one point. We turned no-one away.

Invisibility

Our families came from different ethnic groups from across the world and possessed varying abilities to communicate in English. Several were asylum seekers from war zones, some were refugees and others were materially impoverished. All were housed on the estate; some had lived there for several years. Despite the architect's vision of urban living, with its connotations of close neighbours and neighbourliness, few families knew others on the estate, let alone outside it. Everyone seemed to feel isolated, with many dislocated from their families and cultures. The toddler group became a link between some of them, and a reason to speak with one another at chance encounters.

> One of our group members had seen a pregnant woman at the elevator. When she saw her later with a baby in a pushchair, she told her about the toddler group. Though she had lived in her flat for eight years, Sophia did not know her neighbours and felt isolated. She came to the group but for several weeks remained distant, sitting alone on a bean bag engrossed in the Highway Code. She said she hoped to learn to drive as a way of getting off the estate.
>
> Her toddler, Jeb (17 months) raced around the room grabbing and throwing toys. We tried to engage him in play, commenting on his excitement while encouraging him to pause to explore the toys by modelling curiosity in them ourselves. These attempts to develop a joint focus of attention were punctuated by Sophia, his mother, shouting from her position on the bean bags.

I will focus upon this mother–child couple, who became regular attendees, for the sake of continuity and to illustrate how the situations of individual members were mirrored in the life of the group and the community.

Just as the estate, likened to a centipede, was resisted by the local community at its birth, so the residents, often dislocated from their own family communities, felt invisible and rejected by the wider community within which they found themselves. This appeared to have been so since the estate was erected.

Intrusions

We experienced frequent intrusions into the group. During one session, a woman burst into the hall and shouted at us because lights had been left on the previous night. On other occasions, youths intruded. Youth workers were permanently based in an adjoining office and the youth group used the hall at another time. The turbulence and unpredictability of adolescent life was evident on the estate and in and around the hall.

> The door was thrown open and a hooded youth rode in on his bicycle. Adults and toddlers were startled. Several children ran to their mothers, others further away remained motionless. The leader spoke to the youth, who responded that he was looking for the youth group leader. With relief, she directed him to the office and he rode out, avoiding the toddlers with considerable skill. Attempting to contain the intrusion, she commented on the unexpected nature of the visit, saying to the toddlers that the big boy

had surprised us and had now gone to the office. Mothers complained about the youths on the estate and it was several minutes before the toddlers settled somewhat warily to play.

Graffiti were another way in which the adolescents made themselves known and seen. Gang culture had grown in several estates during the 1990s and had culminated in a murder on this estate in 2001. The graffiti, intimidating for the residents, were the medium through which gang members sought recognition.

When a rival gang member lined out a local youth's "tag", a fight between them ensued resulting in one youth being stabbed and killed within the estate.

The outbreak in the community of actual violence linked with terrifying experiences that some of our parents had lived through in their countries of origin. This was illustrated when another murder occurred on the estate during the life of the group.

"Man stabbed to death in a flat on the estate". Reported in the press under the headline, "Wall of fear blocks hunt for killers", the police were "stone-walled by residents who were terrified of retribution" (*Camden New Journal*, June 2006). The wall (of fear) like the façade of the estate, separated the community from the outside world and represented an impenetrable boundary.

AFC staff arrived unaware of this event. Most families attended this week. Initially, the mothers were subdued while the toddlers were unsettled. The staff commented on the toddlers' excitable and risky behaviours. Gradually, the mothers spoke of rumours about the murder. Each had their own version and their debate about what had "really" happened grew in intensity until their emotions mirrored their toddlers'. Sophia, who had until this time been a disconnected member of the group, disconnected too from Jeb, her son, and became animated by this shocking event. She and another mother argued about the method and motives for the murder. The staff were concerned for the toddlers and reflected with the mothers on their children's understanding; what they were picking up about their parents' anxiety about keeping them safe and their risky behaviour in the group that day. Sophia said that her older children were afraid to walk with her to school and that she felt bad because she could not prevent them from knowing about the violence. She was frightened herself.

Sophia spoke for the first time of her departure from her homeland, describing murders and other terrors she had experienced there. She said she felt no safer here and had difficulty leaving her flat. We were able to think with her about how she successfully managed to take her children to school, bring Jeb to play at toddler group and keep her children physically safe. We began to be able to understand Sophia's difficulties with managing Jeb's ordinary toddler aggression and emerging quest for independence.

The parents were so preoccupied with personal safety that it was sometimes difficult to support them in thinking about how to help their toddlers develop an understanding of others' minds. Frequently, the staff questioned their ability to apply the therapeutic principles that underpin the AFC approach adequately within this context. However, since the parents continued to attend the group, some very regularly, one could speculate that the regularity and provision of a welcoming play "space" within a predictable and psychologically safe environment was "good enough". It felt safe enough for Sophia to talk, albeit fleetingly, about triggered memories of trauma that she thought she had left behind. Perhaps a sense of trust and expectation was conveyed that was helpful to both the parents and the toddlers.

> Gradually, Sophia herself began to play, wearing the dressing-up hats to great effect and fashioning wonderfully delicate items from the play-dough. We admired her creativity and skill, and she drew some of the other toddlers into her play. After she had been coming to the group for some time, she created a figure reclining on a sofa and we reflected on how comfortable the sofa looked and how rested the woman seemed. We wondered whether Sophia had come to think of the group as a place of respite, containment and comfort. Meanwhile, Jeb started to engage, extend and show some imagination in his play.

Being found

A favourite game that gradually evolved in this toddler group was "hide and seek", reflecting the losses, felt invisibility and dislocation experienced by the families, and their wish, perhaps, to be found.

> Jeb often stumbled into the hall, not connecting with the staff, his mother or other toddlers, who continued to be treated as objects from whom he grabbed the toys he wanted. Frequently ignored by his mum, Sophia, except for the occasional shouted reprimand, Jeb was difficult to engage.
>
> During one session, Jeb (2 years 6 months) crouched behind a bean bag. One of the staff noticed him, peeped across and commented playfully that Jeb was missing. Where was he? To her pleasure he popped up and much was made of "finding" him. He bobbed down again several times, laughing loudly as he burst out to surprise us. Lucy, a younger, quieter toddler watched and giggled from the safety of her mother's lap. Lucy had previously been wary of Jeb, who often blundered over her, much to her mother's consternation.

The following week Jeb jumped over the bean bag and hid again. The hide and seek game resumed, much to his delight. This time, Lucy hid too and, helped by the staff, one with each child, they took turns hiding and then seeking. With the adults' support, both children were able to wait a few seconds before being found by the other.

Some weeks later, Jeb and Lucy created their own hide and seek game, just the two of them and in a different area of the room. Jeb was becoming more aware of Lucy as another person and managed to offer her the beloved baby doll for which they both had a passion and whose hair Sophia had brushed and braided. In turn, Lucy was less anxious when Jeb came near and could stand more firmly and laugh with him.

Management at the boundaries

The development of a joint focus of attention, learning about taking turns, tolerating delayed gratification and managing frustration are vital lessons for a toddler. The parent's management of the toddler's intense feelings in a safe, calm way can make the toddler's strong feelings more digestible, and is important if the child is to internalise this process for himself.

Groups that share resources also need to recognise that the other has similar needs and a "mind" that wishes to be thought about. The "parent" institution needs to provide reflective and clear communication across containing but permeable boundaries or, as Roberts (1994) describes, "management at the boundaries".

The youth group moved out one summer. This meant the end of the interruptions by youths but also of the presence of other life in the hall, and there was no longer a cleaner. The hall grew grimy and sometimes hazardous objects, including drugs, were found. The leader visited the Council and Housing Association offices nearby and was advised by each that responsibility for maintenance lay with the other. Since there was no written contract, both the AFC and Sure Start felt in a weak position with regard to insisting upon cleaning. Moreover, no other Sure Start group now used the hall. To minimise health and safety issues for the families, the AFC staff swept, provided toilet tissue and, literally, cleaned up others' excrement and waste. They felt exhausted and angry, and drew parallels with their families' experience of invisibility, neglect and abandonment.

The following spring it became evident that another group was using the hall. Toys went missing or were found broken or in disarray. This was a concern as, developmentally, the older toddlers were beginning to show a capacity to be able to hold people, games and objects in mind, seeking out favourite toys to which they had become attached. As the AFC approach nurtures regularity and consistency to help toddlers, in turn, to feel reassured and held in mind from one week to the next, caring for and preserving a space for the toys, as far as was possible in a busy setting, seemed fundamental to showing care too for our children and parents.

We learned that a council-run Day Nursery now met in the hall for two days each week. We reflected on the issue of sharing toys with a "phantom" sibling group and the frustrations of finding disarray each week. It felt particularly persecuting to find that objects that had been carefully repaired had been broken again and the destruction, though focused on small items, seemed relentless. Our initial feelings of dismay intensified and turned into toddler-like fury! When, at times, the breakages felt like deliberate malice, they engendered such strong feelings that we felt like retaliating. The ongoing difficulties were brought frequently for discussion to the AFC team meeting, whose role, much like that of the parent, was to help with the understanding and regulation of feelings so that these did not become overwhelming and acted on.

> The AFC staff arrived to find that the hall had been vandalised. Broken glass was everywhere, the fire extinguisher had been activated and the lavatories had been "abused". Though both were contacted, no-one from the Council or Housing Association came.

The AFC staff cleaned the hall. They felt that neither organisation wished to take ownership or responsibility, and that each had abandoned the task in the hope of handing it to the other. It felt difficult to create a safe and comfortable place where our parents could be helped to reflect, when external circumstances continually impinged in a way that replicated their real experiences of invisibility and neglect.

Contact was needed between the staff of the two groups with a view to constructing a relationship for, as we know from working with toddlers, it is important that disagreements or mis-attunements are followed up by attempts to understand and make adjustments. A meeting with the Day Nursery staff, together with respective managers from their "parent" organisations, was arranged to discuss joint areas of concern.

The AFC staff did not wish to exacerbate a split between the two groups. When the recent vandalism of the hall was raised it was evident that the other group leader was unaware of this. Their council manager said that she had cancelled their session because of it. It became clear that the AFC staff had been left to find the mess and clean it up. When the issue of sharing the toys was raised, the council manager asked her staff for their key to the toy cupboard, handing it to the AFC leader and saying that the toys should be separated. While this action felt uncomfortable, and indeed increased the splitting of the groups, the AFC leader accepted the offer. This was immediately regretted but, at the time, she had been provoked to the point that she acted on her "toddlerish" desire to possess and protect the toys.

Such regression to earlier ways of being at moments of stress needed to be recognised and managed if constructive relationships were to be built.

> We took the opportunity to reflect with our parents upon our desire to possess our own toys and resist any sharing with the Day Nursery. We likened ourselves to toddlers wishing to be in control and we joked about our feelings of wanting to tantrum. Sophia laughed and wagged her finger at us and said, "you naughty girls, you must share and they must look after". In recent times, Sophia seemed lighter-hearted and also more engaged in managing Jeb. She intervened with him directly, rather than shouting from a distance, and explained to him that other children also wished to play with a toy, and that he might feel cross but he must wait his turn.

Perhaps our recognition of our own toddlerish struggles with sharing helped our parents manage their own feelings of shame when their toddlers, quite naturally, acted out. However, unlike managing the self-centred toddler, whose displays of controlling behaviour and disregard for others are usually interspersed with times of shared pleasure, the competing needs between groups that existed successively provided little opportunity for shared, pleasurable experiences. We only experienced the "fall-out" from the existence of the other and efforts to re-attune relationships needed to be persistently pursued, and supported by the "parent" organisation, or "managed at the boundaries".

Displacement and conclusion

> The AFC staff arrived to find the Day Nursery in situ. Apparently, the Nursery now needed to offer a session at the same time as the AFC group. As the two groups could not both share the hall and the Nursery had no parents present, the AFC staff offered to greet their own parents and toddlers outside and accompany them to the park. As the weather was cold and inclement, the parents with toddlers who attended declined the park and departed.

The AFC staff were concerned that they had not succeeded in preventing the displacement of their group from the hall. They felt dislocated from their base and considered how this mirrored, on a minor scale, the families' dislocation from their cultures and families of origin.

We took the opportunity to speak with the other staff to discuss concerns held in common and in a way that was mutually supportive. Both staff groups were able to acknowledge that there were difficulties for the other in sharing inadequate resources including, now, the same time slot. The leaders agreed that the responsibility for this lay with the council manager.

The latter, with support from the AFC manager, agreed that an alternative solution needed to be found.

Here, the AFC manager adopted her parental role of setting a firm boundary across which clear communication could take place. Just as toddlers need firm boundaries and verbalisation of feelings if they are to learn to modify their behaviour and compromise, management of boundaries together with clear communication is necessary later in life when negotiating relationships between individuals, groups or organisations if social and functional coexistence is to be achieved.

An alternative venue for the Day Nursery was quickly found nearby after this fruitful "clash" between the two groups. The leaders felt more positive and sympathetic to one another. The key to the toy cupboard was offered back to the Nursery.

Some months later:

> Three men with large, unleashed dogs ascended the steps and entered the foyer. They made exchanges and snorted something. The leader was concerned that they might enter the hall and remained where she could see them. Eventually, they left.

The following week, staff arrived to find hooded youths surrounding the hall and negotiated entry with some difficulty.

> The parents and toddlers arrived, disturbed by the presence of the youths who began to run and climb the balcony rails and chimneys. The parents became agitated and the toddlers mirrored the antics of the youths outside. The leader decided to lock the outer door. Sophia then spoke anxiously of a gang of youths who had recently stabbed a man to death while he was bringing in his shopping from his car. He was from her country of origin.

The group's fragile sense of safety and security was revealed in its response to the youths outside. The parents resisted the speculation that they might be "free runners",[10] holding on to their perceptions of the youths' sinister intentions.

Following these incidents our AFC managers decided that the group's safety was at risk and brought forward a planned move to the local Sure Start Children's Centre. Just as those families with resources had departed the estate, so, too, was the group to leave. The staff's feelings of relief and hopefulness were tempered by their sense of failure, guilt and sadness, which perhaps mirrored some of our parents' feelings about leaving their home countries.

I conclude with this contribution by a previous resident of the estate to a local art exhibition. This touches upon the human narratives which are concealed behind walls and impermeable boundaries that separate, but beyond which we all need to reach:

> The sky is grey, flat and empty over (this) estate in London. Weeds are growing out of drains, curtains are closed against the light and the place is deserted. Weirdly, there is no litter and not a bird in the sky. Where have all the people gone? . . . Throughout the 19th and 20th centuries, artists have focused on the urban experience – the street and the train station, the private space of the domestic interior, the space one inhabits and the ways in which the exterior world insinuates itself inside one's head, filling up all the available mental space. The city itself has also become an exterior model of human consciousness – an organism that can never be grasped except incompletely, comprehended only in fragments . . . The relationship of painting and art to architecture is deeply complicated. Most of all, it is a story about people, rather than things and walls.[11]

Chapter 9

Building a toddler group in a hostel for homeless families: An iterative technique

Elspeth Pluckrose

This chapter describes the establishment of a toddler group in a hostel for homeless families. The group offers a weekly drop-in service for residents with small children, many of whom have histories of trauma. It differs from the traditional AFC toddler groups in that it takes place in an institution whose primary purpose is not mental health but the provision of accommodation. It has developed through an iterative process in which my growing understanding of what these particular group members needed informed my practice, which gradually changed accordingly.

Hostel life

The hostel

The hostel is a large institutional building housing more than 100 families with children under 5 years old. The staff worked hard to meet residents' basic needs for shelter and security, but there were disputes in the building and tensions between staff. It was impossible to escape from a sense of neglect, rivalry, powerlessness and hostility in the face of an overwhelming task.

My previous experience as a hostel manager made me aware that institutional dynamics could lead to destructive splitting between the hostel support services, which could impact on the running of the toddler group.

Jacques (1955) described *collective social defence systems* within institutions, whereby individuals use the institution to support their own psychic defences against anxiety, guilt and uncertainty. These defences are incorporated into the systems within an institution and have an impact on the effectiveness of individuals in the completion of routine tasks. Menzies Lyth (1970) used these ideas to understand the defences incorporated within hospital nursing systems. These reduced the hospital's effectiveness in meeting its primary task of patient care, but defended against the primitive anxieties aroused by undertaking tasks which were often frightening or disgusting, and included close contact with dependence and death. Structures within the hostel could be viewed in a similar way: splitting and projection between the different support services worked to defend staff against the anxieties aroused by work with a vulnerable and dependent client group.

Menzies Lyth described how nursing systems attempted to minimise anxiety regarding responsibility and authority. The individual nurse used splitting and denial to project aspects of herself into other nurses. She could project her desire to behave irresponsibly into junior nurses and then treat them with harshness and superiority, whilst projecting the stern and critical aspects of herself into her superiors, from whom she then expected harsh treatment.

Within the hostel, it seemed that both the residents and the two staff teams were subjected to projections of irresponsibility so that they could then be criticised and blamed. Each team held the other responsible for their failure to support residents, while feeling powerless to do this themselves. Each seemed to feel that they had the harder task. The office team worked shifts, collected rents, managed breaches of the tenancy, organised repairs, and managed resident conflicts. The support team were inexperienced in dealing with the complex needs of the client group and focused upon the practical task of re-housing. Both staff teams tended to see the residents as difficult and responsible for their own difficulties; in this way the pain of individual residents' situations could be evaded. However, projection of responsibility and authority into other aspects of the institution also left individual staff feeling powerless and lacking in authority. This was demonstrated when a health and safety inspector telephoned to discuss an inspection: staff argued about who should speak to him and eventually passed the phone to the cleaner. Ultimately, difficulties were seen as due to the individual failings of the hostel manager, who responded by becoming increasingly unavailable.

In these complex ways, the anxieties aroused by the seemingly unmeetable needs of the residents could be projected; guilt at failure to perform repairs could be avoided, as residents seemed undeserving or to blame for their own plight. These institutional defences contributed to the overall feeling of neglect, powerlessness and hopelessness.

Setting up the group within this environment, I endeavoured to build a collaborative working relationship with different staff within the institution, to observe and understand the painful institutional processes without becoming too drawn into them. I was aware of the ways in which the toddler group was measured against other support services, and of the attempts to create conflict between me and other hostel professionals. However, I focused on providing the best possible setting for the families attending the group.

The mothers

Parents bringing up children within a hostel face many challenges. Most of the families come from under-privileged communities with long-term experiences of abuse, addiction, and domestic violence. Many are refugees and asylum seekers bringing experiences of loss and trauma. The hostel meets their basic needs but cannot address underlying difficulties.

During my initial visits, I became aware of the level of deprivation, and understood that it would be important to set up a group that would not stimulate feelings of deprivation. We had a generous budget for toys, but took care to keep some older toys as provision of a 'too good experience' might provoke painful envy and destructiveness.

Even so, something of this dynamic was seen in the early weeks of the group, most notably when mothers commented on the play kitchen and described their longing for "a kitchen like that one". The kitchen reminded many of the refugee mothers of their lost homeland, and foods of their own culture. Their sense of deprivation and loss aroused intense rivalry and they began to argue that the foods from their country were the best.

In the hostel, each family lived in a single bed-sit room with kitchen area and separate shower/toilet. The average stay there was five years, adding to the sense of hopelessness. The mothers seemed exhausted and preoccupied. They had low expectations, demanding little and seeming to feel that nothing could last and that making demands upon us would drive us away.

The toddlers

Long-term hostel living affected the toddlers in various ways. Observing them, I became aware of the impact long-term hostel living had upon them. Many lacked social experiences and found it hard to play. They did not speak and could not communicate their emotional states. They responded with delight to playful interactions, but sharing adult attention was difficult. This was conveyed when, during snack time, I encouraged a child who seemed uninterested in the snack to draw instead. A whole group of children quickly abandoned their food and began fighting to possess individual crayons. The hostel rooms were so small that the toddlers did not have ordinary experiences such as sitting down at the table to eat together. Sitting all together at the group's snack time was therefore a novel experience. Moreover, they had little opportunity to experiment with either physical or emotional distance from their mothers, and so had striking difficulties with experiences of separation.

Klein (1940) linked anxiety about separation with an understanding of early anxieties and defences connected with loss. She linked these to the baby's ordinary experiences of managing the presence and absence of his mother, on whom he is totally dependent. Every time a baby feels the need for his mother and she is absent, she is experienced as "lost" to him. These developments are bound up with weaning, which presents the infant with the reality that he does not exclusively possess mother and an awareness that she can give love and care to others. Over time, in ordinary development, including repeated experience of a good enough mother who reliably returns, the baby may establish an internal picture of his mother which sustains him when she is absent. Where the process goes well, when enough good experiences have been internalised and there is not too much hostility, experiences of absence promote development, and developmental gains help to balance experiences of loss.

However, this process is sometimes complicated by destructive feelings aroused by the infant's inability to tolerate the frustration generated by the experience of being left. These destructive feelings can wipe out a picture of a good mother, leaving the infant in a frightened state. The infant is filled with persecutory anxiety about a mother who is now seen as unloving and inflicting pain, together with persecutory guilt about the damage he fears he has inflicted. The infant feels he has damaged both the external and the internalised mother, turning her into something bad and frightening inside.

Anxiety about separation during the toddler period is thus linked with difficulties in working through experiences of loss and establishing a secure picture of a reliable mother in the toddler's internal world. The toddler has to learn to manage his ambivalence towards the mother he loves, who is also the mother who presents him with painful experiences of her absence.

Within the hostel, the process of separation seemed especially complex. It is difficult to know to what extent the mothers' difficulties (including their own experiences of unresolved loss) complicated the toddlers' problems with separation. However, it became apparent that difficulty with managing separation was present in the majority of toddlers attending the group, even those whose mothers were functioning well. These mother–toddler dyads lacked repeated ordinary experiences of comings and goings, because living in a single room meant that babies and toddlers could almost always see and hear their mothers. This lack of practice meant that within the toddler group, the toddlers panicked if they lost sight of their mothers.

Attending the group allowed space and greater distance to develop between them and enabled some of the essential developmental work of toddlerhood to begin.

The toddler group

The therapeutic frame

In common with all the AFC toddler groups, it has been crucial to provide a consistent reliable setting. However, the hostel setting led to changes in technique, the most noticeable of which was flexibility in the management of group boundaries.

Winnicott's ideas (1960b) about "holding" are useful in thinking about this flexibility. "Holding" is the mother's "live adaptation to the infant's needs": the mother meets the infant's needs in a way which is reliable but not "mechanically reliable", and which "implies the mother's empathy". For Winnicott, maternal holding enables the infant to build up "continuity of being". Its main function is to reduce impingements upon the infant resulting in "annihilation of personal being".

Adaptations to the group frame resulted from my empathetic understanding of the members' particular needs, at this time, in this setting. In practice this meant changes to management of the boundary and adaptations to facilitate attendance and survival of breaks. The group itself began and ended on time, but if someone arrived early they were not sent away. There was no fixed membership. Mothers and children were not excluded, even when the group became very full. Since many of the attending families entered the UK as asylum seekers, they were likely to be particularly sensitive to exclusion and closed doors. In Winnicott's terms, rejection would be "an unbearable impingement".

We also tolerated interruptions by other residents who came through the room to access computers essential for making housing bids. Here, I was guided by my countertransference, or "maternal empathy". Sending intruding residents away might appear protective of the group, but would feel like "mechanical reliability". All the residents shared an experience of homelessness, and toddler group members might have viewed this kind of management of the boundary as a harsh failure to understand the reality of hostel life.

Alongside this permeable boundary, I held an idea of the importance of the containing framework firmly in my mind. I thought of the group as starting and ending at a fixed time, even if some families came into the room before the beginning or struggled to leave at the end. I spoke to the group about intrusions into the group space, trying actively to make sense of them on the group's behalf. This can be equated with Parsons' (2007) description of an "internal analytic setting" held in the analyst's mind during phases of work when unpreventable analytic breaches took place. Parameters and boundaries were held in my mind, and I used my countertransference to inform my understanding and adapt my technique.

In encouraging attendance and management of breaks, my practice was an *extension* of toddler group techniques. I needed to reach out to maintain the link with mothers to help them to attend, to assure them they were held in mind, with letters or sometimes, when I knew them well, by going to knock on doors. Perhaps this too meets Winnicott's description of "empathy" rather than "mechanical reliability".

Breaks were difficult because longer interruptions were experienced as abandonment. The underlying difficulty might be understood in terms of a failure to establish a reliable good object within the internal world, with consequent difficulties in tolerating experiences of separation. Through trial and error, I found that it was unhelpful to give residents the usual notice before breaks because this resulted in confusion, with several families ending their attendance as soon as a break was mentioned. Instead, I wrote individual letters during the last week of the term, encouraging them to come to the last session. During this last session, I talked in the usual way about when we would return. These final sessions were difficult for the mothers and toddlers. I addressed this by giving each toddler a balloon to take with them when they left. This was a response to the toddlers' need to take away something concrete at a time when it was difficult for them to believe that we would return. The balloon, which would not last forever, nonetheless helped mothers and toddlers to stay in touch with a good experience.

Work with mothers

I was quickly made aware of the need to adapt my technique with the attending mothers. From the first week they mostly sat on the comfortable sofas and did not play with their children.

> In an early group, I watched a boy playing alone, glancing frequently towards his mother as she sat on the sofa sending text messages. She did not look at him. I tried to help him gain her attention, but she did not respond. Later I overheard her telling her friend: "I don't know why they think he wants to play with me, he's always with me, he wants to get away from me and play with other people".

Although this comment felt harsh, I could see that it also contained a different truth. This mother, at this time, was unable to give her son the attention he wanted; instead she brought him to a place where someone else might provide this. Indeed, the majority of mothers who attended the group came in order to have some space for themselves as well as to provide something for their children. Understanding their predicament helped me to rethink my role. I gave the mothers equal space in my mind and hoped that by listening to their problems, I might enable them to make more space in their minds for their small children.

> Anwar (2 years) and his mother attended infrequently. I noticed that she was cross with her son and suspicious of me. I concentrated on making them feel welcome, playing with Anwar and allowing his mum space on the sofa. From there she frequently became exasperated, shouting at her son

across the room. One week she seemed especially upset, and confided in me that things were difficult with Anwar's father. She said that she felt judged and criticised by other residents. I understood that she was letting me know that she also feared that I would judge her.

Following this brief moment of emotional contact, she brought Anwar regularly. She spoke more about her marital difficulties, and was critical of her son. She expressed dissatisfaction with him because, like her, he cried easily. She also hated it when his behaviour reminded her of his father; for example when he enjoyed playing in the car or fought with other toddlers, she was reminded of his aggressive car-loving dad.

Although I was protective of Anwar when his mother was directly hostile to him, I concentrated on allowing her to talk about how tired and overwhelmed she was. When she arrived in the group and told me instantly "*today I hate Anwar*", I accepted this as painfully true, and encouraged her to take a break on the sofa, letting her know "*today I will look after Anwar*". I understood that mother and son needed space from each other. When, at other times, she was depressed and self-critical, especially of her parenting, I worked to help her to understand her responses. We observed Anwar together and she began to express her pride at his achievements and skills.

By receiving her overt hostility towards her son, and accepting her hatred as a painful but ordinary aspect of maternal ambivalence, I offered containment to Anwar's mother and created space in the group for him. Not responding in the critical manner she both feared and expected, enabled modification of the harsh superego, which had led her to attack herself for her failings as a mother, and to feel persecuted by her son, who she experienced as sensitive and insufficiently resilient. Since I was able to accept her as an ordinary mother, she could begin to accept an ordinary boy as lovable despite his faults. It became possible to help her to make a home for Anwar in her own mind.

The mothers' vulnerability taught me that my priority should be to offer them a safe space; they were exhausted by their children's demands and needed someone to contain their emotional distress. They could take a break whilst the toddler group team managed difficult situations; not placing further demands on depleted resources, but simultaneously modelling ways of managing toddlers' challenging behaviours.

Work with toddlers

Once a "holding" space was established for the parents, a corresponding facilitating space could be created for the toddlers. In many ways the group leaders' work with the toddlers is similar to that in AFC groups, including facilitating emotional regulation and symbolic play, the active expression of toddlers' emotions, and enjoyment of individual toddlers' development.

However, within this group there has been more emphasis on particular developmental difficulties, especially separation, a difficulty which we came to identify as linked to hostel living.

For Yasmina (16 months) separating from her mother proved difficult; she seemed determined to stay physically in contact with her mother, and cried inconsolably if her mother moved away. Yasmina rejected my attempts to engage her. She cried if she thought I was approaching her and averted her eyes when I spoke. As she grew older the difficulty intensified; she cried angrily and turned to her mother if she noticed me looking at her from across the room. Her mother began to worry about how stuck Yasmina seemed, and so despite feeling increasingly hopeless I persisted in trying to find ways to help Yasmina. I began to talk with her mother, keeping myself at a distance; I was careful not to look at Yasmina although I included her in the conversation. Slowly she grew in confidence, walking into the group ahead of her mum. She began to show interest in toys and other children, but avoided contact with all adults except her mother. One day I noticed her playing with the fierce toy animals, picking them up and roaring at her mum. Standing alongside them, I began to play the same game with her older brother, who then also roared at Yasmina. Yasmina found this funny and made fleeting eye contact with me. The following week this game was repeated, although now Yasmina could occasionally roar towards me. Later, as I sat on the floor playing with other children, she approached my back, tickled me on the neck with a glove puppet and giggled. When I turned around she ran back to her mother laughing and pretending it had not been her. This game was then repeated as she practised moving between her mother and me.

For Yasmina, practising small separations had initially been a daunting task. The group offered her an opportunity to see the advantages of beginning to take steps away from her mother, and to develop the secure knowledge that she would still be there. Her clinging behaviour arose from the hostility and anger engendered by her awareness of her mother's desire to be separate. The games she eventually used to facilitate separation allowed her to express her aggression safely and symbolically; she then felt secure enough briefly to practise leaving mother.

The experience of working with toddlers like Yasmina led me to another variation in technique. Mothers had often asked me if they could leave the toddler group room for "a few minutes". I had usually agreed without fully understanding the significance of doing so. Now these comings and goings could be seen as an opportunity to observe the toddlers' responses and to actively help mothers and toddlers manage experiences of separation.

Becoming a therapeutic group

One of the most challenging aspects of understanding this group's development has been trying to make sense of my experience of it as an ongoing therapeutic group rather than a series of therapeutic encounters. Group theories emphasise commitment and regular attendance as crucial for establishment of a working therapeutic group. However, despite the changing membership, the group leaders have always experienced this toddler group as a therapeutic group. Perhaps we formed a kind of "core group", which held a group frame in mind. Over time, it seemed that the group membership began to form a larger core group of more consistent attenders, which did not always have the same membership, but came to hold some core group functions. This group of leaders and regular attenders created stability, and crucially held aspects of the group's history and experience. The group has thus been able to move towards group therapy as described by Foulkes (1964), whose model is based on the development of a shared network of communication and understanding between members of the group including the therapist. Another way of thinking about this draws on Bion's experience working with groups in the army (Bion, 1961). He observed that, despite frequent changes in membership due to soldiers returning to the war, loyalty to the group and devotion to the group task remained intact. In the hostel changes of membership were less important than the successful continuation of the group.

The painful work of building a network that enables a group to be of therapeutic use is described by Garland, Hume and Majid (2002) in relation to work with refugees. They describe the ways in which experiences of loss can contribute to the tendency of a traumatised individual to "withdraw his emotional connections with the world around him and reinforce his boundaries against penetration by the world". Groups are seen as the treatment of choice for traumatised individuals because they offer an opportunity to become involved in others' lives and difficulties within a safe setting, keeping personal boundaries open and fostering a sense of psychological agency. This is vital for those in whom 'a prolonged sense of helplessness has crushed initiative and fostered unhelpful dependence' (Garland et al., 2002). This "sense of agency" can be recovered through the experience of finding a capacity to extend understanding to others, which involves drawing on the individual's own internal resources, which in turn begins to reduce the sense of helplessness.

Within the hostel group this capacity to make emotional connections was perhaps slowed by the fact that group members were neighbours and needed to be careful about exposing their anxieties. However, it was helped by the links mothers made to similar experiences of motherhood and hostel life, and by the toddlers' capacity to make new relationships.

Gradually it has been possible for group members to develop a sense of agency, and to feel less overwhelmed by powerlessness, both within the group and outside it. It has become possible to provide a space in which organisational issues could begin to be processed. At first, the group simply provided a space in which the state of the hostel was demonstrated or enacted. For example, the group became volatile at a time of changes in hostel management which led to delays to repairs. In the group, the mothers complained and the children became noisy, expressing the institution's edgy mood with increased fighting. The toddler group staff were left feeling hopeless and depleted.

As the toddler group became emotionally connected, it offered a kind of safety valve. During a flood, which led to prolonged power failure in parts of the building, the residents were able to talk and support each other. With our help they began to understand the impact of such disturbances on the behaviour of their children. The group could be used for thinking and the processing of difficulties rather than for enactment.

Further evidence of the group's therapeutic functioning was provided by observation of group members' increasing capacity to offer each other support, no longer seeming to be overwhelmed by rivalry, or fear that there would not be enough to go round.

> Liam (2 years 8 months) had witnessed his mother Zara being attacked in the corridor and the police being called. Zara told me he was constantly talking about the incident and wondered how to help him. In the group Liam played with the police cars, told me about the police coming and said that his mummy had cried. Other mothers began to talk to Zara, expressing both sympathy and outrage. At the end of the group Liam struggled with leaving, but eventually agreed that he would show me the way back to "his house". He was then able to leave calmly, having obtained support in the corridor for them both. In following weeks it was clear that other toddlers understood the importance of the police cars to Liam, collecting them for him, and giving them up from their own games. Liam's need to play with the cars seemed to be implicitly understood and supported by the whole group.

Zara and Liam trusted the group to help them with a traumatic experience and the toddler group as a whole extended thoughtful understanding to them both. This is an example of the development of emotional connectedness within the group and of both mothers and toddlers finding a "*sense of agency*" in this process.

This sense of emotional connectedness is most striking in the toddlers' play. In a very ordinary way the toddlers have come to use the group to address difficulties which they share. Many of their games are attempts to explore problems of both hostel living and the developmental challenges of toddlerhood. Some of these games have gathered emotional significance

within the group, and are then shared and transmitted to become part of group life.

> At "tidy up time", Sanya (2 years 3 months) tried to help whilst Abdul (2 years 6 months) protested loudly. I encouraged them to put away the toy animals. I picked up a lion and in the lion's voice said "goodbye and see you next week", before putting it away. They joined in. At first I spoke in an excited voice but gradually I spoke more gently. Both children followed my lead, and as Sanya spoke I heard the sadness in her voice. When we had put all the animals away both children left calmly. Over the following months this game became an established way of managing the ending. New toddlers were introduced to the game, especially by Sanya, and it began to take place even without her, becoming a part of the culture of the group.

This transmission of games within the group took place when the game captured a shared difficulty. A drumming game became similarly shared (see chapter 3) because it allowed exuberant expression of toddler difficulty in managing anger and aggression.

The group became a place in which central toddler issues of separation and anger were expressed symbolically. Over time the toddlers generated a shared network of communication, expressed safely within play. This in turn added to the sense that a therapeutic group had been established, despite a continually changing membership.

Conclusion

In this chapter I have described the adaptation of the AFC toddler group model to work within an institution accommodating a vulnerable population. These adaptations have developed through an iterative process, gradually and in response to the group's needs. The toddler group now feels securely established. Some toddlers have moved on to nursery or out of the hostel into flats and return to the group to talk about their experiences, confirming its importance to them. It can come as a shock, after a long wait for a flat, to find that they miss aspects of hostel life, including the toddler group, which for some has become established in their minds as a valuable, sustaining place.

Chapter 10

Reaching out to vulnerable parents and toddlers: Establishing a parent-toddler group in a deprived area of South London

Fátima Martínez del Solar

This chapter describes my three-year experience of establishing and running a parent-toddler group in a deprived area of South London. When I left my job as a parent-toddler group leader at the Anna Freud Centre (AFC) to work in a community Child and Family Mental Health Service in South London, I hoped to bring my experience of working psychoanalytically with families to this new context. Having recently arrived from Peru, I did not anticipate great differences between the two areas.

In the event, I encountered very different conditions. I hope to show how, with much thought, I was able to modify my expectations and technique to suit the needs of the families there, and to establish a psychoanalytically informed parent-toddler group in which meaningful change and growth could occur. I will illustrate my work with vignettes and observations of a mother and her daughter Tara.

I hope to demonstrate that a psychoanalytic perspective can be usefully brought to bear in community work with vulnerable populations, and, through this, to encourage professionals in the field to be innovative, develop similar strategies and use psychoanalytic interventions in their work with parents and young children in the most deprived areas.

The parent-toddler group

As an outreach worker, I was expected to engage "hard to reach" families who constantly struggle with practical issues of immigration, housing, social isolation and mental health problems, in addition to parenting their young children. Fear, frequent re-housing, language and culture form barriers to their engagement with formal services. As a result of death, trauma, relocation, loss and deprivation, they have little sense of belonging to a community. They hesitate to form new relationships, since, in their experience, these are unlikely to last. I believed that a parent-toddler group could support such a population.

I hoped the group would be a warm and non-threatening space where parents could come to play with their children. By forming a relationship with the children, I wanted to model interaction and play for the parents, and to help them to understand, think about and verbalise their children's feelings and behaviour. As Zaphiriou Woods (2000) suggests, very vulnerable parents, who are afraid of individual therapy or of accessing other mental health services, might experience a playgroup environment as safer, less threatening and more normalising of their experience. In addition, the group could help to relieve the social isolation faced by so many families in the area, by introducing them to other parents and children, and by linking them to services available in the community.

The playgroup was held in a Community Centre in the heart of a large council estate. We met for one and half hours each week. Initially, I worked alone, but as the group grew, I acquired two assistants. A year later, other colleagues joined.

Development of the group

During the early months, I inundated the community with leaflets and made contact with other practitioners, offering our group as a support for their work. I also approached parents personally and invited them to join.

In the first year, attendance was very poor, with only one or two children and their parents attending each week. Different individuals came to each session, which meant there was no sense of a "group". My assistants and I had to tolerate the frustration of thinking about the children's play and relationships, and of potential interventions, in the knowledge that they might return to the group only weeks later or not at all. At the end of the first year, we had four parent–child couples registered who struggled to come regularly. I struggled to justify this endeavour to my managers, and to lessen my feelings of guilt at spending time and resources on a project that seemed unsuccessful.

These difficulties, together with the parents' lack of interest and participation, often left us feeling useless, confused and uncertain about what we were doing wrong. This was very different from the AFC, where the waiting list ensured a constant supply of new members. Our difficulty seemed to reflect the experience of the parents we were trying to reach and help: they were vulnerable and often struggled, unsupported, in their attempts to deal with life and parent their children.

After some months, it became clear that we would have to adapt both our expectations and our theoretical framework to suit the population we were trying to reach. I realised that I might have been expecting more autonomy and agency than was possible. These parents were preoccupied with urgent practical matters to do with their day-to-day survival. There was little space in their minds for play and their child's emotional wellbeing, for thinking about them as different from themselves. It was not that they did not want to come, but they needed us to go to them and bring them into the group.

We became more active in initiating contact and helping the parents and toddlers to leave their houses. Although this technique compromised the psychoanalytic stance of neutrality, it seemed necessary in order to help such vulnerable parents to engage. The notion of developmental help was useful in convincing us to reach out to them (A. Freud, 1965). Supervision with the AFC consultant[12] was essential in helping us to understand and modify our intervention. At this crucial turning point, we stopped waiting for families to come to us and instead went actively towards them.

Upon receiving a referral, we decided to make home visits to begin to establish a relationship of trust with the parent and child, before asking them to the group. Once the relationship was established, we invited them to the group. When appropriate, we offered to collect mothers from their houses, or organised for them to meet with us at the local shopping centre to walk together to the venue. We sent reminders via mobile phone text messages. We telephoned mothers who were particularly vulnerable and tended to forget from one week to the next. During this initial period, they needed us to be their memory.

In addition to this active recruitment of new members, we modified our expectations further, and accepted that attending irregularly was the best these families could manage. We continued to remind them of our availability whenever they wanted and were able to come, and were always happy to receive them even if they had not come for a long time. Over time, our steadfast commitment, flexibility and readiness to adapt to the needs of the parents and toddlers resulted in better participation.

During these first three years, we were so invested in generating a sense of belonging to a group that we did not realise this was not easily attainable for people from divergent cultures and experiences. We needed to start from scratch, to build a different kind of group experience, made up of the little contributions that each parent and child provided with their presence. The group slowly became more coherent as members started attending more regularly. A few members attended weekly while others came about every three weeks, but over a long period of time.

Referrals and population

Initially our members came from other CAMHS (Child and Adolescent Mental Health Services). In time, referrals started to come from GPs (general practitioners) and health visitors, social services, adult mental health and paediatric services. Issues that families face include anxieties about their child's development and behaviour, parent mental health problems, domestic violence and social isolation. A high proportion of mothers who attend the group are on antidepressant medication and have a history of mental illness. Some have experienced severe trauma. The group caters for asylum seekers and refugees, many of whom are victims of war, and for illegal immigrants, who are unable to access services and benefits. Most have no family nearby and some live in temporary accommodation, with a high rate of re-allocation.

About 60 per cent of the population are of black and ethnic minorities. For the majority, English is not their first language. Currently we have people from six African countries and three European countries, as well as Caribbean, Latin American and Chinese members. White English members are in the minority.

In order to describe the approach and style of our intervention, a case example is included to illustrate how we worked towards building a therapeutic relationship that enabled the mother and child to become members of the group and benefit from the experience.

Case example

Tara (11 weeks) and her mother were referred to our Child and Family Service by their midwife. Her mother needed individual support due to severe post-natal depression. Aged just 21 years, she was a mixed-race illegal immigrant from North Africa. She had come to the UK when she was 16, and remained after her visa expired. She had no rights to benefits or housing, and her relationship with Tara's father had ended. She had one sister in the UK, with whom she had no contact, and very few friends.

Individual sessions

In our first meeting, Tara's mother said that she felt depressed and angry. Her accent made angry sound like "hungry" and I often found it difficult to understand which she was. She seemed to have amalgamated the two words to express that she was both angry *and* hungry. In the countertransference, I felt inclined to offer her some of our biscuits to satisfy her hunger. She told me how distressed she was.

> "I feel angry with myself when I look in the mirror; I hate myself, my face, my hands, my nails. Since having the baby, I feel I've turned horrible, ugly. I wasn't like that. I know it's not her fault. I'm happy she is here, but I can't wait until she grows up." (Tara 11 weeks)

She was reluctant to leave the house and to be seen. She sometimes wore a wig or a cap, which prevented me from seeing her face and gave her a strange appearance. She was unwilling to speak about her history, particularly her parents, saying, "It puts me down to think about them." She said she had a loving grandmother in her home country whom she sometimes telephoned.

From the beginning, the quality of her interaction with Tara was concerning.

> Mother was playing with Tara while speaking. She teased her by putting her lollipop in Tara's mouth, pulling it out when she tried to suck it. (Tara 11 months)

During the same session, she stood Tara on her feet and said, "Walk, come on, walk. I cannot bear her cries and feel like covering my ears when she is crying." She referred to Tara as a selfish and clingy baby who wanted everything for herself. At the same time, she said she wanted Tara to have a different life from her own, but did not know how to achieve this.

Mother had suicidal thoughts, but thinking about Tara stopped her acting on them. Thinking she needed medication, I referred her to her GP, who thought she was not depressed, but manipulative.

Mother and baby were living at a friend's house, but needed to move, as the friend could not continue accommodating them. They became homeless when Tara was 4 months old. They were found one night crying at a train station by a woman who offered them shelter for the night. They stayed with her for two months, until they found new accommodation.

They lived on half of the maintenance money that Tara's English father received from the government, while he kept the other half. Tara's mother was impoverished and living on the periphery of society. Preoccupied with her survival and fighting with Tara's father, she was so depressed that she had little capacity to relate to others. Sometimes during sessions, she spoke aloud, as if I were not there. When I responded, she said, "Sorry, I was speaking to myself." Sometimes, she arrived unkempt and dirty. At these times I found it difficult to be with her: she managed to provoke in me the disgust she felt towards herself.

> Mother looked dirty today. She spent much of the session pulling lice from her hair. She said, "I have not washed my hair for a long time." (Tara 11 months)

I felt desperate, overwhelmed by this mother's disturbed and disturbing presence and by her impact on Tara. During the first seven months of our contact, she attended only one in four individual appointments, which left me feeling impotent. I frequently spoke to her midwife, who thought she might be involved in prostitution and drug dealing. My attempt to refer her to social services was unsuccessful as her illegal status made her ineligible for help. Although initially I was very concerned when she failed to attend appointments, I gradually realised that she always returned.

Joining the parent-toddler group

Mother saw a leaflet advertising my parent-toddler group and asked if she could join. She started attending when Tara was 10 months old. They came about once a month initially, sometimes disappearing for a month or two. I continued offering individual appointments, but to my surprise mother said, "I prefer the playgroup. I don't want to speak about those things, Fatima – you know I don't like speaking." I therefore stopped offering individual appointments and instead supported her attendance at the group. I sent text messages or phoned to remind her. The group setting enabled her to regulate the contact she had with me: not too close or personal, and not too distant.

Tara starts walking, mother walks towards us

In the group, we initially observed mother sitting to one side, looking very depressed. She complained of headaches and hay fever and kept herself to herself. In contrast, Tara was interested in the new environment and enjoyed being with people. At 11 months, she would dance in the baby bouncer while babbling and smiling to others.

When Tara started walking, her play became rough. She pushed the buggy, screaming, walking clumsily over things, falling frequently. She seemed to lack a sense of space and awareness of other people. Finding her difficult, mother turned to us for help. She asked us to intervene. It was as if once Tara started walking, mother also began to walk towards us and embrace the group.

Informing and normalising

Tara's ability to walk away from her mother and exercise her independence initiated a change in their relationship which mother found difficult. By exerting her age-appropriate mobility and autonomy, Tara became less compliant and more challenging.

We used these changes to inform mother about what could be expected from her child at different ages, making links with her feelings and anxieties. We explained that her emotional availability and acceptance of Tara's new independence was fundamental for her development (Mahler et al., 1975). Despite being generally withdrawn, Tara's mother was receptive. She was relieved that much of the behaviour that she found unacceptable in Tara was part of normal development and that it could be observed in other children in the group.

Containing mother

My assistant and I took turns to be with mother or play with Tara in every session they attended. We wanted them to feel welcome, to strengthen their relationship with us, so that mother would come more regularly. It was a difficult task: when asked how things were going mother typically said that things were the same, she was struggling as always. We felt that we needed to contain her distress and conflicted feelings towards her daughter (Winnicott, 1988) and were often left feeling concerned for and preoccupied with them both. However, we believed that the experience of being wanted and accepted when they came to the group would make it easier for mother to accept our help.

As Tara continued to make demands and assert her autonomy, mother continued to feel depressed and "horrible". She reported huge power struggles. She said she wanted time for herself away from Tara, whom she described as "very selfish and lazy". I spoke to mother about how difficult it was for her to attend to Tara's needs, because she had her own needs and wanted to be looked after herself. She nodded silently. I said, "Tara is not happy because mother is not happy." I said she wanted to be a good mum to Tara, but it was so difficult to explain things and address Tara's feelings, when she was feeling depressed and probably needed an explanation of why her own life was so difficult.

Acknowledging mother's own needs, and her wish to provide her best for her child, made her feel understood instead of criticised. This seemed to have a therapeutic effect, and we started observing mother smiling and playing with her daughter. We thought that because mother felt accepted and understood by us, she could begin to accept and enjoy greater closeness with Tara. However, we observed that the play was often rough as well as loving.

Containing Tara

We worked at giving mother a rest, and tried to engage Tara, in the hope that the space created would relieve the tension between them. It was difficult to relate to Tara; she made little eye contact and seldom responded to our attempts to play with her. She moved aimlessly from toy to toy, picking one up, dropping it, and suddenly moving on. Our attempts to join her usually ended in her biting, spitting or throwing a huge tantrum. We spent a great deal of time after the group thinking about how to intervene more effectively.

Tara's exuberance and activity suggested that she enjoyed the space and the people in the group, but she often caused trouble, by snatching toys from other children or hitting them. Mother tended to intervene after the problem had occurred, and then only to scold her. On these occasions, we tried to normalise Tara's behaviour, talking about "toddlers' struggles". Mother remained critical and rejecting of her daughter.

> Mother was aggressive and dismissive of Tara today. "She is horrible," she said to me in front of Tara, who became upset. Her play became frenetic and she shouted frequently. Later, she fell from a seat, hitting her head badly, but hardly cried. It was painful to watch mother's inability to respond and comfort her. (Tara 14 months)

We tried to help mother communicate with Tara. We could see she was an intelligent child who needed to be considered as an individual with her own mind. We suggested that she needed things explained and her feelings verbalised to feel more in control (Katan, 1961).

> At the end of the group, mother approached Tara and tried to put her coat on. Tara reacted violently and ran away. Mother became upset and tried to force her to put on the coat. This interaction ended with Tara crying and mother extremely angry. I said that Tara found it difficult to end something she was enjoying and maybe mother could warn her a few minutes in advance that the group would be ending shortly, and they would be leaving. (Tara 16 months)

Tara continued to find it difficult to leave, but when we prepared her by talking her through the departure calmly, she managed better.

Because of our continuing concerns about Tara, I occasionally offered mother an individual appointment. She accepted the appointments but never came, saying that she fell asleep or forgot. Individual attention seemed to overwhelm her and make her feel worse about her mothering.

Becoming part of the group

After almost a year of erratic attendance, mother and Tara (18 months) began to attend fortnightly. Mother had started working using false documents. On one occasion she brought professional studio photos of the two of them. Perhaps she wanted to show me that she had positive feelings towards her daughter and the two of them as a family, not just the negative feelings she tended to express.

Mother became friendly with another young, single mother, who had a daughter the same age as Tara. We observed them leaving the group together, and talking about their activities during the week. We actively supported this developing relationship. When the two little girls started playing together, mother and Tara began to attend the group regularly. They seemed to have developed a sense of belonging, which enabled us to work with them in more depth.

A happier relationship

Mother appeared more comfortable, both with herself and with other group members. She and Tara spent time together at the painting table. Tara played with the paints and mother painted her own pictures. There was a sense of companionship as they played in parallel and enjoyed the time together. Mother's drawings revealed that she had considerable artistic talent. The group seemed to have provided a space for the child within Tara's mother. It allowed her to express her infantile needs, "painting her own picture", while Tara expressed hers. Under these conditions, mother was able to take pleasure in being with her daughter. We praised her, pointing out that Tara was calmer and more able to settle.

Thinking about Tara

Feeling happier with Tara, mother was able to think about her more empathically. She told us, "She is so rough, I'm worried she's a bully and that people don't understand her." We wondered how much of this was an accurate description of Tara's behaviour, and how much a projection onto Tara of her mother's own feelings and experience. I suggested to her that perhaps when Tara was so "rough" towards us, she worried that we would not understand or like either of them.

We showed mother that her efforts to connect with Tara were helping her to progress developmentally. We emphasised that Tara responded well when treated respectfully, and modelled this in our handling of both of them. A male colleague and I decided to give Tara some individual attention every week. Tara enjoyed and was responsive to his attention.

> Halfway into a session mother became very angry with Tara who had wet herself, despite being asked if she wanted to use the toilet. Mother did not have spare trousers. She said, "She does it on purpose to bother me," and wanted to take Tara home as punishment. As they were leaving, my colleague intervened. He said to mother, "Let's think about this together. Please don't go now." He explained that accidents are to be expected during toilet training. We lent her some pants and she stayed. Tara returned happily to her play. Mother and toddler both seemed relieved. (Tara 19 months)

Mother, like Tara, responded well to explanations that helped her to understand how and why things happened. She became less spiteful towards Tara, who in turn became calmer. The tensions between them gradually lessened. Though Tara remained active and inclined to be clumsy, mother and child were less entangled in constant battles.

We tried then to support mother's maternal feelings and self-esteem. Tara typically ran to hug my colleague and me when she arrived at the group. Mother seemed to accept that Tara was affectionate towards us, but we remained concerned that she might feel jealous or rejected. We pointed out that she was the most important person for Tara, who preferred playing with her mum. Mother's self-esteem was so low that she did not believe us. She was convinced that Tara rejected her when she attempted to play with her. We hoped that if we created a space for her to speak more about herself and her feelings, a space might arise for her to think more about Tara and their relationship.

Depression and anger

> After a long Easter break, mother was quiet, depressed and angry. She blamed Tara, saying that Tara had been naughty and selfish during the break. She felt overwhelmed by Tara's neediness and, as a result, Tara had become more clinging and aggressive. Mother felt lonely and disappointed. A vicious cycle had become established: mother projected her anger and depression on to her daughter, who responded by becoming uncontained and fragmented. Her frenetic play expressed how unsupported she felt by her mother and her difficulty in receiving her mother's projections.
>
> Mother told me she was concerned about Tara's aggression and spitting after the break. She said, "She's terrible now, I'm finding it difficult to be with her. I see her need. I don't know how to do it. It's been hard these weeks." (Tara 20 months)

We thought that both mother and Tara had reacted very strongly to the break, feeling overwhelmed by their needs and their anger at being abandoned by us. Mother made hurtful, aggressive comments towards her child. Tara responded with aggression towards other children and her play became fragmented. We wanted to help them verbalise their feelings, in the hope that this would alleviate their need to enact the feelings in play and in their relationship.

> Tara was pulling a toy from another little girl. I said to her, "I think you are angry about the long time you have not come to the group. You must have missed your group. You are finding it difficult to share with the other children, because you have forgotten that we share the toys here." She spat at me. I said in a kind but firm voice, "We don't spit here." (Tara 20 months)

Since Tara was only able to express her anger by spitting, we addressed her feelings while at the same time setting boundaries to her behaviour. We also talked to mother about having missed the group and displacing her angry feelings onto Tara. Their regular attendance at the group was useful in helping us to provide emotional containment, while also modelling appropriate limit setting.

Progressive and regressive behaviour

Recognising Tara's infantile needs and regressive behaviour and helping mother to accept them as part of normal development enabled mother to become more flexible and tolerant, and not to react aggressively as she had done in the past. It also allowed Tara to regress and play at being a baby again.

> Tara was trying to climb into a baby bouncer. I said, "Do you want to play that you are the baby?" She replied, "Yes." She fastened the safety belt and started to rock herself. I said, "It's nice to be a baby, it feels good. Growing up and becoming a big girl is more difficult." She continued rocking herself. I called mother and said, "Have you seen? She wants to be your baby." Mother smiled. (Tara 2 years)

I spoke to mother about children's wish to be their parents' babies. I said, "It's a human need. Even when you are older you want to know that you are still your mum's child." Mother pulled a face, dismissing my words. Later in that session she joined me in the kitchen, as I washed the coffee mugs. We were alone. She told me that her mother had abandoned her at birth, but kept her twin sister. She met her mother for the first time when she was 12 years old. It had taken almost two years for mother to tell me about this part of her life. I felt tremendous compassion for her. I understood her difficulties better and valued her efforts more.

We spoke at length about how difficult it was for Tara's mother to be a mother when she had not had a mother herself (Martínez del Solar, 2003). We talked about Tara's need to be a baby and I suggested that if mother could accept Tara's infantile needs, Tara might find it less difficult to grow up. I said, "To be able to grow up, you need to be a baby first."

Two years after joining the group, mother and Tara's attendance became reliable. When they could not attend, mother called me or sent a text message. She knew she was a valued member of the group and proud that, as its longest attending member, she had earned a place in the group. There were continuing difficulties, but Tara no longer disrupted the group. She played and had a good time with her mother. Although I knew they still needed help, I was less concerned about them. I sensed that there was an incipient strength in their relationship, albeit a fragile and vulnerable one; it had helped them find a way to survive so far.

Postscriptum

Tara and her mother stopped attending regularly when Tara, aged 3 years, started nursery. We continued to have occasional contact with them, when they visited the group during nursery school breaks and holidays. When Tara turned 5, they arrived with a birthday cake to celebrate with us, confident that we would be welcoming. Mother still suffers from depression and finds things difficult, but Tara is doing well at school. Mother still occasionally drops in on the group without Tara. She sits alone and paints.

Our group today

The group has now been running for over six years. We have approximately 20 families that come (some regularly, some irregularly). The average attendance per week is 15–17 couples.

Over the years the nature of the group has changed, as we receive more referrals from peri-natal, adult mental health and social services. Current referrals are predominantly of parents with acute mental health problems, and we have become a specialised group focusing on severe difficulties within the parent–child relationship. We have a permanent waiting list and no longer need to advertise the group to the community. The group is now co-managed by Adult and Child Mental Health Services, having been initially managed by Children's Services only.

In 2007, we were awarded a Highly Commended Distinction for Clinical Governance Award by our local trust. The project is currently being evaluated for replication in other Children's Centres in the borough.

Chapter 11

Integrating parents and toddlers with special needs: Parent-toddler groups in St. Petersburg[13]

Valentina Ivanova and Nina Vasilyeva

This chapter presents over ten years' experience of running toddler groups in St. Petersburg. Alongside mothers and toddlers showing the usual developmental challenges of that period, the groups include families identified as being at risk: the toddlers have special needs (due to Down's syndrome, cerebral palsy, impaired hearing, etc.), or the mothers are orphanage graduates (young women who were separated at an early age from their parents, brought up in institutions and deprived of secure and satisfying relationships with their birth parents). Despite the special needs and vulnerabilities of individual participants in the groups, the groups focus on what unites them – typical toddler-age problems and the parent-toddler relationship – rather than the differences.

Historical background

The first Russian parent-toddler groups were started in April 1997 by several members of the St. Petersburg Society of Child Analysis. The idea of fostering the emotional development of toddlers arose out of a series of seminars conducted in St. Petersburg by Anna Freud Centre Child Psychotherapists. We began implementing their psychoanalytic principles by creating psychoanalytic toddler groups at a time when psychoanalysis was little applied in this field in Russia. Ms Nancy Brenner, a parent-toddler group leader at the Anna Freud Centre at the time, provided ongoing supervision and organisational support. The toddler groups in St. Petersburg led to similar services developing in other parts of Russia. At present there are three toddler groups in St. Petersburg, three in Voronezh, and one in Moscow, all of which were established with our help.

The St. Petersburg professionals who established the first parent-toddler groups also worked at Centres implementing programmes of early intervention for children with special needs (Muhamedrahimov, 1995, 1997), which included promoting their integration into everyday life (Pastorova, 2002).[14] This revolutionary approach to children with special needs shaped our toddler groups, which became integrative in the broadest sense: they were attended by children who would previously have been hidden away in institutions as a result of their special needs, and by mothers who had grown up in institutions and received inadequate parenting. These mothers were now involved in programmes designed to support their parenting (Zamaldinova, 2000). A toddler group place was offered to any toddler displaying the typical challenges of this developmental phase, and the groups focused on these shared problems and on supporting the parent–child relationship.

At the time of their inception, the form of early intervention offered by the toddler groups was very different from what was being offered in Russia to young children and their families. Psychoanalytic ideas focusing on understanding relationships as the crucial context in which a child develops were at variance with prevailing ideas favouring the use of medication and of active educational stimulation during early development. Such ideas continue to prevail in Russia today, where parents still tend to consult a medical doctor, usually a neurologist, and to resort to medication to deal with early difficulties such as toilet training, temper tantrums, anxieties, aggressive behaviour, disturbed sleep and feeding difficulties, etc. There is also a strong tendency to try to accelerate early intellectual development.

Creating a psychotherapeutic space

A toddler group can be regarded as a psychoanalytically oriented form of group work that helps to establish trust and facilitates every aspect of the child's early development (Zaphiriou Woods, 2000). A limited number of participants (4–8 mother–child pairs), regular attendance, and constant time and place of sessions conducted by highly trained professionals are all features of the psychotherapeutic space of the toddler groups. Traditional principles of group psychotherapy that are used by the toddler group leaders include a non-judgemental attitude, acceptance, empathy, readiness to talk and discuss and the attempt to distribute attention equally among all the members of the group (Rudestam, 1982). We also actively introduce information about the social-emotional development of toddlers. For instance, we talk about ways in which children express their experience through play or behaviour, why it is important to talk to children about their feelings, the toddler's struggle between the wish for closeness and need for independence, etc. In the course of a session – usually at tea time – we introduce group discussions on topics that may be of interest or importance to the parents. Frequently discussed issues include battles over toilet training, difficulties in establishing firm boundaries without resorting to aggression or threats and weaning difficulties (it is not unusual for children to be breast-fed up to 2½ to 3 years of age). The mothers are given the opportunity to share their doubts and concerns, learn different points of view and clarify their own opinions. Since these discussions take place in the presence of the children, it is crucial that the professionals attend to both mothers and children, and try to reflect the feelings of all participants.

As a variation of group work, toddler groups therefore have a number of particular features. In the absence of the 'traditional circle' which provides an opportunity for ongoing discussion, there may be several discussions and interactive sub-groups of children and adults occurring at the same time. There may also be individual mini-consultations to some mothers. It is important for the leader to remain mindful of the entire group experience, its culture and history.

Mothers who are graduates of orphanages

Graduates of orphanages are regarded as hard-to-reach, because of their difficulties in accessing and accepting help (Radina, 2004). Children enter institutions because they are abandoned by their parents or are removed from them following parental alcoholism or neglect. Alternatively, their parents may have died or been imprisoned. At the age of 18 years, they begin independent life, having only ever lived in an institution. These youngsters typically suffer from post-traumatic disorders, low self-esteem and social competence, poor education and minimal financial support from the state (Dementyeva, 1992; Radina, 2004). Even if they are aware of needing help, their social isolation, together with the system of permanent guardianship and control by state caregivers, makes accessing support very difficult. They lack the financial resources to pay for traditional psychological support. Most importantly, they often perceive help as another painful impingement on their world, which was repeatedly invaded in the institution, and which they now desperately seek to protect. Consequently, orphanage graduates who start their own families are at high risk of repeating their traumatic relationships with their parents and/or their experiences in the institution. Another common outcome is that they reject their parental role, placing their children in the care of the institution where they themselves grew up (Radina, 2004; Zamaldinova, 2000).

Because of these particular difficulties, a programme to support graduates of orphanages was created and launched in St. Petersburg (Zamaldinova, 2000). It enabled those of them who became mothers to attend toddler groups with their young children. Some of them settled rapidly in the groups, establishing relationships with the other mothers and becoming responsive to their toddlers. However, we often had difficulties engaging them and some found it impossible to continue attending the groups, despite our best efforts.

We frequently encountered difficulties in the initial stage of inviting these mothers to participate in a toddler group. The usual method of telephoning mothers, informing them about the group and arranging a preliminary meeting, was often not sufficient to enable them to attend. If they did come, they appeared uneasy and were very reserved. They played and talked little with their children. This is illustrated by a 20-year-old mother and her 2½-year-old son Misha.[15]

> During the initial telephone call, Misha's mother did not express any interest in attending a toddler group, but agreed to receive one of the group leaders into her home so that her son could be "seen by a specialist". Mother appeared depressed and withdrawn, while Misha appeared neglected, precociously independent and unusually attentive to his mother. Mother was concerned that Misha's speech was delayed. After the visit, we thought about ways of reaching out to, and working with this mother and her son. With her permission, we arranged for Misha to see a speech therapist and offered to accompany them to the appointment. She accepted this offer of support. Among other things, the speech therapist recommended that the experience of communicating with other children in a toddler group would benefit Misha.
>
> Following this visit and noting that Misha's mother remained withdrawn, we offered to accompany her and Misha to their first toddler meeting. We were aware that mother might experience our initiatives as persecuting and controlling, but by remaining open, attentive and unintrusive – for instance, we did not expect her to respond verbally to what we said – we managed to remain in contact with her.
>
> In the group, she was noticeably different from the others. It was as if she tried to make herself invisible by always sitting in the same place, in the same position, not talking to anyone including her son. It was extremely painful for us to watch the happy toddler running to his mother to share his delight, and getting no response. We tried to find the optimal balance of closeness and safety in our contact with this mother. Our guiding principle was to attend equally to all members of the group, so that each could decide what level of participation she wanted. From time to time we addressed Misha's mother directly, asking her how she was and drawing her attention to touching signs of her son's love for her. He often demonstrated the height-ened awareness and concern for his mother, shown by children whose mothers are depressed and insufficiently sensitive to their child's needs (Crittenden & DiLalla, 1988; Pleshkova, Muhamedrahimov, & Crittenden, 2008; Radke-Yarrow, Cummings, Kuczynski, & Chapman, 1985). For instance, we observed Misha interrupting his play to approach his mother and waiting until she acknowledged him with a glance or nod, before resuming his activity. He did not turn to his mother when frustrated by a toy or an interaction with another child. He showed little distress or aggression and chose to give way rather than stand up for himself.
>
> After toddler group meetings, the leaders regularly met to discuss the group and the range of emotions elicited by Misha's mother. This enabled us

to cope with our strong countertransference feelings, and to resist acting on them by, for instance, competing to be better mothers for Misha. We were encouraged in our approach by Misha and his mother's regular attendance and their return to the group after breaks for Misha's illnesses. This suggested that the group sessions were important to Misha's mother, and felt worthwhile, even though she never told us directly.

The other mothers were initially discouraged by their unsuccessful attempts to engage Misha's mother. However, their attitude gradually changed once they found common ground and a way of communicating with her. They asked after Misha's health and shared their experiences of treating their own children's illnesses. They were friendly and patient, despite her detachment. Perhaps our careful persistence in finding a way to relate to her in a sensitive and respectful manner was a model for them. In time, Misha's mother built a stronger relationship with Misha and learned to communicate with him, even though she remained reserved and withdrawn in relation to the rest of the group.

Children with special needs in the toddler group space

The separation-individuation process is inevitably complicated for a child with special needs (Sinason, 1992, and see also chapter 7). The mother often feels a complex combination of guilt, shame and grief, which impacts on her relationship with her child, the child's subjective experience and the environment in which the child develops. In some cases, the mother's anxiety about having a child with special needs becomes so unbearable that family relationships deteriorate, to the point that the child is institutionalised. Parents often then continue to visit the child in the institution, thus retaining a relationship.

Since children with special needs were traditionally institutionalised in Russia, a significant change in attitude was required before this trend could be reversed. At the end of the 1990s, work aimed at creating respect for children and adults with special needs began, in order to encourage families to keep their disabled children within the family, and integrate them in society. As a result of this work, the Russian people have become more tolerant and children and adults with special needs are now seen in public places such as entertainment centres and leisure resorts. Russian families have started adopting children with special needs, something that was unheard of even five years ago. Parents of children with special needs have become active, and united in organisations offering social support. When their children are toddlers they are more likely to join an integrated toddler group rather than a specialised one. Despite these very positive changes, the birth of a child with special needs is a tremendous challenge for any family, which each family deals with in its own way, as illustrated by Olga, born with Down's syndrome.[16]

At her father's insistence, Olga was placed in a Baby Home soon after her birth. Olga's mother visited her regularly for two years, during which time she consulted a Counsellor about her daughter's development in order to understand her better. Mother wanted to take Olga home, once her divorce was finalised and she had organised her housing, but she was apprehensive about this decision. The Counsellor suggested that she could meet with Olga outside the Baby Home, at a weekly parent-toddler group, where they could get to know each other better. They joined the group when Olga was 2½ years old.

In the group, Olga and her mother sometimes kept themselves apart, but at other times they interacted more. The mother shared happy and sad moments from her everyday life with the leaders, and talked with Olga and other members of the group. She became friends with one mother who supported her decision to take Olga home. Olga took time to settle in the group, but she came to enjoy playing with sand and water and observing the other toddlers playing.

The trips to and from the toddler group, as well as the sessions themselves, functioned as a transitional space that enabled this mother to make the decision to take her child back home. We made no attempt to influence her decision in any direction. However, our attitude of acceptance and, just as importantly, experiencing the other participants' acceptance of her and her daughter probably contributed to the restoration of their relationship. It enabled Olga's mother to feel capable of mothering her child and to see her daughter as not only manageable, but also accepted and loveable.

The following vignette describes our work with Kostia, a 3-year-old boy who suffered from cerebral palsy, and his mother.[17]

Kostia had had very little experience of being with peers who were developing normally. He found it extremely difficult to walk and manage his involuntary movements. Kostia's challenging behaviour easily provoked his mother – who had been abused as a child – to respond punitively. Rehabilitation measures aimed at compensating for his cerebral palsy became a battlefield for re-enactment. His mother's attempts to teach him how to master various movements often deteriorated into harsh drilling.

Painful feelings were frequently discussed in the group. Mothers spoke of feeling ashamed and guilty after being rough with their child. They admitted losing their self-control at moments of great stress and spoke of the importance of receiving support so as not to resort to behaving cruelly to their children.

The leaders often acted as mediators in the children's interactions, reflecting their feelings, helping the parents to set limits and providing information about the other children's experience. Kostia was eager to talk with the other children, but communicating with them excited him, which increased his chaotic movements and frightened the other toddlers. We explained to Kostia and the other children that Kostia expressed his feelings through movements that he had difficulty controlling.

Conclusion

The presence of children and parents with special needs may create an extra tension, especially in the early stages of forming a parent-toddler group. Anxiety, fears, unprocessed losses and trauma may be re-activated in other members of the group, when they come into contact with children who have special needs. The experience of containing, managing and regulating these emotions in the group creates a context for more trusting relationships, and may be the basis for containing the ambivalence which is characteristic of toddlerhood.

Chapter 12

Integration, sharing and separation: Introducing the concept of toddlers and toddler groups in Greece

Evanthia Navridi

I was introduced to the idea of toddler groups at the Anna Freud Centre in London. The popularity of their toddler groups, their contribution to the toddlers' development and their caring support of the family gradually led to the idea of starting a similar programme in Greece. The challenge was to adapt the Anna Freud Centre approach to a different society and culture.

The Toddler Group Programme started in Greece in 2004 and was hosted at a Community Mental Health Centre in Athens. It began as an unofficial pilot, while we made the necessary adjustments to the needs of the local Greek community. Since then, it has run as an integral part of the Centre's services.

To introduce such a novel programme it was necessary to give some thought to the cultural context. In the first place, there was a strong prejudice against mental health services and a belief that they exist exclusively for dealing with psychopathology. A service targeting the "normal" child had to be differentiated and such preconceptions questioned in order to attract interested parties.

A further concern was whether Greek families, given their extended nature, needed the support of toddler groups. In Greece, relatives participate in the family, alongside parents and children, with grandparents, aunts and uncles closely linked and often co-existing in the family nucleus. These "third" parties very often play a decisive role in the children's upbringing, contributing their wisdom and experience during the initial difficult years.

Perhaps the greatest hurdle was that there is no word for "toddler" in the Greek language, even in specialist vocabulary: all children aged 1 to 5 are generally referred to as "preschool". The non-existence of the word underlines the lack of an equivalent concept in Greek culture and consequent lack of awareness of the significance of this particular developmental stage with its specific developmental tasks, behaviours and milestones and the crucial importance of the relationship with the parents.

Taking all the above into account, it became clear that we needed to do some groundwork to prepare the way for starting a toddler group. Our goal was to demonstrate the uniqueness of the toddler stage to parents and professionals and at the same time to counter prejudice so that normal children could become involved in a mental health process.

The Centre that was to house our first Toddler Group was a Community Mental Health Centre in an area of Athens traditionally inhabited by middle- to lower-income families. The Centre's extensive experience in primary intervention, prevention and family support programmes, and the support of its professionals[18] for the idea of a toddler group made it ideal for our project.

The implementation of the toddler group project

We began by educating both the scientific community and the local community about the developmental stage of toddlerhood and the function of toddler groups.

The briefing of the scientific community, which includes mental health specialists as well as professionals involved in the growth, development and education of children, i.e. teachers, child minders and paediatricians, was conducted in two phases. We began by informing them in person through meetings in the Community Mental Health Centre or at their own offices, where we presented and then discussed the programme. Following that, we organised a symposium entitled "Psychological and Emotional Development in Early Childhood", where we presented the particularities and characteristics of the preschool age group, with emphasis on the toddler period. Our main speaker, Marie Zaphiriou Woods, was invited to present the Toddler Group programme operating at the Anna Freud Centre in London. The symposium attracted considerable interest: about 300 mental health professionals, i.e. psychologists, psychiatrists, social workers as well as psychology and education students attended the meeting.

The next stage was to inform the local community where the programme was to operate. Printed material was developed and distributed to local residents, private and professional, in homes, mental health centres and nursery schools. The information included a leaflet presenting the programme and its goals, the target group it was addressing and a short description of the toddler stage of development. We also circulated a questionnaire[19] designed to raise awareness of typical toddler issues and their impact on the parents. Finally, a poster was displayed in all nursery schools and childcare centres and published in the local newspaper.

The Greek family's need for such a programme soon became evident. In the first year, referrals came from local paediatricians or from within the Centre to which they had been referred for other reasons. In the second year, we began receiving referrals specifically for the toddler group.

In our initial pilot year, we did not feel that we could ask parents to commit for a year. Instead we requested a commitment to a series of just six weekly meetings, which could be renewed. This flexibility turned out to be unhelpful, raising rather than reducing the parents' anxiety. Therefore, from the second year, we made commitment for one year a prerequisite for participation.

Description of the Greek model

Our theoretical approach is psychoanalytic in its manner of conceptualising and understanding the child's emotional development, his/her relationship with the parents, as well as the dynamics of the group. Technically, we follow the Anna Freud Centre's approach according to which toddler groups occupy an intermediate space between therapy and education (Zaphiriou Woods, 2005).[20]

Modes of intervention in the group are various and are realised at numerous levels. On the first level, in working with the children, the focus is on toddler issues, such as tackling aggression, strengthening boundaries, and helping them learn to share. On the second level, in working with the parents, they are encouraged to learn from each other, to converse amongst themselves, and share their concerns and experiences. At the same time, they are helped to find alternative ways of dealing with difficult situations and to discover enjoyable exchanges and activities with their children. The third level of intervention focuses on the child–parent relationship. We speak to the parents on behalf of their children in an attempt to communicate and express thoughts and feelings which are difficult for the parent or child to put into words. Finally, we try to connect the external reality of the group, that is, what happens in the group, with the internal reality of the members, that is, with their feelings and concerns which may be expressed in action, e.g. when jealousy and sibling rivalry regarding a new member lead to difficulties playing together.

The setting: Creating a space for the group

The space allotted for the running of the toddler group programme was a big room used by other groups during the week as well as for the storage of old furniture. To conduct our group we had to reorganise the room each week, pushing the furniture against the walls in order to create space in the middle. After the first year we gradually disposed of superfluous furniture, so that four years later, all that remains are a few sofas that have become an integral part of the setting. When not in use, our other equipment is now safely stored in a separate room.

Despite these initial difficulties, we have managed to create a safe, stable and warm environment, appropriate for toddler-age children and their parents. The room has to be tidied and set up before and after each meeting.

Children aged between 1 and 3½, with no psychopathology diagnosis, are accepted in the group, which usually consists of 5–6 child–parent pairs. The group is co-ordinated by two psychologists, who are themselves under psychoanalytical supervision[21] once a week. The group meets once a week for 90 minutes. It takes place in the afternoon at a time when many parents finish work.

The toddlers are mostly brought by their mothers, but some fathers join as well. In some cases, fathers substitute for the mother on a regular basis. There are also instances where both parents take part as a family, bringing along more than one child. The parents are asked to commit to participating in the group for at least one academic year, until their child reaches the age of 3½. Departures from the group coincide with the summer holidays and the end of the school year.

Integration, sharing and separation in toddler groups

During toddlerhood, the child seeks separation and autonomy while continuing to feel dependent on the mother. This process of separation-individuation generates considerable anxiety because of the toddler's unconscious wish to merge with mother while also fearing being devoured by her and therefore losing him/herself (Mahler et al., 1975). The mother is correspondingly deeply involved in a similar process because of her dependence on her child, and her relationship with her inner child[22] and her inner mother–child relationship (Navridi, 2007).

The toddler groups aim to provide support to toddler-aged children, their parents, and the parent–child relationship, at this critical developmental stage. However, by its very nature, a group arouses a degree of ambivalence in its members. As Foulkes (1948) pointed out, individuals have a more or less unconscious fear that the group may deprive them of their individuality. It therefore represents a danger as much as a promise of much-needed support. This is inevitable as the group becomes an organism, as it were, with an existence over and above that of the individuals who make up its composition. There are therefore echoes of the conflict between dependency and separation in the parent–child relationship, and many group interactions and events can be seen as attempts to deal with the anxiety arising from such contradictory feelings, as will be illustrated below.

The process of sharing is clearly manifested in the toddler group. We share space, toys and snacks as well as our thoughts, worries, and feelings. Furthermore, participants – both parents and children – are expected to share not only the material objects of the group but also the therapists. Therapists, in turn, are called upon to share the practicalities of arranging and tidying the space, as well as working and thinking together for the group, thus also promoting a model of co-operative partnership. This process of sharing takes place at both conscious and unconscious levels and aims at strengthening the attachment between toddlers and their parents and the interpersonal relationships within the group, as well as supporting the process of separation and autonomy. As Marie Zaphiriou Woods observes, during toddlerhood: "attachment and separation are interrelated, so interventions will often impact on both, even though the primary intention may be one or the other" (Zaphiriou Woods, 2005).

Life begins through a process of sharing. Each one of us comes to life because someone else, that is our mother, managed to tolerate sharing her being and her body with us during pregnancy. Likewise, in order for a group to exist, according to Anzieu (1975), its members must fantasise it as an ideal human unity, which contains them. Interestingly enough, Foulkes (1964) called this deeper psychological web of human group unity "group matrix"[23], a term evocative of pregnancy. In other words, at a deeply unconscious level, there may be a unifying force which is felt to be physical.

Sharing and the parent–toddler dyad

The toddler group setting consists of a series of constants: the room, the toys, the therapists, and the other participants, but also some routine activities such as eating a snack in the middle of the session or tidying up the playroom at the end. In the group, the participants are expected to share all the above and it is through sharing that they negotiate important emotional issues. Parents are given the opportunity to play or learn to play with their children by sharing the toys available amongst themselves.

Activities with toys contribute to the process of separation-individuation because they promote the notion that parents and toddler have separate thoughts and feelings, which can be safely communicated through play. As children are invited to share toys, activities and other things in the group a process takes place which contributes to the dissolution of the magical omnipotence, which is so characteristic of toddlers' thought, and enables autonomy rather than egocentrism (Pretorius, 2004).

How does this take place? The child learns to perceive that an object, thing or activity has significance for others as much as for himself. A toy, for example, can be seen as the vehicle of others' projections, metaphorically as well as literally. The symbolic value of the object is therefore not determined solely by the individual child. This process forms the basis of the child's awareness of other people's minds and subjectivity.

Within the group there is a continuous give and take of objects, which resembles a silent dialogue amongst the participants. In a way, it is as though emotions are transferred through this dialogue, with a particular play material used to communicate unspoken messages.

> Ionas (2 years 7 months) and his mother are playing with plasticine. This is their game: He cuts the plasticine in neat little pieces and gives them to her.

She, in turn, joins the pieces into one sausage which she gives back to Ionas. He then starts to cut it up again into smaller pieces which he calls "carrots" and gives to his mother to "eat".

In this particular example, parent and toddler are not only sharing the plasticine, but a whole lot more within the therapeutic context of the group. This harmonious trade can be seen to represent a dynamic interpersonal process between them. Through cutting and rejoining the pieces of plasticine, it is as if mother and child act out the separation-individuation process. The play material provides them with the means to work out their related anxieties. The message they share is that by dividing into separate entities, like the plasticine, they can exist independently without becoming "amorphous" or disappearing.

The use of plasticine to denote separation in this mother and child's play suggests the following meanings: that separation is something malleable rather than rigid; that it can be "eaten" and "digested", i.e. internalised and not merely introjected as something foreign and threatening; that one can play with it and its transformations. Introducing the mother and the child pair to the field of metaphor and metonymy (Chouvier, 2002), the plasticine game enables and eases communication and the elaboration of the emotional turmoil of separation.

In other cases, the separation-individuation process does not take place so smoothly, and sharing is not feasible because the anxiety it generates makes the subject unable to use[24] the object (Winnicott, 1971).

> Tonia (3 years 2 months) is participating along with her sister Fivi, aged 13 months, and both parents. In this particular session, the mother was continuously preoccupied with the sister (a frequent occurrence) and the father was playing with Tonia and another child, Stefanos, aged 2 years and 5 months, helping them to construct a railroad and its surroundings (signs, trees, etc.). At some point, Tonia knocked everything down and re-arranged it in her own fashion. Her father scolded her but continued the play. After a while, Tonia started snatching the trees from Stefanos as soon as he was about to place them around the railway. The boy started crying, demanding the toys, while Tonia's parents told her off severely, making her cry bitterly.

Sharing is difficult for Tonia. She seems to experience it as "there is nothing left for me". When she was born, her mother had a serious accident. Tonia had to be looked after by her grandparents for a couple of months. By the time she had recovered, mother was pregnant again but had to remain in bed from the fifth month onwards. When her sister was born, Tonia was again sent to her grandparents, receiving only visits from her parents. She was not given the chance to form a secure attachment with her mother, through which she would have been able to build self-confidence and move towards greater autonomy. The birth of her sister when she was 2 and her parents' difficulty in meeting both children's emotional needs further compromised the process of separation-individuation, and her ability to share. Consequently, Tonia struggles to share her parents with her sister, as well as to play co-operatively and share her father and the railway game with someone else. For Tonia, a playmate in the game with her father becomes a rival, threatening the relationship with father, and arousing intense anger and jealousy.

In the illustration above, it seems that the railway game acquires a role in the transference and comes alive through the projections it gathers. The trees take the form of parents who cannot "stand by" both children simultaneously; the children have to "make them stand" differently, each one in their own way, in order to possess them. Again, the play materials mediate between parent and child, but also within the group amongst its members, transferring emotional messages. In this case, the message is about the impossibility of sharing when you feel deprived and anxious about the survival of those on whom you depend.

Besides the toys and play materials, the group members are expected to share the therapists, who also constitute usable objects for the participants, mediating within and between the parent–toddler dyads. Sometimes, the therapist functions as the mediator, offering his/her senses as a bridge between parent and child. At these moments, a third person appears to be needed to help them fill the gap between themselves, that is the "potential" space which, according to Winnicott (1971), is created during the separation of mother and infant, in order to turn separation into communication.

> Socrates (17 months) turned the desk into a little house and crept underneath. His parents were focused elsewhere and did not see him. Looking at the therapist, he called: "Mummy". The therapist repeated this while looking at the mother who, however, answered: "He means you".

In Socrates' case, his gaze appeared insufficient to bridge the distance between his mother and himself. The therapist had to mediate: by transferring her gaze from Socrates to his mother, she also transferred his gaze onto her. In this incident, the therapist's gaze appears to be more than a purely personal action. Crossing the boundaries of the strictly personal space, it can be shared by the members of the group.

In another instance, the therapist was called upon to use her sense of smell to convey a message in the form of smell from one participant to another:

> The mother of Pericles (27 months) was having trouble potty-training him. One day, she told the therapist: "If you smell something, please let me know because my nose is blocked so I can't tell."

Pericles' mother had great difficulty in allowing him to take responsibility for his body. She often complained about no longer being able to lay him down to change his nappies. By asking the therapist to inform them when Pericles needs a nappy change, it was as though she was expressing her need for support to eventually hand over responsibility to the boy himself. A triangle between the therapist and the mother–toddler pair was created: mother and therapist shared responsibility for Pericles' body in order for him to gradually come to share the responsibility with them, and mother and child shared the therapist's sense of smell, to ease the transition to his achievement of greater bodily independence and ownership.

Sharing the group as a collective subject

As well as being a collection of people, each with their own subjectivity, the group becomes a "collective subject", with its own characteristic procedures, its history, culture and character. Kaës (1976) describes the group as an organ of connections and transitions of the members' internal realities. The transition is from the member's personal reality to one that is experienced as shared. This sharing is often expressed by one member of the group, who at a certain moment appears to take responsibility for the group and to represent it. The group can then express its emotional need through that person.

> It is snack time. Everyone is seated at the table, except Lydia (2 years 3 months), who refuses to sit with the others and continues to play with her toy. At some point, she asks the therapist to help her. The therapist responds to her call and then returns to the table. She leaves again when Lydia again asks for help. Within a few minutes everyone has got up and the snack framework has collapsed.

The example above took place in one of the first group sessions, when group activities caused considerable anxiety to the individual members. Snack time, when everyone is asked to sit together around the table, was one of these activities. By repeatedly distracting the therapist, little Lydia managed to destroy the group activity, and so provided a "solution" to the group's anxieties. Identifying perhaps with the group's projections, the therapist disrupted the structure. In doing so, she helped the group to avoid a situation that caused them anxiety.

At other times, the anxiety is not voiced by any single member; rather a shared emotional mood develops which is expressed beyond words and "speaks" for the conscious or preconscious preoccupations of the individual participants. It is as if the crisis the group undergoes at a collective level is internalised by each member, becoming a silent personal crisis.

In this session, we welcome a new couple-member to the group. Despite careful preparation for this event in previous sessions, the newcomers' arrival causes great tension. The children are unable to share the toys or play together. There are constant fights and crying, as they grab toys from each other. At the same time, the parents are also having trouble getting on and joining all together in a conversation. Each one attempts to monopolise the therapist's attention, excluding the others. One mother actually said: "We are divided like we're at war."

In the above group, it seems impossible for the participants to share anything, be it a toy or a topic for discussion. It seems that the arrival of the new member in the group triggers off a situation of sibling rivalry, which overwhelms the group as a whole.

Another example:

In this particular session, the group will meet the new therapist who will replace the current one for a period of two months. Only one mother–toddler pair has come. Throughout the session, Mihalis (2 years 7 months) plays with the same toys and in the same way as one of the absent boys (Andreas), filling the boot of the big car with the toy animals, and making and cooking fresh plasticine peas, both of which were favourite activities of Andreas in recent weeks. Moreover, his mother Fay treats him the way Andreas is usually treated by his mother, even using the same expressions.

Mihalis and his mother seem to be playing out the group's preoccupation with the replacement of their therapist, by replacing the absent participants themselves and by keeping them present at a representational level. The group's anxiety about survival was also reflected in the absence of the other group members and in Mihalis' play; every time he played a little more roughly with a toy, he anxiously took it to his mother to check if the toy was all right or if it had 'broken'.

There are periods in the group process when participants seem to silently agree to exchange ideas on a particular subject. At first sight, it may appear that this subject has no connection at all with what is taking place in the group, but in reality it is closely linked to the group's immediate emotional present, to the here and now of the group (Navridis, 2005).

The group is going through a period of preparation in order to be separated for some time from one of the two therapists. In this particular session, one mother talks about holidays in view of Christmas which is approaching, saying how difficult it is for her to spend this time alone with her children since she is divorced. A little later, a father starts talking about his work. He says his colleague is absent on "sick leave" and as a result he has twice the amount of work and is having a hard time. In addition he talks about the uniform he wears at work which is plastic and makes him sweat, thus risking illness. Still later, a toddler who is playing with his mother and one of the therapists, asks the second therapist to join in and play with them.

In this particular group, the dominant themes are the difficulties caused by someone's absence or departure. The topic of discussion constitutes a transformed and metaphorical means for the group to speak about or enact their current concern, consciously or preconsciously: the departure of their therapist and their worry about whether they will be able to survive without her. This was interpreted to the group at a suitable moment.

Conclusion

The toddler groups provide a transitional space between the toddler and the mother, where "there is trust and reliability in order to create a potential space which can become unlimited separation space . . . that the toddler and the adult can creatively fill with play" (Winnicott, 1971, p. 189). As a framework directed towards prevention, the toddler groups constitute a developmental space between the healthy and pathological. With regard to ways of intervening, they belong to the intermediate space between therapy and education (Zaphiriou Woods, 2005).

The sharing process in this group experience materialises in the transitional space that exists amongst participants. It is a process that takes place at a conscious and unconscious level, in the space between the inside and outside of the individual members (Winnicott, 1971), sometimes strengthening the bond amongst them and at other times contributing to the separation and individuation process. According to Kaës (1987), group clinical work is in itself a transitional experience, in the sense that it forms a common creative ground, ensuring for each individual member of the group a play area, between what is his and what transcends him, between what makes him unique and what he shares with others.

Chapter 13

Finding our own path: Engaging working parents in a toddler group in Peru

Ana María Barrantes and Elena Piazzon

A visit to the Anna Freud Centre parent-toddler groups in 1999[25] fuelled our desire to work in a similar way with small children and their parents in Lima. We began to establish this work and called our group Carretel – meaning "Cotton Reel", which refers to one of the first symbolic interpretations of a toddler's play: the Fort-da game (S. Freud, 1920, p. 15).

The prevailing culture

In Peru, the rearing of children under 5 focuses primarily on performance. Nursery schools and places that offer early stimulation for babies emphasise cognitive and academic progress, promising to produce talented children, but arguably neglecting the child's developmental emotional needs. The emphasis on performance encourages some parents to pay for structured, achievement-oriented programmes in order to teach themselves how to train their own children, and may interfere in the development of natural, spontaneous relationships. Some parents are concerned that their child will not perform adequately in an increasingly competitive society. It is often these parents who struggle most to understand and relate to their child as a small individual who is separate from themselves.

Parents also send their young children to early academic programmes, because they are led to believe that their child needs to learn socialising skills in a formal setting. This overlooks and undermines the appreciation that socialisation begins in the home, within the protected family environment. The importance of the parents and family is further undermined by another tendency in Peruvian culture, to delegate the main aspects of child rearing to others, regardless of the socio-economic level of the family. We find this very concerning. In the upper socio-economic classes, children have nannies even if the mother does not work. As a result of delegating child care to others, many parents who consult us do not feel that they know their child. They struggle with the "to and fro" of daily life, because it is usually taken care of by others. For example, in Ana María's Nursery School, the psychologist recently organised a workshop for parents to discuss toilet training. Only five mothers attended, even though the workshop was scheduled in the evening, when mothers might be free to attend. Thereafter, the workshop was scheduled in the morning, directly after the children were brought to the nursery, in the hope that this might be a more convenient time. This time, only four mothers attended. When a workshop was organised for nannies, more than 30 signed up and many had to be turned away!

In the lower socio-economic classes, older siblings, other relatives or neighbours typically care for young children, while their mothers work or are occupied by domestic matters. There are some public childcare centres, like Wawa Wasi in Quechua, where mothers in the community are paid and supervised by the state to care for the children of working mothers. The children of middle- and upper-class families are seldom sent to daycare centres, as a nanny usually looks after them in the home. Some working mothers, however, do use daycare if they are worried about leaving their child at home with a nanny or if they seek a more stimulating environment for their child.

The healthcare system in Peru deals only with acute medical problems. Some people have private medical insurance, while others have no insurance at all. There is no organised system for referring children to our parent-toddler group or to other organisations where families might receive psychological and emotional support.

After several years of working with children and their parents, we became aware that adults in our culture tend not to speak much to small children, apparently not regarding them as thinking individuals with separate minds. This, and the fact that a nanny is often present, makes it difficult for parents to internalise an image of their toddler as an individual who appreciates verbal communications and explanations. Young children do not seem to be credited with much awareness of their surroundings. Parents often take children from one activity to another without warning or explanation and restrict their communications to commanding and informing the child. While some parents are very good at reading their child stories, they may not engage the child in a two-way conversation. Some mothers have shared their concern that their child's language development might be delayed, without being aware that a child learns to speak by being spoken to.

The following two clinical vignettes illustrate the prevailing manner of relating to and communicating with toddlers:

> Michelle's mother was concerned that her daughter (18 months), could not speak yet. While the mother became upset telling us, Michelle approached her with a plastic strawberry. She showed it and gave it to her mother, uttering a long babbling phrase. "See what I mean?" the mother said, quite upset. She told her child, "Michelle, I cannot understand you, speak to me clearly". We pointed out that Michelle already knew the melody of speech, but needed help to learn the words.

This vignette shows the child's intention to communicate with her mother. Language is an intersubjective process that involves an encounter between at least two subjects. For it to develop, the child's effort needs to be met by a mother who is thinking of her child as a developing being. We find that adults in our culture have difficulty acknowledging young children as "others" with their own minds. As the example above shows, we frequently observe parents saying things about their toddlers as if they were not present, or were unable to hear and understand what is being said. They may then miss their children's communications – whether through babbling (above) or play (below).

> The mother of Isabella (almost 3 years old) spoke aloud about not wanting to have any more children. She said she was not made to be a mother. Isabella made a bed for her doll. She gave her mother the doll. While holding the doll, the mum said, "I do not want her to get all worked up about this baby game; I don't know how Isabella plays so well at being a mother". We suggested that Isabella might have learned it from her mum and that she wanted her mother to be happy playing "mummy, her mummy". This had a powerful impact on the mother, who was more gentle and tender with her daughter, in subsequent sessions.

Introductory workshops

In Peru, Nursery Schools compete to offer new programmes. They are perceived as more attractive if they are imported from a sophisticated country or a well-known school. Fee-paying primary schools offer places to increasingly younger children, without being qualified to address their emotional needs. We felt the need to create a space to reflect on the place that children occupy in our lives and society and to think about and discuss the needs of young children. Consequently, when we started our parent-toddler group in 2000, we also organised fortnightly workshops entitled "Working with Toddlers" based on Erna Furman's (1992) model. We invited nursery school directors and psychologists, speech therapists, paediatricians and other professionals in related fields. Approximately 20 professionals from various institutions met to talk about clinical material and review relevant literature. Children with language difficulties and the process of mourning in a child who had lost one parent were two issues we discussed.

Starting Grupo Carretel

The first few months were spent reviewing the literature, drawing on our related and complementary professional backgrounds. Since we did not yet have our own premises, our "virtual" organisation, called Grupo Carretel, met in our private consulting rooms or at Ana María's Nursery School.

We tried every way we could think of to advertise and get a group started. We distributed flyers and brochures to colleagues and nursery schools throughout Lima and spoke to paediatricians and professionals. Very few referrals came from the paediatricians and it took eight months before we found six children to start a group.

One mother, who was eager to start the group, started speaking to others. This "word of mouth" method proved the most successful in recruiting new members. Those interested were mostly young couples who were searching for the latest innovations in child activities and stimulation. They seemed mistrustful of written material and glossy brochures, but became interested when they heard about something that sounded selective, exclusive and not widely advertised; they were curious and keen to be included in what they thought might be the latest trend.

The parent-toddler group met in Ana María's Nursery School, which is located in a middle-class neighbourhood of Lima. A classroom was adapted to make it suitable for toddler-aged children. The room led onto a patio where there were moving toys like cars and tricycles. There were caged animals in the garden, such as rabbits, a baby alpaca, parakeets and a squirrel. The children interacted with the animals and brought carrots from home to feed them.

One of us meets briefly with a parent before they start attending the group. We explain the group to them, try to find out about their expectations and ask them to complete a simple application form. We charge a moderate fee. One or two observers are usually present in the group to help us reconstruct the group process and to train as future leaders. We chose to run the group on Saturdays from 09:00 to 10:30am, since parents who work or delegate childcare are more likely to be free to attend with their toddlers at this time. To our surprise, five of the six children came with both parents! A few of these children also attended the nursery school (without their parents). Initially this was confusing for them, but we helped them to work through and understand it.

Our journey

Leaving the dyadic work of the consulting room to begin to work with a group of toddlers and their parents was not easy for us. To complicate things further, since most toddlers came with both parents, we were working with triads. Our initial anxiety about beginning this new experience was compounded by the parents' anxiety about meeting and getting to know each other, watching their child in relation to other children and adults and – most crucially – the anxiety arising from the chaos and uncertainty of free play. We found it very difficult to contain the group process and the anxiety generated by the lack of structure. The parents, who were looking for the latest innovative programme, seemed puzzled and uncomfortable. They seemed to be thinking, "Is this all there is to it?" and to be wondering whether we could maintain a safe atmosphere. It was a new experience for us all. Although we managed to engage them in talking and playing and snack time proceeded fairly well, we did not know how we would get to know each family. After the first group session, we felt overwhelmed by the whole experience.

The parents' apprehension and our own insecurity impelled us to reassure each parent about the benefits of this activity. We lacked confidence initially that we could contain their anxieties within the group setting and feared that they would stop attending. We discussed this extensively amongst ourselves, evaluated the tension and hesitation we sensed and decided to offer each family an individual appointment. We announced this at snack time during the fourth group session. We each met three couples individually, and we repeated these meetings two months later. These two individual meetings helped us to develop a working alliance with each family and gain insight into their particular expectations. Discussions with the Anna Freud Centre toddler group leaders were helpful in highlighting the need to contain and work through the anxieties in the group. We were increasingly able to do this as we gained experience and confidence. Most families in that first parent-toddler group continued to attend and work with us for one and a half years.

When we started a new group in the second year, the situation was very different, as we had become known to the community for more than a year. The conferences and workshops that we had organised had made people interested in and appreciative of the value of a space to play. Despite all the parents and toddlers being new, starting this second group went very smoothly. Of the eight families that joined the group, six of the mothers were professionals, working in child-related fields, and two had adopted children. Thus, we seemed to have successfully reached professionals in related fields, but we had not yet successfully introduced our ideas to the community in general. Increasing public interest in our ideas remains one of our major concerns.

Clinical material

Camila (1 year 4 months) attended the group with both her parents, during the first year of our work. Her case illustrates the difficulty we experienced in establishing a working relationship with some families. Although on the surface our connection was friendly and fluid, at a deeper level we experienced them as withholding and keeping their doubts and concerns to themselves.

Camila's mum had helped to spread the word and get our first group started. Both Camila's parents were young, successful professionals, who described their daughter as strong-willed and decisive during the initial meeting. They said that they wanted the best for her and perceived our toddler group as offering the latest "fad" in child-rearing. Camila's mother stopped working when Camila was born, but some months later, she enrolled her in a daycare centre so that she could start part-time teaching at a university. Apparently, Camila settled there "without difficulty". When Camila was moved to a second daycare centre, her parents were surprised that she had difficulty separating from her mother. Unsure of how to help Camila, they approached us.

Camila arrived at the first group meeting with both parents. She clung to her mother, hiding her face in her mother's neck and whining "Mummy, mummy, mummy," as if her mother were absent. She showed no interest in the toys or other children. Contrary to her parents' perception of her, we observed a very anxious little girl. Her parents were surprised by her behaviour and linked it to her unhappy experience at the second daycare centre, which she no longer attended. We noticed that mother also found it difficult to settle, after she arrived at the group. She walked around the room wearing her coat, carrying Camila and her handbag. We felt it was important for us to welcome the three of them and help them settle at the beginning of each group meeting.

During their first individual meeting, these efficient professionals revealed that all aspects of their personal and professional lives were planned and that they disliked situations they could not control. They were struggling to create a space for Camila in their busy lives. It emerged that they seldom talked to Camila about matters that related directly to her. We reminded them of an event in the toddler group when the father had asked for directions to the bathroom. We had asked him if he had told Camila he was leaving the room. He had said he did not think it necessary, as she was playing by herself. In the course of the meeting we encouraged them to think of Camila as a unique person with a mind of her own. Camila's father commented that when he first met his wife, they talked a lot, went out together and something slowly developed between them. He then asked if we were suggesting that he do the same with Camila. He said that he had thought that that process was already complete as she was his own flesh and blood. The parents seemed to become more aware that relationships need space, time and imagination to develop.

A few months later, the mother told us that she was pregnant, but that Camila did not yet know. They said that they thought it would be better for Camila to start toilet training so that she could enjoy the summer and her second birthday free of diapers, before they told her about the pregnancy. They seemed to want Camila to achieve their expectations, before breaking the news about the new baby. It was difficult for them to imagine that she was already picking up clues that something was happening in the family and that this might complicate the toilet training.

In subsequent weeks, Camila's early separation difficulties were played out in the toilet training. One day Camila arrived clinging tightly to her mother's leg, as if she wanted to merge into her body. We welcomed them and spoke directly to Camila saying, "It's difficult to come in today". Camila did not respond. Mother entered, dragging her leg and the clinging child. Once inside the room, Camila sat on mother's lap. Again we spoke to Camila saying, "Perhaps you need some time to settle and see what you feel like doing". She started wriggling on her mother's lap, and then suddenly wet herself. As she was taking her to the bathroom, her mother said very calmly to her, "Your pee has come out," as though this had nothing to do with Camila. While mother changed her, Camila started naming the drawings in the changing area. She seemed to be trying to deny the discomfort and overcome the humiliation of having lost bladder control by finding an area of competence her mother approved of. One of us wiped up the mess in the playroom, as if to protect Camila. When they returned, mother commented that Camila never asked to go to the toilet and that the adults constantly asked her if she needed to go. We addressed mother and child saying, "Perhaps we can help Camila to begin to recognise the messages that come from her body?" Mother said that when she wet herself, her nanny became upset and scolded her. We said, "Camila might think that it is the adults who are in charge of her body."

The second clinical example is taken from our second group which, as mentioned above, started smoothly and harmoniously. Unlike the parents in the first group, these mothers had a good understanding that the group provided a space to play and relate. They were in tune with our aims and were eager to attend. The members interacted freely and a very open atmosphere developed quite quickly. It took us some time to become aware of the specific difficulties that existed amongst these young professionals.

Fernanda (1 year 4 months) was an observant, verbal child who enjoyed a very close, interactive relationship with her mother. Mother's attunement with her daughter impressed us from the beginning: she waited and calmly followed her daughter's play. However, she found it difficult to let Fernanda enjoy her increasing autonomy and Fernanda seemed anxious about her. On their first day, Fernanda picked up a story book called "Mummy is having a baby". Mother became anxious, interrupting her reading to tell Fernanda, "It is for older children," and did not finish reading the story. Fernanda continued to pick up the same story book, each time they attended the group. When the mother noticed this, she became uncomfortable and talked it over. She confessed that Fernanda's wish was to have a baby brother or sister; this was painful for her as she had had fertility difficulties. Once this was understood, they were able to finish reading the story. Fernanda then began bringing her mother two or three dolls saying, "You take care of them". Fernanda instructed her to feed the baby dolls and to do things for them. This kept her mother very busy, while Fernanda went off to play away from her. Mother recognised Fernanda's need to separate, commenting with a laugh that, "Fernanda seems more ready to be away from me, than I am to be away from her". She told us that her own mother had died when Fernanda was less than a year old. She was deeply affected by her mother's premature death, as she had enjoyed a close relationship with her. Knowing about this bereavement helped us to understand why it was so difficult for her to facilitate her daughter's growing independence. She was aware of her periods of sadness and was concerned about the effect on her child.

Three months after joining the group, mother unexpectedly became pregnant. She had needed fertility treatment to conceive Fernanda and had mixed feelings about this new pregnancy. Though she was happy to have conceived naturally, she did not feel ready to have another child. When she eventually found the courage to tell Fernanda about the pregnancy, Fernanda started expressing some hostility towards her mother. She sometimes refused to play with her at home or demanded to be carried around, which mother seemed to accept. They then missed the group for three weeks, because mother was in bed with a threatened miscarriage. The three-week mid-year holiday followed. When they returned to the group, we learned that mother had lost the baby. She had not managed to come to terms with this loss, nor had she been able to tell Fernanda or explain why she had spent time in bed. After talking with us about it, mother and father explained to Fernanda at home, "Mummy was in bed, because the doctor was not sure if the baby is coming and he finally told us that the baby is not coming". This clear explanation seemed to calm Fernanda. Mother reported that Fernanda settled better at bedtime and was less tearful when she went to work. In the group she gradually recovered her creative and joyful pretend play. She was joined in this by a new boy who was the same age as her, and they began to play collaboratively together.

Current situation

After six years of running the parent-toddler group, we are now reviewing and reformulating our approach. We have become aware that the physical location of the group in the nursery complicates the referral process and interferes with the children attending the nursery. As there has been no space exclusively dedicated to the toddler group, the room has had to be set up and tidied away each week, which is very inconvenient. We have also struggled to maintain a constant flow of new members wishing to join the group. We are in the process of finding a space that will be exclusively dedicated to the parent-toddler group and addressing the other challenges.

Part III

Research and evaluation

Introduction

Kay Asquith

The University College London Master of Science degree in Psychoanalytic Developmental Psychology is based at the Anna Freud Centre (AFC) and has enduring links to the parent-toddler groups. A central element of the MSc is the observation of children in naturalistic settings, with a compulsory weekly observation of a parent and infant in the home, continuing for one year. Students may also choose to observe toddlers once a fortnight, recording and presenting their observations for discussion in small groups, which are facilitated by the toddler group leader. Observing the toddler AFC groups allows students to follow the developmental stages of toddlerhood and to see normal parent–child interactions. This makes their theoretical learning "come alive". They also observe the toddler leader and assistant interacting with the children and parents in "therapeutic" ways. Honing their observational skills and being exposed to psychoanalytic practice greatly facilitates the development of those students who choose to continue on to a clinical career.

The toddler groups also provide an important setting in which students may undertake research. Every MSc student undertakes a substantial piece of independent research and some elect to work with the toddler groups. Such projects may involve quantitative or qualitative analyses or a combination of both. Relevant and mutually interesting research questions are developed in consultation with the student's individual supervisor and the toddler group staff. In this way the students work on clinically relevant material and their findings can be fed back into the thinking and practice of the groups. Past research topics have included interviewing mothers about how attending a toddler group helped their child's transition to nursery school and exploring parents' feelings about attending a sheltered group run for toddlers with special needs (see chapter 7).

In order to give a flavour of the projects undertaken, and how particular research questions require different methodologies, the following chapters describe three projects in more detail. The first is a qualitative investigation of parents' thoughts and feelings about attending a psychoanalytic toddler group. This is followed by a quantitative study based on coding parents' interviews for reflective functioning capacity at the time they joined a toddler group, and again upon leaving. It investigates whether attendance impacted on parental ability to reflect about their own and their toddler's emotional experience. The final chapter is an observational study, describing how "snack time" in a group was used by parents and staff to encourage socially appropriate mealtime behaviour.

Chapter 14

A qualitative study of the experience of parents attending a psychoanalytic parent-toddler group[26]

Annabel Kitson, María Luisa Barros and Nick Midgley

Over the last 20 years there has been an upsurge of interest in and development of early intervention services in the field of mental health (Kassebaum, 1994; Zigler & Styfco, 1995). Today, it is widely recognised that early interventions are essential to help mitigate emotional and behavioural difficulties in children, which can lead to emotional disturbances, pathological behaviour and social problems if not attended to (Fonagy, 1998; Green Paper, 1999). As part of the ten year childcare strategy, UK government initiatives in health and education (National Service Framework NSF, Every Child Matters) have tried to implement whole system reforms to provide young people with the best start in life (HM Treasury, 2004). By offering more integrated multi-agency services to children through the development of Sure Start Children's Centres, the initiatives seek to increase the percentage of 0–5 year olds showing age-appropriate levels of personal, emotional and social wellbeing. Since there is recognition that services that are solely aimed at children are not enough to address the issue, national policy has placed greater emphasis on primary prevention programmes and early interventions, to support parents, children and their families (Department of Health, 2004). The current focus on universal and targeted services aims to support parents of pre-school children in order to minimise risk of poor outcomes. For example, by providing additional support to parents whose children are at risk (Department for Education and Skills, 2006) and enhancing appropriate parenting styles, such programmes foster children's healthy development into adulthood (National Service Framework, Department of Health, 2004, p. 9).

Many preventative strategies for parents and children have been developed and are now on offer. The Early Years Foundation Stage (Department for Education and Skills, 2007) helps guide all early years providers, as they set out a structure of learning, development and care for under-fives, providing a range of activities including parent-toddler groups. There has been little research looking into the effectiveness of such interventions. Some early studies in "at risk" populations found that parent-toddler groups offered parents a chance to learn from each other about parenting, health, education and children's developmental needs (Palfreeman, 1982). More recently, analysis of community-based Sure Start Local Programmes (SSLPs) in disadvantaged areas has been evaluating the impact of a range of services offered to families, including toddler groups, parenting programmes and other provisions. The work carried out by the National Evaluation of Sure Start (NESS) found that in over 9,000 families in 150 SSLP areas, parents attending SSLPs were more likely to engage with services, be warm and accepting of their children and show less negative parenting, compared to families in similarly deprived areas with no SSLP (NESS, Belsky & Melhuish, 2008). These parenting styles were found to benefit the children, who, at 3, demonstrated improved social skills and positive behaviour, as well as greater independence and self-regulatory capacities in comparison to children in non-SSLP areas (National Evaluation of Sure Start Research Team, 2008).

These impact studies have yielded important results, but little is known about parents' experiences of attending toddler groups, especially the specialist psychoanalytic toddler groups that are part of the Anna Freudian tradition, which were established with the explicit aim of enabling parents and toddlers to establish trusting relationships, and of promoting toddler development (Zaphiriou Woods, 2000).

The study

Despite a growing body of clinical knowledge built up over 25 years, the Anna Freud Centre parent-toddler groups have been under-used as a setting for formal research studies and little formal research has been done exploring the experience of service users. The study reported here aims to understand in greater depth what characterises such a service, from the parents' own perspectives. The sample was small, allowing for an in-depth analysis of the interviews, and the study was exploratory, trying to map out for the first time some key aspects of the experience of attending a psychoanalytic toddler group from the perspective of parents. Given the importance of service-user involvement in the evaluation of early intervention services, and the increasing emphasis on evidence-based practice, it is vital to understand from families themselves what they consider to be the distinctive features of a psychoanalytically informed parent-toddler group.

Methodology

The study made use of a qualitative research methodology – Interpretative Phenomenological Analysis (IPA) (Smith & Osborn, 2003) – that requires an in-depth analysis of data from a small number of participants. We interviewed six mothers and one father who attended with their toddlers for a period of a year and whose children had recently left the toddler groups, asking them about their experiences of the group. All the parents but one were first-time parents, in their early thirties; only one single mother was in her forties. They were all middle-class European parents, except for one who came from an Asian background.

A semi-structured interview was devised using open-ended questions in line with the principles outlined by Smith (Smith & Osborn, 2003). Consent was sought and given for the interviews to be transcribed verbatim and then analysed using IPA (Smith, Osborn, & Jarman, 1999).

Results

The researchers' analysis of the data led to three "superordinate themes", each of which captured certain aspects of the parents' experiences of attending the Anna Freud Centre toddler groups. Our presentation of the findings of the study is organised around three broad areas that parents spoke about as significant to them:

- the setting of the toddler groups;
- the experience of the parents themselves;
- the experience of the group for the toddlers.

We will briefly highlight some of the findings within each of these areas, with extracts from the interview data to help illustrate the themes.

The setting of the toddler groups

Almost all of the participants commented on the setting of the toddler groups in terms of the regularity and predictability they offered: the same room, familiar toys, a "serene" atmosphere (although not all the time!) and certain "rules of conduct" laid out by the toddler group leaders. This seemed especially important for families who had histories of loss, sudden transitions and unpredictability. As one parent put it, when talking about her son's experience of the groups: "I think that what he really lacked, until we started going there, was a routine and I noticed that from going there, how much he liked that, and he liked that everything was in the same place every week, you know, and the same people are there. And you can find the same book that you want and he really, really liked that." Some of the parents appreciated the structure this predictable setting gave, while others felt more ambivalent: "There was this feeling of making a commitment which I think is absolutely right, but I think all of those things could frighten some people . . . because I know what it's like to be a young parent, I think those things might have been quite scary."

Participants commented on other aspects of the setting as being poten-tially off-putting for families. One was the fact that observers (students who are learning about child development) attend the groups, which was described as "quite weird" or "odd" by parents; another was the fact that the groups take place as part of a Centre which is known as a "child mental health/psychoanalytic" setting, which could be a source of support (knowing that this was a place where people understood about families and the difficulties they go through) but also a source of anxiety.

The combination of these factors made one parent feel considerable pressure to "behave well", because she felt people were watching to see if she was doing "really crap parenting". Such anxiety was particularly marked when parents described how they felt before attending the groups for the first time; once they had begun to attend most parents felt that the atmosphere was non-judgemental: "It is an environment where you can be natural, you don't have to be embarrassed." This seemed particularly important for parents who felt very ashamed of their toddlers' "naughty" behaviour, which sometimes prevented them from mixing with other families.

The experience of the parents

For parents who were often socially isolated and/or newly-arrived in the UK, for whom the experience of being a parent was often "miserable", the toddler groups offered them a place to socialise with others. "It was more like a family for me," explained one parent, who had recently arrived in the country, while several commented on the feeling of being supported themselves by attending the group, as it had a "sort of containing kind of familiarity . . . in terms of being structured, boundaried".

Parents raised some issues about how it felt for them, as parents, to approach the Anna Freud Centre asking to attend a group. For example, one mother talked about how she felt she "ought to somehow make a case" for her child to attend a group which might primarily be for parents who have some concerns about their toddler's development. Yet conversely, others pointed to the difficulty a parent might have asking for help – perhaps because of how painful it might be for a parent to feel that something is wrong with their child's development or wellbeing, or how hard it might be to acknowledge that they themselves were struggling with being a parent.

For some, part of the value of attending the group was the chance to have a break from their own child, and to allow someone else to play with their toddler, knowing that they were in a safe setting. One parent spoke about her sense of being "stressed and bored", a "24-hour slave" to her children, spending most of her time "supervising" and trying to prevent her two children from "killing each other". She said that the toddler group was one of the few spaces where she could escape from this feeling. Most parents emphasised their appreciation of the opportunity to share and learn from the experiences of other parents who were experiencing similar difficulties with their children, such as sleepless nights or fights over food. Seeing other toddlers' behaviour could also help to reduce the stigma associated with difficult behaviour. As one parent put it, "Knowing that your child is not abnormal because she is doing this and that, cos all the other children are doing the same so, then you think, 'Well, you know, it's a child thing'."

An important issue for some parents was a feeling that they were "under pressure to play" with their toddler all the time. Being observed in the group appeared to stir up feelings of being criticised for some of those interviewed, whilst others felt that this encouraged them to observe their child from a different perspective. For these parents, it was as if being observed played a part in the reaffirmation and development of their own identity as a parent, enabling them to step back and observe their child and recognise his or her own individual needs.

Perhaps more than any other theme, parents spoke of the importance of the relationship to the toddler group leaders. While one of the parents spoke of ways in which she felt criticised and her child was misunderstood, all the others emphasised how valuable it was to have such an opportunity to be listened to, given advice and perhaps most importantly to be offered a different way of thinking about their child. As one parent put it, "She advised me to listen to what [my child] had to say, listen to her side of the story and that was such a foreign concept to me, because in my country you don't listen to a toddler, you just discipline them."

Several other parents echoed the value of coming to see their child as a person with thoughts, feelings and emotions: "I would explain to [the toddler group leader] and she would [tell me that] maybe there is something she, my child, is trying to express and she can't, she's frustrated, and you know, I tried, I started looking at my child as a, you know, as a little person, as opposed to a child or a baby, and started putting myself in her shoes . . . to be a little part of her and try and understand her more because it's amazing how much they do understand and how much they do take in."

The leader's emphasis on boundary-setting was complemented by the importance of positive regard and encouragement, as well as their direct interaction with the toddlers' unacceptable behaviour. One parent described it in this way: "If my child was doing things that he shouldn't then [the toddler group leader] would tell him in no uncertain terms to stop it," said one parent, while another described how "the leader really taught [us] how to say 'No, I don't like that when you grab that or when you push me' or something".

The experience of the toddlers

The toddler hut where the groups meet is well equipped with books and age-appropriate toys, and there is space for the children to move around inside and outside, which was especially important for families living in very cramped housing conditions. Sometimes, the toddler group was the first space outside the home that these toddlers had got to know well – "it's like a piece of territory", explained one parent. She added that her daughter's attitude appeared to be "this is my space and I'll play with what I want to". The participants felt that their children not only had a chance to feel some ownership of this space, but also to grow and develop within it: "She really got to explore – the toys but also explore herself with other children, with other parents."

Several parents commented on the changes that they could see in their child over the course of the year, for example in relation to their child's growing independence, especially where there had been separation difficulties. Such changes were seen as important in aiding the successful transition to nursery.

Parents did not see every aspect of the experience as positive for their children, however. Ambivalence about attending a group where the majority of children had overt behavioural problems was highlighted a number of times. One parent described how "It was quite shocking, with missiles being thrown and heavy things with balls being kicked . . . [one of the other toddlers] would kind of build up into a frenzy of just lashing out all over the place, and I suppose if I wasn't the kind of parent I am I might say that I don't want [my child] to be around that sort of stuff." Yet some parents also admitted relief at knowing that other children could also behave badly, and found hope in the fact that such behaviour could be tolerated and yet also dealt with firmly and appropriately.

Conclusions

Parent-toddler groups are an integral part of local provision outside the home for pre-school children in the UK. However, little systematic research has been done into the impact of these groups and what they can offer to families. While this study was small in scale, it does provide a rich account of parents' experiences of attending a parent-toddler group, and alerts professionals to potential issues of engagement or disengagement in such a service, which is crucial when offering early intervention services to parents and toddlers.

Overall the study confirmed how important it is for early interventions to address the needs of both parent and child, and support both. One parent described the group as "an emotional support for [her child] and for [herself]". Similar feelings were manifest in the accounts of other parents who talked about the group leader providing a key "holding role" for them. In many ways the effectiveness of the toddler group as an intervention rests in the capacity for the toddler group to focus on the needs of the parent *and* child – as well as the relationship between the two. The findings of the study appear to support the belief that such groups must provide maternal and paternal functions to parents and children at a time when they are particularly needful of positive input (Zaphiriou Woods, 2000).

In general the Anna Freud Centre toddler groups were perceived as a nurturing and "stable environment" that functioned symbolically as a secure base (Bowlby, 1988). This stability and safe atmosphere appeared to facilitate parents' reflectivity and fostered trusting relationships and attunement between mother and toddler, through talk and play. The groups laid great emphasis on mother–child play as a means of developing their relationships and stimulating play. While this was confirmed in this study, for some parents coming to the group offered an opportunity for their child to play with other adults and toddlers, developing their social skills that way, while they socialised and shared experiences or rested.

Most parents felt that the group enabled them to express some of the ordinary difficulties of parenting, such as the gradual process of separation and moving onto nursery, as well as giving them an opportunity to think about the feelings their toddlers aroused in them, including the negative ones. Sharing these feelings appeared to help parents feel less anxious, ashamed and alone, and to become more emotionally engaged with their children. Parents learned how to comprehend their children's minds by trying to look at things from a child's perspective. In particular, the psychoanalytic approach taken by the Anna Freud Centre meant that the focus was not on teaching "parenting skills" or offering "strategies", but on encouraging parents to get in touch with their own children's emotional lives and, in doing so, give their behaviour meaning. The study emphasises how important it is for early interventions to address the needs of both parent and child, and that when such interventions are successful they can make an enormous difference. This valuable lesson might also be applicable to many other early intervention settings.

To give the final word to one of the parents taking part in the study: "Places like that toddler group are little gems, and it's so important that there are those things."

Chapter 15

Thinking about my toddler: Can a psychoanalytic toddler group enhance reflective functioning capacities in parents?

Carolina Camino Rivera, Kay Asquith and Anna Prützel-Thomas

The concept of Reflective Functioning

Reflective Functioning (RF) is the disposition to understand one's own behaviour and the actions of others in terms of underlying mental states, such as thoughts, feelings, and wishes (Fonagy & Target, 1997). This capacity evolves gradually in the context of the parent–infant relationship and depends fundamentally on the parent's capacity to contain the child's affects and to anticipate and adjust to the infant's physical and psychological demands (Fonagy, Steele, & Steele, 1991). The caregiver's capacity to acknowledge that the infant possesses a psychological experience of his or her own and to respond to and reflect upon this mental activity allows the child to develop an understanding of his or her own emotions, promotes self-regulation and ultimately helps the child to develop a reflective functioning capacity.

The importance of a reflective capacity was first identified by Fonagy and colleagues in a study using attachment measures with parents expecting their first child (Fonagy et al., 1991a). Expectant parents were interviewed about their own childhood experiences with their parents using the Adult Attachment Interview (AAI) (George, Kaplan, & Main, 1985). This hour-long, semi-structured, semi-clinical interview focuses on early experiences and their effects. The interviews were transcribed and coded on a scale for Reflective Functioning that had been developed for the study (Fonagy et al., 1998). When the first-born children were approximately 1 year old the quality of their attachment relationship with the parent was assessed. A significant level of agreement was found between the parents' attachment classifications, their capacity to reflect on their childhood experiences, and their own child's attachment organisation. As a result, the study concluded that the intergenerational transmission of a secure pattern of attachment might depend on the caregiver's capacity for RF (Fonagy, Steele, Moran, Steele, & Higgitt, 1991b).

Appreciating the link between reflective capacity and a more secure parent–child relationship, Arietta Slade shifted from retrospective consideration of "being parented" (as measured by the AAI) to contemporary consideration of "being a parent" (Slade, 2005). She developed the "Parent Development Interview" (PDI) (PDI: Aber, Slade, Berger, Bresgi, & Kaplan, 1985; PDI-R2-S: Slade, Aber, Berger, Bresgi, & Kaplan, 2003/2005a; PDI-R2: Slade, Aber, Berger, Bresgi, & Kaplan, 2003/2005b) which measures the parent's representations of herself as a parent, her child and their currently developing relationship. In addition, Slade and colleagues developed a scale to measure RF within this setting (Slade, Bernbach, Grienenberger, Wohlgemuth Levy, & Locker, 2005a). Slade, Grienenberger et al. (2005b) found that high maternal RF scores coded in this way were linked to infants classified as securely attached, whereas low maternal RF scores were correlated to children being identified as insecurely attached. They hypothesised that the parent's capacity to reflect upon her own child is the variable that more accurately links adult and infant attachment organisations and better explains the transmission of (in)security of attachment from one generation to the next.

Thus, reflective capacity appears to be related in important ways to a mother's behaviour with her child, and in turn to the child's developing models of attachment. Given that secure attachment tends to predict more positive outcomes for children, intervening to enhance RF in parents could potentially promote more positive attachment relationships and better outcomes for the children.

Enhancing Reflective Functioning

Slade (2003) suggested that the knowledge gained in attachment research could be applied in preventive interventions dedicated to the improvement of RF in parents of infants and toddlers. A number of subsequent studies have investigated the impact of various interventions on maternal reflective capacity (e.g. Goyette-Ewing et al., 2003; Reynolds, 2003; Slade, Sadler et al., 2005c).

In a small-scale study of 15 incarcerated mothers and their infants, Baradon and colleagues (Baradon, Fonagy, Bland, Lenard, & Sleed, 2008) used an attachment-focused intervention, which positions the baby as an active partner, to enhance the quality of parent–infant interactions. The programme of eight two-hour sessions demonstrated a significant increase in the mean overall level of RF. After the course, mothers were able to reflect more freely on how their emotions and behaviours might affect their infants, and the mothers were able to attribute their own and their infant's behaviour to internal mental states more accurately.

These limited findings suggest that maternal RF capacities may improve with an appropriate intervention. Broadly, programmes dedicated to the enhancement of RF capacities in parents focus on the parent–child relationship and tend to include a modelling approach. The psychoanalytic approach used by the Anna Freud Centre (AFC) parent-toddler groups emphasises identifying and thinking about feelings (both conscious and unconscious) in promoting parental understanding of their toddlers' behaviour. These groups offer an ideal space for fostering the enhancement of RF capacities in parents.

The present study

The study sought to address the following research question raised by the AFC parent-toddler clinicians: do RF capacities in mothers change in the course of their participation in psychoanalytic parent-toddler groups?

Parents attending the AFC toddler groups were asked to take part in a PDI at the time of joining the group, and again at the end of their period of attendance, in order to investigate any possible change in reflective capacity. Parents were interviewed by the toddler group leader. The interviews were audio-taped, transcribed and coded. The entry interviews were completed between 2003 and 2005 and the exit interviews between 2004 and 2007. All the participants were mothers ($N = 12$) ranging in age from 29 to 39 years (Mean = 34.17, SD = 3.973). Sixty-seven per cent ($N = 8$) had boy toddlers and 33 per cent ($N = 4$) had girl toddlers. The toddlers were between 12 and 32 months old, with a mean age of 19.92 months (SD = 5.76) at entry, and a mean age of 34.50 months (SD = 5.52) at exit. Some mothers reported having more than one child and most of them were of White ethnic origin. By contrast, half of the toddlers were of mixed ethnicity.

Both entry and exit PDIs were coded for RF using the Slade, Bernbach et al. (2005a) coding system. This coding system results in a global RF score ranging from bizarre, anti-reflective statements (-1) to high RF ($+9$) which is full or exceptional reflective statements of a personal nature (Slade, Bernbach et al., 2005a). Consistent normal/ordinary reflective statements received a rating of 5.

Results

Entry RF: The RF scores obtained by parents in the entry PDIs ranged between 2 and 3 (Mean = 2.58, SD = .515). According to the RF coding scheme, a score of 2 corresponds to interviews containing vague or inexplicit references to mental states that are too limited and inexplicit to be considered even "low RF". A score of 3 entails questionable or low RF capacities showing that although parents made use of language associated with mental states they were not able to demonstrate that they really understood the implication of their statement. These ratings indicate that the parents manifested a lack of awareness of the characteristics and nature of mental states, and had difficulty in establishing links between mental states and behaviour or between different mental states. Maternal entry RF was not related to the age of their child (N = 12, rho = −.099, p = .760), their own age (N = 12, rho = −.245, p = .589) or to the number of children they had (N = 12, rho = −.245, p = .442).

Exit RF: The mothers' exit PDIs reported RF scores from 2 to 5 (N = 12, Mean = 3.58, SD = .996), that is, fluctuating between vague or inexplicit references to mental states and definite or ordinary RF. A score of 4 indicates the use of mental state language in a slightly more sophisticated manner than in a response that would be considered questionable or low RF. However, the links between mental states or between mental states and behaviour are rudimentary or inexplicit and are not elaborated or convincing enough to be considered a definite or ordinary RF. A score of 5 which is "definite or ordinary RF" denotes that the interviewee has a consistent model of the mind making sense of her experience in terms of thoughts and feelings. Nevertheless, the model is restricted and does not allow the regulation of more complex experiences (like conflict and ambivalence).

Change in RF over time spent attending toddler group: The analysis of the difference between entry and exit PDI-RF scores indicated that the average of the scores obtained in the exit PDIs (N = 12, Mean = 3.58, SD = 0.996) was higher than the average of the scores achieved by parents in the entry PDIs (N = 12, Mean = 2.58, SD = 0.515), and this difference was statistically significant (N = 12; Z = −2.521; p = 0.012, 2-tailed).

Length of time spent attending a toddler group and the improvement in RF scores: Mother–toddler dyads varied in the length of time they attended a group and there was a strong, statistically significant, positive correlation between the length of time spent attending a group and the level of the mother's reflective functioning at the time she left the group (N = 12, rho = .691, p = 0.013). The longer the mother–toddler dyad attended the group, the higher the level of maternal RF when they left the group. Length of time in the group was also related to overall improvement in RF scores (N = 12, rho = .776, p = 0.003). So the longer the mother attended the group, the greater the improvement in her overall levels of RF.

These findings suggest that, on average, maternal RF significantly increased during time spent in the toddler group and that this increase was related to the length of period of attendance. There was also a statistically significant relationship between change in RF scores over the course of attendance at a toddler group and the child's age at the time of leaving the group (N = 12, rho = .779, p = 0.003) (although not to the child's age at entry).

Controlling for the influence of toddler age: The relationship between exit RF and length of attendance was further analysed by controlling for any potential impact of the child's age (and development). The relationship between improvement in RF and the length of time the mothers had attended the toddler group dropped to just below statistical significance (p = 0.051) once we controlled for toddler age at exit. This suggests that at least some of the improvement in RF could be accounted for by the child's age at the time they left the group.

Conclusions

The lack of a control group in this study and the possibility that other variables may have influenced RF during the course of attending a toddler group make it impossible to conclude categorically that attending a toddler group caused the improvement in average maternal RF. Nonetheless, the results suggest a trend that should encourage further investigation of the topic. On average, maternal RF did increase during the period that mothers attended the toddler group, and the magnitude of this increase was related to the length of time spent in the group. Mothers who attended for the longest showed the greatest increase in RF scores. This association was complicated by the child's own development, as higher RF at exit was also related to the child's age. Older toddlers' mothers showed higher RF at exit. However, even when the influence of child age was held constant, the relationship between time spent in the group and improvement in maternal RF fell to only just below statistical significance.

It would seem that a psychoanalytic parent-toddler group, led by an experienced Child Psychotherapist and assistant helping mothers think about their toddlers' thoughts and feelings and modelling appropriate responses, may positively influence a mother's capacity to reflect on her child's behaviour.

This preliminary exploratory study suggests that there is scope for further work in this area, including a larger study involving a control group which would allow for more sophisticated statistical modelling techniques, with the aim of more definitively unravelling the influence of group attendance and child age.

Chapter 16

Snack time at an Anna Freud Centre parent-toddler group: Microanalysis of social eating in toddlerhood

Joshua Holmes, Anna Prützel-Thomas and Kay Asquith

Acknowledging the "common feeding difficulties which occur in everyday life of otherwise normal children", Anna Freud describes a developmental line "from sucking to rational eating", culminating in the child being able to "*regulate* his own food intake actively and rationally, quantitatively and qualitatively, on the basis of his own needs and appetites and irrespective of his relations to the provider of the food, and of conscious and unconscious fantasies" (Freud, 1963, p. 251). Furman (1992) notes that the "social graces" of snack time – such as asking for plates of food and remaining seated while they eat – are, at first, "new and hard" tasks for toddlers (Furman, 1992, p. 27). She describes toddlers at snack time as a "bundle of drives being reined in by the attendant parents and other adults". Furman describes the sense of achievement felt by the toddler at the mastery of self-feeding and links it with the ever-present "admiring support of mother".

At the Anna Freud Centre parent-toddler groups, eating is a lesson in socialisation. "Snack time" is one of the few elements of structure in the groups. Sandwiched between periods of free play, toddlers and their parents are encouraged to sit around a table together. They are offered plates of "finger food" – slices of banana and apple, raisins, grapes and grissini. These plates are communal but each toddler has her own plate on to which food can be transferred. Drinks are similarly offered in communal jugs and then poured into individual cups.

Typically an inner circle of toddlers forms, surrounded by an outer circle of parents and adults. Sometimes parents sit at the table next to their child. More usually they sit directly behind, or behind and slightly to the side of, their child. Some toddlers require much persuasion to join the snack table, while others gravitate to the table as soon as the first morsels of food are laid out.

Since 2005 weekly group meetings have been videotaped, with participants' consent. The camera is mounted in the ceiling, and focuses automatically on particular areas of the room, including the snack table, for specific periods of time. This resource allows the opportunity to examine to what extent the theoretical assumptions of Freud and Furman can actually be observed in interactions around snack time. The data for this research comprised recordings of snack-time sessions made during 2005. DVDs were first scanned to identify snack-time footage, then subjected to analysis of the selected sequences in the following stages:

a)   Watching complete sequences and making broad notes.
b)   Identifying "event boundaries", that is to say, beginnings and endings of loosely co-ordinated activity. For example, off-screen noises some-times distracted those sitting at the snack table, thus creating such a boundary.
c)   Transcribing observations – including verbal and all non-verbal inter-actions.

Transcribing the sequences in minute detail then allowed a more inter-pretative analysis based on Interpretative Phenomenological Analysis (IPA, Smith & Osborn, 2003) to draw out the main themes commonly seen to occur within this broader, general framework.

Three super-ordinate themes emerged from the data analysis:

1.   snack time as an affectively laden experience;
2.   parental regulation vs self-regulation at snack time; and
3.   snack time as a period for observation and learning.

1. Snack time as an affective experience

For all its participants, snack time is a time of high and changeable emotion. Two affective situations were recurrently observed: anxiety and closeness/comfort-seeking.

This observation shows how eating is inhibited when potential threat arises:

Extract 1
49:16 There is a sound away from the snack table. Yasmin, 18 months old, stares in the direction of the sound for around ten seconds. She sits still. She stops chewing the food in her mouth. Then she starts to chew slowly, still staring at the same place. Then she turns back to the table. (Transcript 3, lines 68–72)

Oral comforting behaviour is common at times of stress, such as during the celebration of Amanda's second birthday when she touches her mouth with her finger almost constantly, and at one point:

Extract 6
49:00 . . . Her whole right hand is in her mouth. (Transcript 2, lines 89–90)

As well as non-eating and self-soothing oral behaviour, another frequent reaction was the seeking of proximity of a secure figure (usually mother, occasionally a group leader or assistant). It was common for mothers, sitting close to their toddlers at the table, to lean in or touch their child on the arm or the cheek. Here we see how a toddler seeks and wins proximity from a mother who appears initially reluctant to give it:

Extract 7
56:19 Amanda, age two years and four months, turns from the snack table with her hand outstretched toward mother. Mother, arms folded, does not respond. Amanda turns back to the table for a few seconds then moves her hand back towards mother. Mother leans close to Amanda. Amanda grabs mother's hand and takes it on to her lap. She turns back to the table, then back to mother again. Apparently in response to her child's prompting, mother moves her chair about a foot forward so that she is now much closer to Amanda and the table. (Transcript 5, lines 108–120)

Here it seems that Amanda feels anxious about the potential physical distance between herself and her mother, triggering "babyish" behaviour:

Extract 5
55:09 Amanda's mother sits on a chair near the snack table. As she sits down she pulls out a chair for Amanda in front of her that is directly at the snack table. Instead of sitting on it, Amanda moves, indicating she wants to get on her mother's lap. (Transcript 5, lines 80–83)

As well as arousing anxiety, social eating in the toddler group is regularly a time of laughter, joy, amusement, and pleasure. The next observation shows how adults' laughter at someone singing away from the table is picked up and reflected by a toddler at the table:

Extract 8
53:50 Somewhere else in the room someone sings "if you see a crocodile don't forget to. . .". All the adults look away from the table. The group has been smiling at the game and now turn back to the snack table. Melanie, one year and 11 months, then looks towards the mother sitting at the head of the table. She holds her fingers out in front of her face. She has her cheeks stuffed with food. Her lips are pursed. She

points and smiles with her eyes closed. Melanie moves her head as if in laughter for a couple of seconds. (Transcript 1, lines 43–56)

2. Parental regulation vs self-regulation

Snack time provides an arena in which the conflict between parental regulation and control on the one hand, and the toddler's search for autonomy and self-expression on the other, is played out.

Mothers sometimes regulate their toddler verbally by "correcting" their way of asking for things, and emphasising the importance of "manners":

Extract 14

54:24 John, age two years and eight months, points at the jug of juice and says, "I want that one". His mum picks up the jug and pours some for him. As she's pouring Stella, age two years, points at it and says "more", holding out her mug. Stella's mother says, "more juice *please*". (Transcript 5, lines 71–78)

Many examples were observed of toddlers' burgeoning independence expressed through preference and claiming behaviour. This observation shows Stella and her mother in conflict over choosing where to sit:

Extract 20

52:46 Stella, age two years, and her mother walk into shot. Mother says, "come here – Stella sit here. Stella sit here". Stella looks at her mother and tentatively sits at the chair at the opposite end of the table. Mother has one hand on the chair which she wants Stella to sit in. She is looking at Stella. Mother comes to the end of the table where Stella sits. She bends down and reaches for her arm with her right hand and Stella's plate with her left. Stella resists and shakes her arm free of mother's grip. (Transcript 5, lines 2–6)

Rewards for complying with parental requests, usually physical (in the form of a touch of the arm or a pat on the back), or verbal (in the form of praise), are affect regulating. When Stella finally agrees to sit where her mother desires:

Extract 15

53:54 She walks past the toddler leader who touches her back as she goes past. When she reaches the other side of the table, mum helps her into her seat with both arms. (Transcript 5, lines 50–53).

3. Observation and learning at snack time

Group members watch one another closely at snack time. Toddlers regularly observed mothers, leaders, and other toddlers. Mothers often observed their toddler while the toddler was seemingly not focused on their mother, the observer. At times, observation instigated mirroring behaviour:

Extract 22
54:23 Amanda, age one year and 11 months, puts something in her mouth. Mother puts something in her mouth. Amanda walks away. (Transcript 1, lines 87–89)

Sometimes mothers mirrored their toddler, as though to say "well done", "that's my girl", and also to create a happy playful atmosphere. More commonly toddlers mirrored the behaviour of other toddlers or adults. Here one toddler clearly mirrored the behaviour of another whom she was observing:

Extract 23
54:07 Stella, age two years, stops drinking. She looks at John, age two years eight months, who is still drinking. Stella resumes drinking. John is not looking at Stella. Stella watches John drink from his cup and put it on the table. She copies this exactly. John points at the jug of juice and says "I want that one", his mum picks up the jug and pours some for him. As she's pouring Stella points at it and says "more", holding out her cup. (Transcript 5, lines 65–75)

Discussion

1. Affect regulation and snack time

Qualitative microanalysis suggests that snack time in the toddler group is (a) inherently social and interactive and (b) steeped in affect. From a psychoanalytic point of view toddlers are still at a stage in which mother and food are linked in their mind (A. Freud, 1963). Clearly food intake, in itself essential to survival, is linked with the positive reinforcers of pleasure and enjoyment. In addition, social eating is associated with positive affect in that it creates strong links between those that share food together. A number of potential negative affects are also associated with eating for both toddlers and their parents. Food is necessary – but will I (or my toddler) get enough to satisfy my (his/her) hunger? Will I (or my toddler) get the "best bits"? Is it safe to eat, or might some danger supervene while I am (he/she is) concentrating on eating? Will I (or my toddler) break group norms by appearing "greedy" or failing to share, and have to suffer the consequences of group disapprobation?

Children gradually learn to regulate these affects (Delaney, 2006): to contain hunger, wait for the signal that eating is now allowed to begin, enjoy sharing food with their family and friends. In addition, they have to learn how to enjoy eating, that a phased and gradual intake will be associated with greater pleasure and positive social reinforcement than "grabbing and guzzling". Initially, and certainly still at the toddler stage, these affects have to be "regulated" with the help of an adult.

Adults form a "circle of security" in order to ward off the anxiety, whether internal or external in origin, that eating may arouse in their toddlers. Parents help their toddlers manage the anxiety associated with group eating through a combination of physical proximity and emotional accessibility. This is consistent with the attachment view that these two factors are the main ways in which a parent provides a secure base for his or her child (Ainsworth, 1982; Bowlby, 1988).

Extract 31

56.21 Ben, age two years 10 months, stands near his brother. The other children are already seated, all with mothers placed behind them in the "circle of security". Ben then goes around the table pushing past another mother (not his own). As soon as he sits down he turns around and says something to the toddler leader, who is preparing food by the sink. She kneels close to him and listens. (Transcript 5, lines 101–106)

During the above observation, each other toddler is sitting with their parent behind them in the "circle of security". Ben shows signs of a secure attachment pattern by recruiting, in the absence of his primary attachment figure, an "alloparent" (Hrdy, 1999) in the toddler leader. He unconsciously "knows" that he will not be able sufficiently to relax in order to eat unless he has a protective adult in close attendance. No less than negative affect, pleasure needs to be "held" and regulated by parents, such as when Melanie smiles and plays after a period of adult laughter (Extract 8), as though she is checking that it is still all right to eat and enjoy herself.

2. Parental regulation vs self-regulation

Learning to manage the affective experience of eating is a joint effort between mother and toddler and part of the process of separation-individuation, although of course each is coming from a different perspective. Mother is able to draw on her own capacity for affect regulation to help her child do so. A second key finding of this research confirms Anna Freud's view that the separation-individuation process plays itself out during snack time, and that a successful and ego-syntonic mode of operation involves a fine balance, from mother's perspective, of "being there" and "letting be".

This often takes the form of the "oughts" and "shoulds" in relation to eating, such as Stella's mother's insistence that she says "please" after requesting some juice (Extract 14). Stella's want for juice is not simply met, but it *may* be met if she conforms to social norms of politeness. Mothers want their children to be fed, but they also want their child to be socially successful. This means an ability to share, a lack of explicit greed, and adhering to "table manners".

Toddler inner regulation takes place a) through internalisation of maternal regulatory capacities and b) direct modelling (peers, parents). The toddler is learning to master anxieties associated with eating, and to modulate his or her pleasures through self-control. Thus eating is directly pleasurable through oral satisfaction, but also "anally" in terms of controlling one's own wants, leading not only to greater social acceptability, but also to emotional self-sufficiency and independence.

3. Observation and learning

Just as the mother helps her toddler with snack-time anxieties, so when necessary the group leader helps to alleviate maternal anxieties. The group leader and assistant strive to make the toddler group a safe space. This leads to the snack time "circle of security" providing affective safety. This safety facilitates mirroring and modelling between toddlers and other toddlers, toddlers and adults, and mothers and leaders.

4. Implications

This study suggests that group eating is an important part of learning to regulate affect in a social context. As a child learns to regulate the desire to eat, this could lay down a pattern for regulation of desire more generally which would then apply to sexuality and indeed other "sublimated" cultural phenomena such as participation in sport or artistic activities.

Furthermore this study strongly suggests that affect regulation is interpersonal. Mothers regulate their own affects (e.g. holding back so as to "let be" the toddler's autonomy) and help regulate the toddler's feelings (being there in case of anxiety; directly insisting that they observe social norms); the toddler then begins to internalise the pattern which is picked up in part from this interpersonal "dance", in which she/he plays a part, e.g. recruiting the mother or alloparent to provide the security needed for eating to begin, or pushing an over-anxious parent away as a bid for independence.

Conclusions

Microanalysis of the minutiae of parent–toddler interaction at snack time provided a rich resource for understanding the developmental processes associated with eating. Social eating in toddler groups is an intensely affective experience, both negative (anxiety about whether it is safe to eat, and whether the need for nutrition can be reconciled with the requirement to share with others) and positive (pleasurable, both individually and socially). Toddlers experience a mixture of adult-aided and self-regulation of such affects.

As predicted by Anna Freud (1946), battles for autonomy and separation-individuation are typical of eating behaviours in toddlers. Social eating is also a time of intense mutual observation, modelling and learning for toddlers, and, to some extent, for their mothers. This provides the opportunity for therapeutic intervention: the structural elements of snack time support toddlers and their parents, particularly via the "circle of security", and through the group leader's presence and availability. Close observation suggested individual differences in parent–toddler interactive styles. The theoretical and empirical investigations of the developmental origins of eating disorders, initiated by Anna Freud, are extended by this and possible further studies.

Chapter 17

Conclusion

Mary Target and Elizabeth Allison

It is a real pleasure and honour to conclude this lively, absorbing and inspiring book. We have been taken clearly through the rationale and several adaptations of the toddler group model, from its beginnings as an off-shoot of the growing field of child psychoanalysis within the Anna Freudian tradition. As has been so well described, the model enables the study and developmental support of toddler-age children and their parents. We have been introduced to a burgeoning variety of applications of this psychoanalytic approach to some very challenging contexts, across sections of British society and across cultures and countries.

We see this book as evidence for Anna Freud's view that the *direct study* of normal development is a vital supplement to information reconstructed from later child or adult clinical material, and for her view that the second year of life is "all important for the child's essential advance from primary to secondary process functioning; for the establishment of feeding and sleeping habits; for acquiring the rudiments of superego development and impulse control; for the establishment of object ties to peers" (A. Freud, 1978a, p. 731). Those (e.g. Green, 2000) who reject the value of direct observation of infants for the building (and testing) of psychoanalytic theory should read this book.

In chapter 2, Marie Zaphiriou Woods offers a concise but rich description of toddlerhood that insightfully condenses vital discoveries about human development derived from psychoanalysis, broader developmental theory and intensive, sustained and systematic observation:

> Toddlerhood begins when an infant takes his first faltering, but independent steps. This maturational achievement, occurring usually at around one year, ushers in a surge in the developmental advance towards "intrapsychic separateness and, eventually, individuation, identity and autonomy" (Blum, 2004, p. 542). This is a lifelong task which is never fully completed (Stern, 1995). During toddlerhood, this progressive thrust culminates in the toddler achieving inner images of his mother, and of himself in her absence (A. Freud, 1965; Mahler,

Pine, & Bergman, 1975), that are integrated and stable enough to enable him to manage himself (his body, thoughts and feelings) without her constant availability or that of a mother substitute, in a nursery school for instance. This usually occurs at around 3.

This definition reminds us that the experience of agentive selfhood and the establishment of object constancy are two closely interrelated developmental achievements. The book's exploration of the developmental leaps involved in toddlerhood, which make the phase potentially a crisis, shows us that toddlerhood is just as vital and precarious a phase as adolescence, probably more so, although adolescence is often seen as the most troublesome and risky period of ambivalent dependence. Although toddlers are small enough to be physically controlled and directed (generally speaking), the passion, aggression and conflict inherent even in perfectly normal development are most vividly and often movingly described in this book, and the ways in which psychoanalytic developmental theory can both explain and gain enormously from close-up observations are also crystal clear.

Marie's contributions, together with others' in the book, also highlight our understanding that the development of a capacity for mental representation (stable inner images of both mother and self in a relationship) is crucial in enabling the child to reach the milestones of toddlerhood and the preschool period. The work of Anna Freud and her colleagues on the vicissitudes of development (e.g. Edgcumbe, 1981; A. Freud, 1965; Katan, 1961) has played a vital role in helping us to appreciate that we are not born with our capacities waiting to be expressed. These capacities grow along developmental lines (A. Freud, 1963), along which progress may be delayed or derailed by internal or external factors, especially within the closest, attachment relationships. A key aspect of mental and emotional development is the ability to recognise what is in our own minds, and also understand others' behaviour in terms of intentions and feelings. We have tried to describe how this ability gradually takes shape through phases of development from birth to adulthood (Fonagy, Gergely, Jurist, & Target, 2002). The gradually and sometimes painfully acquired ability to recognise emotional states and wishes is critical in enabling us to regulate our emotions, tolerate separations and experience a sense of agency. The development of this capacity depends on interaction with more mature and sensitive minds. There is a vital synergy between attachment processes and the development of the child's ability to understand behaviour and relationships in terms of feelings, attitudes and wishes. We hear from the colleagues running a toddler group in Greece:

> Activities with toys contribute to the process of separation-individuation because they promote the notion that parents and toddler have separate thoughts and feelings, which can be safely

communicated through play. As children are invited to share toys, activities and other things in the group a process takes place which contributes to the dissolution of the magical omnipotence, which is so characteristic of toddlers' thought, and enables autonomy rather than egocentrism.

(Pretorius, 2004)

How does this take place? The child learns to perceive that an object, thing or activity has significance for others as much as for himself. A toy, for example, can be seen as the vehicle of others' projections, metaphorically as well as literally. The symbolic value of the object is therefore not determined solely by the individual child. This process forms the basis of the child's awareness of other people's minds and subjectivity. Toddlerhood is a critical period in the development of this awareness, and we can clearly see how the "developmental help" of the toddler group setting and play space fosters it, along with affect regulation and the direction of attention.

Many of the observations gathered naturalistically and through a psychoanalytic lens in this book are supported by empirical studies. Thus, research confirms that it is during the second year of life that children begin to understand that they and others have intentions which explain their actions (Wellman & Phillips, 2000) and that their actions affect how other people think and feel, as well as causing physical effects (e.g. by pointing, Corkum & Moore, 1995). These capacities in toddlers have been shown to reflect their prior and current relationship with their primary caregiver, as we have seen amply described in this book (Calkins & Johnson, 1998). This is also the time when children begin to acquire a language for internal states such as feelings, and the ability to think and talk about feelings and desires in others in ways that begin to extend beyond an egocentric point of view (Repacholi & Gopnik, 1997). Somewhat paradoxically, this has been shown to lead not only to an increase in joint goal directed activity, such as play, "cooking", tidying up, etc., but also to teasing and provocation of others including younger siblings (Dunn, 1988).

However, the toddler is not yet able to differentiate mental states from physical reality without a lot more help and development in the years up to four (Flavell & Miller, 1998). There is no room yet for alternative perspectives: "How I see it is how it is". This can make the world a pretty frightening place, including the immediate world of other people, to whom the toddler is almost completely vulnerable. He tends to experience fantasies as too real, whether they are fantasies or wishes of his own or ones attributed to someone else. Some of the examples described so beautifully in this book illustrate the intensity with which emotional states are experienced in this stage of development.

Being able to pretend, and play, is an essential counterbalance and relief from the grip of reality. Nevertheless, while Winnicott did more than anyone else to show us how essential playing is for small children and their growing sense of reality, he also made it clear that it too is mentally and emotionally risky, especially until play has been formalised in structured games. "Games and their organisation must be looked at as part of an attempt to forestall the frightening aspect of playing. . . The precariousness of play belongs to the fact that it is always on the theoretical line between the subjective and that which is objectively perceived" (Winnicott, 1971, pp. 58–59). The toddler thus relies on a sensitive adult – a parent and if he is lucky a toddler group leader! – who is able to think about both their own and the toddler's internal world, and help him to differentiate internal from external and self from other. Throughout toddlerhood, he remains dependent on his caregivers to help him to gradually develop and maintain his awareness of his internal world as distinct from but significantly related to the external one.

This volume brings this critical developmental stage vividly to life. The beautiful vignettes captured from the psychoanalytic parent-toddler groups run at the Anna Freud Centre and in various outreach settings can leave the reader in no doubt of the intense and visceral emotional states encountered at this stage of development, as well as in intensive and prolonged psycho-analytic work with older children and adults. The book also amply and intricately shows how our capacity as adults to be able to think about our own minds and the minds of others, which can provide such relief in times of emotional turbulence, has to be nurtured in the emotional relationships and exchanges in these early years. We have been treated to many striking illustrations of the toddler's need for the caregiver to scaffold this nascent capacity at times when he would otherwise be overwhelmed by his violent passions of love, hatred, jealousy, passionate excitement and rage.

Sometimes parents may find it difficult or impossible to provide this necessary scaffolding, perhaps because of a lack of provision of such support in their own early life or because their current adverse circumstances mean that their resources have to be focused on physical survival rather than psychic development. They may be consciously or unconsciously drawn to parent-toddler groups such as those described in this book, in the hope of being helped to manage not only their toddlers' emotions but also their own. There are many examples throughout the book that show how the adults as well as the toddlers can be helped with this task, which is a challenge for every human being at times, in a way that is tactful and always respectful of their need to feel capable, and gradually empowers them to feel more so.

The chapters on application of the model in deprived settings, especially chapters 8, 9 and 10, convey a sense of how difficult it might be to avoid presuming that development in this area is more advanced than adverse social circumstances have actually permitted. The leaders of these chal-lenging groups describe their initial frustrations and bewilderment leading to gradual realisation of how much help these parents needed just to establish and hold on in their own minds to a sense of the group as a space that was reliably available for them and their toddlers and that they could afford to feel attached to. We see how, little by little, the provision of a consistently available secure space offering both parents and toddlers experiences of having their minds held in mind, perhaps for the first time, provided a matrix where the ability to reflect on their feelings could gradually develop in and come to be valued by the group members. In her chapter on running a toddler group on a housing estate, Lesley Bennett writes somewhat apologetically:

> The reader may feel that I am focusing too heavily on describing the external situation rather than what happened "inside", and I would say here that it is often difficult to reflect upon the internal world without first thinking about those external features that can be "defined", in order to create a sense of a safe space within which to think and function.

Her extraordinary descriptions of the challenges she faced in trying to hold onto the group space, both concretely and metaphorically, leave no doubt as to the importance of the real, external setting. The book as a whole is a testament to the fact that we can only discover our internal worlds and be helped to feel that it is safe to inhabit them through our encounters with other minds. Understood in this sense, the external is not peripheral but actually fundamental to establishing the possibility of an experience of psychic reality.

Towards the end of the book, examples are given of imaginative evaluations which retain the spirit of psychoanalytic observation, especially the methods of Anna Freud and her colleagues. The research chapters represent the effort to make contact with the unconscious inner world underlying subjective experience, using a disciplined and systematic framework of theory and method, while also retaining an openness to being surprised and taught by a child.

The psychoanalytic parent-toddler groups at the Anna Freud Centre can be viewed as part of the Anna Freudian tradition of developmental help, which comprises interventions providing support for development, prevention of developmental disturbance and treatment to try to get things back on track when development has gone awry. As Rose Edgcumbe has noted, "[Anna Freud] herself seemed, to many of those who worked with her, doubtful whether these innovations could be considered a legitimate part of the main body of psychoanalytic technique. Instead, she considered them to be a useful extra tool for patients not suited to 'proper' psychoanalysis" (Edgcumbe, 2000, p. 2). The work described in this volume is a powerful argument that developmental help from a sensitive and attuned caregiver is necessary for all of us in our early years in order for the internal world of representations – that may later become the psycho-analyst's concern – to be established. The work with parents also shows that many of us are likely to continue to need help in this area at certain challenging times in our lives, such as our own children's early years. The very moving observations in chapters 6 and 7 of some parents' commitment in the face of their own and/or their toddlers' disabilities show both the need for highly sensitive help and the extraordinary, humbling and proud efforts parents can make to help their small children to develop mentally and physically.

Ultimately, the book leaves the reader with a feeling of hope that in cases where everything seems stacked against the parent and toddler, appropriate support can still have a powerful positive effect. As such, these groups deserve to be recognised and embraced as a legitimate, lively and enlightening part of the psychoanalytic tradition.

Appendix

Marie Zaphiriou Woods

The AFC parent-toddler group service

- Two parent-toddler groups meet at the AFC.
- Two more meet in local outreach settings (a hostel for homeless families described in chapter 9 and a Children's Centre).
- In previous years there was a third specialist toddler group that met at the AFC (see chapter 7), and a different outreach toddler group in the tenants' hall of a local council estate (see chapter 8).
- The groups meet weekly during term times (without half-term breaks).
- Each meeting consists of 1½ hours of free play, with a mid-session snack (morning or afternoon).

Structure

- The service is currently managed by a Child and Adolescent Psychotherapist (IMP) who also runs a toddler group.
- Each AFC parent-toddler group is run by a leader and an assistant.
- The leader is usually a Child and Adolescent Psychotherapist (or related professional with an understanding of psychodynamic thinking).
- The assistants have usually completed the AFC-UCL MSc in Psychoanalytic Developmental Psychology or an equivalent degree.
- The staff forms a team that meets weekly at the AFC to discuss referrals, management and clinical issues.
- The former manager (MZW) consults to the staff team once a term and provides supplementary supervision to outreach group staff when required.
- MZW offers individual sessions to toddler group parents who require more support than can be offered within the group.

The groups at the AFC

- The groups are small, with a consistent membership of up to eight parent-toddler couples.
- They are open to any parent with a toddler who wishes to attend, though priority may be given when there are overt concerns.
- Toddlers are brought by mother, father, or another close family member.
- They are aged between 1 and 3 years, with a balance of boys and girls in each group.
- The groups are rolling: when a toddler leaves, usually for nursery, he/she is replaced by a toddler aged between 1 and 2 years.

Referrals

- Most parents refer themselves, having learned about the groups from flyers posted locally, the internet, or from other parents.
- Some are referred by Health Visitors, Social Workers or GPs.
- A significant number (up to half) come from within the Centre, especially from the Parent-Infant Project.
- For vulnerable traumatised parents who have attended other services, the parent-toddler groups may provide a halfway station that enables them to take the next step of joining an ordinary nursery school.

Presenting problems

- Some toddlers come with already identified difficulties (e.g. developmental delay, aggressive behaviour, feeding and sleeping difficulties, history of health problems).
- Most parents' explicit reasons for joining a group are a wish for support and for their toddlers to mix with other children.
- Their struggles with their growing toddler usually emerge gradually.
- Traumatic histories, involving psychiatric problems, loss, domestic violence, illness and disability, are frequent and perhaps unconsciously drive these parents' choice of a parent-toddler group attached to a child psychotherapy service.
- Many parents have relocated from their country of origin and lack ongoing support from their extended families.
- Parents who are aware of their own difficulties sometimes express concern about the impact of their mental state on their toddlers.

Ground rules

- Parents are asked to commit to regular attendance for a year.
- They are responsible for their children's safety at all times.

- They are asked to contribute financially according to a sliding scale related to ability to pay.
- Parents are invited to speak to the group leader about any concerns they may have about their child.
- The leader agrees to raise any concerns that develop (or occur) about the parent and/or child.

Observers

- Students studying for the AFC MSc in Psychoanalytic Developmental Psychology observe fortnightly (2 in the room, 2/3 in an observation booth).
- They record and discuss their observations in weekly seminars with the toddler group leader and assistant.

Research and evaluation

- The Parent Development Interview (PDI) is administered at the beginning and end of attendance in a toddler group (see chapter 15).
- Feedback questionnaires are sent out at the end of attendance in a toddler group.
- Qualitative research is conducted by MSc students (see chapters 7, 14 and 16).

Notes

1 Nancy Brenner, Marie Zaphiriou Woods, Pauline Cohen, Pat Radford and Anne Hurry are thanked for their insightful reading of this chapter.
2 For the sake of clarity and convenience, I generally refer to the toddler as "he" and the parent as "she".
3 This chapter draws on an unpublished paper by Nancy Brenner, Justine Kalas-Reeves, Valli Kohon, Jenny Stoker and Marie Zaphiriou Woods given at the First International Anna Freud Centre Toddler Symposium. The author of this chapter is grateful to her co-writers for their contributions, and for their helpful discussions.
4 Nancy Brenner, Valli Kohon, Evi Vasilakaki and Marie Zaphiriou Woods are gratefully acknowledged for their valued contributions to this paper. An earlier version of this paper was published as: Pretorius, I.-M. and J. Wallace (2008) Being seen to be able: the impact of visual and motor impairment on the relationship between a father and his daughters. *Child Analysis*, 18: 41–67.
5 The Inman Trust is a fund administered by the British Psychoanalytical Society set up by the estate of William Inman (1875–1968) for work on the links between emotions and disorders of the eye.
6 The author is grateful for the assistance of Marielle Davis, Elena Borras and Midge Arroll.
7 The interview was later coded for reflective functioning (Fonagy, Target, Steele, & Steele, 1998; Slade, Bernbach, Grienenberger, Levy, & Locker, 2004).
8 The author gratefully acknowledges Susanna Riesz-Neurath for the observations she has contributed.
9 Social housing complex built by local councils.
10 A form of urban acrobatics practised in city environments.
11 Article on Archpeinture exhibition, Camden Arts Centre, September 2007, by Adrian Searle, Guardian.co.uk.
12 Marie Zaphiriou Woods was the AFC supervisor and Consultant.
13 We are grateful to Rose Edgcumbe, Caroline McGaffin (Essenhigh), Nicky Model, Pat Radford, Gemma Rocco, Jenny Davids, Tessa Baradon and other specialists at the Anna Freud Centre for training, supervision, and for organisational and emotional support.
14 St. Petersburg Institute of Early Intervention and Centre of Integrative Education.
15 Misha and his mother attended a parent-toddler group facilitated by V. Ivanova and A. Pastorova.
16 Olga and her mother attended a parent-toddler group facilitated by V. Ivanova and A. Pastorova.

17 Kostia and his mother attended a parent-toddler group facilitated by V. Ivanova and N. Pleshkova.

18 The successful realisation of the Toddler Groups would not have been possible without the support of the scientific personnel of the Centre as a whole and particularly of the director of the Child and Adolescent Unit, Dimitris Anagnostopoulos and also Eleni Lazaratou, Effie Layiou-Lignos, Aggeliki Christodoulou, Julia Papadaki, and Pavlina Lascaratou.

19 Questions included: "Does your child go to bed easily?", "Do you feel mealtime is a difficult, time-consuming procedure?", "Does your child cling to you and find it difficult to be separated from you?", "Does he/she have tantrums?", and so on.

20 The Anna Freud Centre in London has supported and contributed to the development of the Greek Toddler Group programme. Marie Zaphiriou Woods played a significant role in the early stages of implementation, supporting and supervising the procedure.

21 The psychoanalytic Supervisor of the toddler group programme is Effie Layiou-Lignos who is a psychoanalytic psychotherapist for children and adolescents. Her vast clinical experience played an important role in the implementation of the toddler group programme.

22 The inner child stands for the internal object. According to the psychoanalytical literature, internal objects constitute emotional representations of external objects that have been introjected. Internal objects are unconscious emotional images apparent through fantasies to which we react as "real" (Rycroft, 1968).

23 "The Matrix is the hypothetical web of communication and relationship in a given group. It is the common shared ground which ultimately determines the meaning and significance of all events and upon which all communication and interpretations verbal and non-verbal rest" (Foulkes, 1964, p. 292). Additionally, Nitsun (1996) writes that "the matrix has the properties of a container, symbolically linking to the mother or specifically to the womb through its generative capacity . . . It provides a context for transformation of both the individual and the group . . . This aspect has been associated with Winnicott's notion of the transitional space (1953), in which the space within the group circle becomes a projective screen, a practising ground for early interaction, an intermediate area of play and discovery, and a place for everyday creativity" (p. 22).

24 Winnicott distinguished object-usage from object-relating. He believed one has to relate to an object before one can make use of it. In order to use an object, it must be "real" and belong to a shared reality, not a series of projections.

25 We observed the group of Valli Shaio Kohon.

26 An earlier version of this chapter appeared in *Early Child Development and Care*, vol. 178, no. 3, April 2008, pp. 273–288.

References

Aber, J. L., Slade, A., Berger, B., Bresgi, I., & Kaplan, M. (1985). The Parent Development Interview (Unpublished Manuscript).

Ainsworth, M. D. S. (1963). The development of infant-mother interaction among the Ganda. In B. M. Foss (Ed.), *Determinants of Infant Behaviour* (Vol. 2, pp. 67–112). New York: Wiley.

Ainsworth, M. D. S. (1982). Attachment: Retrospect and prospect. In C.M. Parkers & J. Stevenson-Hinde (Eds.), *The Place of Attachment in Human Behavior* (pp. 3–30). New York: Basic Books.

Ainsworth, M. D. S., Blehar, M. C., Waters, E., & Wall, S. (1978). *Patterns of Attachment: A Psychological Study of the Strange Situation.* Hillsdale, NJ: Erlbaum.

Anzieu, D. (1975). *Le groupe et l'inconscient. L'imaginaire groupal.* Paris: Dunod.

Balbernie, R. (2001). Circuits and circumstances: The neurobiological consequences of early relationship experiences and how they shape later behaviour. *Journal of Child Psychotherapy, 27*(3), 237–255.

Baradon, T., Fonagy, P., Bland, K., Lenard, K., & Sleed, M. (2008). New Beginnings – an experience-based programme addressing the attachment relationship between mothers and their babies in prisons. *Journal of Child Psychotherapy, 34*(2), 240–258.

Bates, E. (1990). Language and me and you: Pronominal reference and the emerging concept of self. In D. Cicchetti & M. Beeghly (Eds.), *The Self in Transitions, Infancy to Childhood* (pp. 165–182). Chicago: University of Chicago Press.

Bates, E., O'Connell, B., & Shore, C. (1987). Language and communication in infancy. In J. Osofsky (Ed.), *Handbook of Infant Development* (pp. 149–203). New York: Wiley.

Belsky, J. (2001). Emanuel Miller Lecture: Developmental risks (still) associated with early child care. *Journal of Child Psychology and Psychiatry and Allied Disciplines, 42*, 845–859.

Belsky, J., & Melhuish, E. (2008). Early intervention for young children and their families in England: The Sure Start journey over the last decade. In U. V. d. Leyen & V. Spidla (Eds.), *Voneinander lernen – miteinander handeln: Aufgaben und Perspektiven der Europdischen Allianz f\r Familien (Shared experience, concerted action: Ideas and perspectives in the European Alliance for Families).* Baden-Baden: Nomos-Verlag.

Bergman, A. (1978). From mother to the world outside: The use of space during the separation-individuation phase. In S. Grolnick & L. Barkin (Eds.), *Between Reality and Fantasy* (pp. 147–165). New York: Jason Aronson.

Bergman, A. (1999). *Ours, Yours, Mine: Mutuality and the Emergence of the Separate Self*. Washington: Jason Aronson.

Bergman, A., & Harpaz-Rotem, I. (2004). Rapprochement revisited. *Journal of the American Psychoanalytic Association, 52*(2), 555–569.

Berkow, R., & Fletcher, A. J. (2002). *The Merck Manual* (18th edition). Rahway, NJ: Merck & Co.

Bion, W. R. (1961). *Experiences in Groups*. London: Tavistock.

Bion, W. R. (1962). *Learning from Experience*. London: Heinemann.

Blos, P. (1967). The second individuation process of adolescence. *Psychoanalytic Study of the Child, 22*, 162–185.

Blum, H. P. (2004). Separation-individuation theory and attachment theory. *Journal of the American Psychoanalytic Association, 52*(2), 535–553.

Bowlby, J. (1969). *Attachment and Loss, Vol. 1: Attachment*. London: Hogarth Press and the Institute of Psycho-Analysis.

Bowlby, J. (1988). *A Secure Base: Clinical Applications of Attachment Theory*. London: Routledge.

Brenner, N. (1988). The third decade (1978–1988). *Bulletin of the Anna Freud Centre, 11*, 189–294.

Brenner, N. (1992). Nursery school observations – to learn, to teach, to facilitate growth and development. *Journal of Child Psychotherapy, 18*(1), 87–100.

Bretherton, I. (1992). Social referencing, intentional communication, and the interfacing of minds in infancy. In S. Feinman (Ed.), *Social Referencing and the Social Construction of Reality in Infancy* (pp. 57–77). New York: Plenum.

Brown, J. R., & Dunn, J. (1991). "You can cry, mum": The social and developmental implications of talk about internal states. *British Journal of Developmental Psychology, 9*, 237–257.

Burlingham, D. (1979). To be blind in a sighted world. *Psychoanalytic Study of the Child, 34*, 5–30.

Burlingham, D., & Freud, A. (1942). *Young Children in War-time. A Year's Work in a Residential War Nursery*. London: Allen and Unwin.

Calkins, S., & Johnson, M. (1998). Toddler regulation of distress to frustrating events: Temperamental and maternal correlates. *Infant Behavior and Development, 21*, 379–395.

Castelnuovo-Tedesco, P. (1981). Psychological consequences of physical defects: A psychoanalytic perspective. *International Review of Psycho-Analysis, 8*, 145–154.

Chouvier, B. (2002). Les fonctions médiatrices de l'objet. In B. Chouvier et al. (Eds.), *Les processus psychiques de la médiation*. Paris: Dunod.

Coates, S. W. (1997). Is it time to jettison the concept of developmental lines? *Gender and Psychoanalysis, 2*, 35–53.

Cohen, P., & Grant, B. (1985). Observations of a toddler during a crisis. *Bulletin of the Anna Freud Centre, 8*, 275–281.

Corkum, V., & Moore, C. (1995). Development of joint visual attention in infants. In C. Moore & P. Dunham (Eds.), *Joint Attention: Its Origins and Role in Development* (pp. 61–83). New York: Erlbaum.

Crittenden, P. M., & DiLalla, D. (1988). Compulsive compliance: The development of an inhibitory coping strategy in infancy. *Journal of Abnormal Child Psychology, 16*, 585–599.

de Marneffe, D. (1997). Bodies and words: A study of young children's genital and gender knowledge. *Gender & Psychoanalysis, 2*, 3–33.

Delaney, K. (2006). Following the affect: Learning to observe emotional regulation. *Journal of Child and Adolescent Psychiatric Nursing, 4*, 175–181.

Dementyeva, I. F. (1992). Sotsialnaya adaptatsiya detey-sirot: problemy i perspektivy v usloviyah rynka. *Sotsis, 10*, 62–70.

Department for Education and Skills. (2006). *Sure Start Children's Centres Practice Guidance*. London: DfES.

Department for Education and Skills. (2007). *Early Years Foundation Stage*. London: DfES.

Department of Health. (2004). *The National Service Framework (NSF) for Children, Young People and Maternity Services*. London: DoH.

Dunn, J. (1988). *The Beginnings of Social Understanding*. Oxford: Basil Blackwell Ltd and Cambridge, MA: Harvard University Press.

Edgcumbe, R. (1981). Toward a developmental line for the acquisition of language. *Psychoanalytic Study of the Child, 36*, 71–104.

Edgcumbe, R. (2000). *Anna Freud: A View of Development, Disturbance and Therapeutic Techniques*. London: Routledge.

Emde, R. N. (1980). Emotional availability: A reciprocal reward system for infants and parents with implications for prevention of psychosocial disorders. In P. M. Taylor & F. Orlando (Eds.), *Parent-Infant Relationships* (pp. 87–115). New York: Grune & Stratton.

Flavell, J. H., & Miller, P. H. (1998). Social cognition. In W. Damon, D. Kuhn & R. S. Siegler (Eds.), *Handbook of Child Psychology* (5th edition) (pp. 851–898). New York: Wiley.

Fonagy, P. (1998). Prevention, the appropriate target for infant psychotherapy. *Infant Mental Health Journal, 19*, 124–150.

Fonagy, P., Gergely, G., Jurist, E., & Target, M. (2002). *Affect Regulation, Mentalization and the Development of the Self*. New York: Other Press.

Fonagy, P., Steele, H., Moran, G., Steele, M., & Higgitt, A. (1991a). The capacity for understanding mental states: The reflective self in parent and child and its significance for security of attachment. *Infant Mental Health Journal, 13*, 200–217.

Fonagy, P., Steele, H., & Steele, M. (1991). Maternal representations of attachment during pregnancy predict the organization of infant-mother attachment at one year of age. *Child Development, 62*, 891–905.

Fonagy, P., Steele, M., Moran, G. S., Steele, H., & Higgitt, A. C. (1991b). Measuring the ghost in the nursery: A summary of the main findings of the Anna Freud Centre/University College London parent–child study. *Bulletin of the Anna Freud Centre, 14*, 115–131.

Fonagy, P., & Target, M. (1996). Playing with reality: I. Theory of mind and the normal development of psychic reality. *International Journal of Psychoanalysis, 77*, 217–233.

Fonagy, P., & Target, M. (1997). Attachment and reflective function: Their role in self-organization. *Development and Psychopathology, 9*, 679–700.

Fonagy, P., & Target, M. (2007). Playing with reality: IV. A theory of external reality rooted in intersubjectivity. *International Journal of Psychoanalysis, 88*(Pt 4), 917–937.

Fonagy, P., Target, M., Steele, H., & Steele, M. (1998). *Reflective-Functioning Manual, version 5.0, for Application to Adult Attachment Interviews*. London: University College London.

Foulkes, S. H. (1948). *Introduction to Group-Analytic Psychotherapy*. London: Heinemann.

Foulkes, S. H. (1964). *Therapeutic Group Analysis*. London: Allen & Unwin.

Fraiberg, S. (1959). *The Magic Years: Understanding the Problems of Early Childhood*. London: Methuen.

Fraiberg, S. (1977). *Insights from the Blind*. London: Souvenir Press.

Fraiberg, S. (1980). *Clinical Studies in Infant Mental Health: The First Year of Life*. New York: Basic Books.

Fraiberg, S. H., Adelson, E., & Shapiro, V. (1975). Ghosts in the nursery: A psychoanalytic approach to the problem of impaired infant-mother relationships. *Journal of the American Academy Child Psychiatry, 14*, 387–422.

Freud, A. (1936). *The Ego and the Mechanisms of Defence*. New York: International Universities Press, 1946.

Freud, A. (1946). The psychoanalytic study of infantile feeding disturbances. *Psychoanalytic Study of the Child, 2*, 119–132.

Freud, A. (1951). Observations on child development. *The Psychoanalytic Study of the Child, 6*, 18–30.

Freud, A. (1952). The role of bodily illness in the mental life of children. *Psychoanalytic Study of the Child, 7*, 69–81.

Freud, A. (1958). Child observation and prediction of development. *The Psychoanalytic Study of the Child, 13*, 92–116.

Freud, A. (1963). The concept of developmental lines. *The Psychoanalytic Study of the Child, 18*, 245–265.

Freud, A. (1965). *Normality and Pathology in Childhood: Assessments of Development*. Madison, CT: International Universities Press.

Freud, A. (1966). A short history of child analysis. *The Psychoanalytic Study of the Child, 21*, 7–14.

Freud, A. (1967). About losing and being lost. *The Psychoanalytic Study of the Child, 8*, 9–19.

Freud, A. (1976). Psychopathology seen against the background of normal development. *British Journal of Psychiatry, 129*, 401–406.

Freud, A. (1978a). Edith B. Jackson, In memoriam. *Journal of the American Academy of Child and Adolescent Psychiatry, 17*, 730–731.

Freud, A. (1978b). A study guide to Freud's writings. In *The Writings of Anna Freud (Volume 8)* (pp. 209–276). New York: International Universities Press, 1981.

Freud, A. (1983). The past revised. *Bulletin of the Hampstead Clinic, 6*, 107–113.

Freud, A., & Burlingham, D. (1940–45). Reports on the Hampstead nurseries. In *Infants Without Families and Reports on the Hampstead Nurseries 1939–1945* (pp. 3–540). London: Hogarth Press (1974).

Freud, A., & Burlingham, D. (1944). Infants without families: The case for and against residential nurseries. In *The Writings of Anna Freud (Volume 3)*. New York: International Universities Press, 1973.

Freud, S. (1905). Three essays on the theory of sexuality. In J. Strachey (Ed.), *The*

Standard Edition of the Complete Psychological Works of Sigmund Freud (Vol. 7, pp. 123–230). London: Hogarth Press.

Freud, S. (1909). Analysis of a phobia in a five-year-old boy. In J. Strachey (Ed.), *The Standard Edition of the Complete Psychological Works of Sigmund Freud* (Vol. 10, pp. 1–147). London: Hogarth Press.

Freud, S. (1920). Beyond the pleasure principle. In J. Strachey (Ed.), *The Standard Edition of the Complete Psychological Works of Sigmund Freud* (Vol. 18, pp. 1–64). London: Hogarth Press.

Friedmann, M. (1986). Alice Goldberger. *Bulletin of the Anna Freud Centre, 9*, 313–314.

Friedmann, M. (1988). The Hampstead Clinic Nursery: the first 20 years (1957–1978). *Bulletin of the Anna Freud Centre, 11*, 277–287.

Furman, E. (1978). The use of the nursery school for evaluation. In J. Glenn (Ed.), *Child Analysis and Therapy* (pp. 129–159). New York: Jason Aronson.

Furman, E. (1982). Mothers have to be there to be left. *Psychoanalytic Study of the Child, 37*, 15–28.

Furman, E. (1992). *Toddlers and Their Mothers.* New York: International University Press.

Furman, E. (1994). Early aspects of mothering: What makes it so hard to be there to be left. *Journal of Child Psychotherapy, 20*, 149–164.

Furman, R., & Katan, A. (1969). *The Therapeutic Nursery School.* New York: International Universities Press.

Galenson, E., & Roiphe, H. (1971). The impact of early sexual discovery on mood, defensive organization and symbolization. *Psychoanalytic Study of the Child, 26*, 195–216.

Galenson, E., & Roiphe, H. (1974). The emergence of genital awareness during the second year of life. In R. C. Friedman (Ed.), *Sex Differences in Behavior* (pp. 223–231). New York: Wiley.

Garland, C., Hume, F., & Majid, S. (2002). Remaking connections: Refugees and the development of "emotional capital" in therapy groups. In R. K. Papadopoulos (Ed.), *Therapeutic Care for Refugees: No Place Like Home.* London: Karnac.

George, C., Kaplan, N., & Main, M. (1985). The Adult Attachment Interview. Unpublished manuscript, Department of Psychology, University of California at Berkeley.

Gergely, G. (1997). *Margaret Mahler's developmental theory reconsidered in the light of current empirical research on infant development.* Paper presented at the Mahler Centennial Conference, Sopron, Hungary.

Gergely, G., & Watson, J. (1996). The social biofeedback model of parental affect-mirroring. *International Journal of Psychoanalysis, 77*, 1181–1212.

Goyette-Ewing, M., Slade, A., Knoebber, K., Gilliam, W., Truman, S., & Mayes, L. (2003). Parents First: A Developmental Parenting Program (Unpublished Manuscript). Yale Child Study Center.

Green Paper. (1999). *Supporting Families: A Consultation Document.* London: HMSO.

Green, V. (2000). Therapeutic space for re-creating the child in the mind of the parents. In J. Tsiantis (Ed.), *Work with Parents: Psychoanalytic Psychotherapy with Children and Adolescents.* London: Karnac Books.

Greenacre, P. (1953). Certain relationships between fetishism and faulty development of the body image. *Psychoanalytic Study of the Child, 8,* 79–98.

Greenacre, P. (1957). The childhood of the artist – libidinal phase development and giftedness. *Psychoanalytic Study of the Child, 12,* 47–72.

Greenacre, P. (1958). Early physical determinants in the development of the sense of identity. *Journal of the American Psychoanalytic Association, 6,* 612–627.

Hellman, I. (1983). Work in the Hampstead War Nurseries. *International Journal of Psychoanalysis, 64,* 435–439.

Herzog, J. M. (1982). On father hunger: The father's role in the modulation of aggressive drive and fantasy. In S. W. Cath, A. R. Gurwitt & J. M. Ross (Eds.), *Father and Child* (pp. 163–174). Boston: Little, Brown.

HM Treasury. (2004). *Choice for Parents, the Best Start for Children: A Ten Year Strategy for Childcare.* London: HMSO.

Hobson, P. (2002). *The Cradle of Thought: Explorations of the Origins of Thinking.* Oxford: Macmillan.

Hoffman, L. (2003). Mothers' ambivalence with their babies and toddlers: Manifestations of conflicts with aggression. *Journal of the American Psychoanalytical Association, 51,* 1219–1240.

Hoffman, L. (2004). When daughter becomes mother: Inferences from multiple dyadic parent–child groups. *Psychoanalytic Inquiry, 24,* 631–658.

Hrdy, S. (1999). *Mother Nature. Maternal Instincts and How They Shape the Human Species.* New York: Ballantine Books.

Jacques, E. (1955). Social systems as a defence against persecutory and depressive anxiety. In M. Klein, P. Heimann & R. Money-Kyrle (Eds.), *New Directions in Psychoanalysis.* London: Tavistock.

James, J. (2005). Analytic group psychotherapy with mothers and infants. In T. Baradon (Ed.), *The Practice of Psychoanalytic Parent Infant Psychotherapy: Claiming the Baby.* London: Taylor & Francis.

Joyce, A. (2005). One to two years old: Junior toddlers. In E. Rayner, A. Joyce, J. Rose, M. Twyman & C. Clulow (Eds.), *An Introduction to the Psychodynamics of Growth, Maturity and Ageing* (4th edition) (pp. 71–95). London: Routledge.

Kaës, R. (1976). *L'Appareil Psychique Groupal. Construction du Groupe.* Paris: Bordas.

Kaës, R. (1987). La malaise du monde moderne et l'experience transitionnelle du groupe. *Revue de Psychotherapie Psychanalytique de Groupe, 7–8,* 147–163.

Kassebaum, N. L. (1994). Head Start: Only the best for America's children. *American Psychologist, 49,* 123–126.

Katan, A. (1961). Some thoughts about the role of verbalization in early childhood. *The Psychoanalytic Study of the Child, 16,* 184–188.

Kennedy, H. (1978). The Hampstead Centre for the psychoanalytic study and treatment of children. *Bulletin of the Hampstead Clinic, 1,* 7–10.

Kennedy, H. (1988). Thirtieth birthday celebrations of the Anna Freud nursery school. *Bulletin of the Anna Freud Centre, 11,* 271–275.

Kennedy, H. (1995). Interviews. *Journal of Child Psychotherapy, 21*(3), 347–359.

Kernberg, P. F. (1984). Reflections in the mirror: Mother child interactions, self-awareness, and self-recognition. In J. D. Call et al. (Eds.), *Frontiers of Infant Psychiatry, Vol. II* (pp. 101–110). New York: Basic Books.

Klein, M. (1930). The importance of symbol-formation in the development of the ego. In *Contributions to Psychoanalysis, 1921–1945*. New York: McGraw-Hill, 1964.

Klein, M. (1935). A contribution to the psychogenesis of manic-depressive states. In *Love, Guilt and Reparation: The Writings of Melanie Klein, Volume I* (pp. 236–289). London: Hogarth Press (1975).

Klein, M. (1940). Mourning and its relation to manic-depressive states. In *Love, Guilt and Reparation: The Writings of Melanie Klein Volume I* (pp. 344–369). New York: Macmillan, 1984.

Klein, M. (1946). Notes on some schizoid mechanisms. In M. Klein, P. Heimann, S. Isaacs & J. Riviere (Eds.), *Developments in Psychoanalysis* (pp. 292–320). London: Hogarth Press.

Lacan, J. (1964). *The Four Fundamental Concepts of Psychoanalysis*. New York: Norton, 1978.

Lamb, M. E., & Billings, L. A. L. (1997). Fathers of children with special needs. In M. E. Lamb (Ed.), *The Role of the Father in Child Development* (pp. 179–190). New York: Wiley.

Lieberman, A. F. (1992). Infant-parent psychotherapy with toddlers. *Development and Psychopathology*, *4*, 559–574.

Lieberman, A. F. (1993). *The Emotional Life of the Toddler*. New York: The Free Press.

Lieberman, A. F., & Pawl, J. (1993). Infant-parent psychotherapy. In C. H. Zeanah (Ed.), *Handbook of Infant Mental Health* (pp. 427–442). New York: Guilford Press.

Luiser, A. (1980). The physical handicap and the body ego. *International Journal of Psychoanalysis*, *61*, 179–185.

Lyons-Ruth, K. (1991). Rapprochement or approchement: Mahler's theory reconsidered from the vantage point of recent research in early attachment relationships. *Psychoanalytic Psychology*, *8*, 1–23.

Mahler, M. S., Pine, F., & Bergman, A. (1975). *The Psychological Birth of the Human Infant: Symbiosis and Individuation*. New York: Basic Books.

Main, M., & Weston, D. (1981). The quality of the toddler's relationship to mother and to father: Related to conflict behavior and the readiness to establish new relationships. *Child Development*, *52*, 932–940.

Marmot, M. (1998). Improvement of social environment to improve health. *Lancet*, *351*, 57–60.

Marmot, M., Bobak, M., & Davey Smith, G. (1995). Explanations for social inequalities in health. In B. C. Amick, S. Levine, A. R. Tarlov & D. C. Welsh (Eds.), *Society and Health*. New York: Oxford University Press.

Martínez del Solar, F. (2003). Toddlers' Group? Se puede ser mamá sin haber tenido una mamá [Toddler Group: Is it possible to be a mother without having had one?]. *Transiciones*, *6*, 89–105.

Mayes, L., & Cohen, D. (1993). Playing and therapeutic action in child analysis. *International Journal of Psychoanalysis*, *74*, 1235–1244.

Meaney, M. J., & Szyf, M. (2005). Environmental programming of stress responses through DNA methylation: Life at the interface between a dynamic environment and a fixed genome. *Dialogues in Clinical Neurosciences*, *7*(2), 103–123.

Menzies Lyth, I. E. P. (1970). *The Functioning of Social Systems as a Defence against*

Anxiety (Tavistock Pamphlet No.3). London: Tavistock Institute of Human Relations.

Mitchell, J. (2003). *Siblings*. Cambridge: Polity Press.

Money, J., & Erhardt, A. A. (1972). *Man & Woman, Boy & Girl*. Baltimore: Johns Hopkins University Press.

Moran, G., & Berger, M. (1980). Report of the Study Group on Psychological Problems of Diabetic Children. *Bulletin of the Hampstead Clinic, 3*, 235–245.

Muhamedrahimov, R. (1995). *Development program for infants with special needs*. Paper presented at the Psychology in Changing Europe: The first east-west conference in general psychology organised by the British and East European psychology group (August).

Muhamedrahimov, R. (1997). Infant mental health in Russia. *The Signal Newsletter of the World Association for Infant Mental Health, 5*(2), 4.

National Evaluation of Sure Start Research Team. (2008). *Early Impacts of Sure Start Local Programmes on Three Year Olds and Their Families. Report 027*. London: Department for Education and Skills.

Navridi, E. (2007). Toddler groups: A transitional context for a transitional age. *Child and Adolescent: Mental Health and Psychopathology, 9*(2), 73–82.

Navridis, K. (2005). *Group Psychology, a Clinical Psychodynamic Approach*. Athens: Papazisis.

Niedecken, D. (2003). *Nameless: Understanding Learning Disability*. Hove: Brunner Routledge.

Nitsun, M. (1996). *The Anti-group. Destructive Forces in the Group and Their Creative Potential*. London: Routledge.

Novick, K. K., & Novick, J. (2005). *Working with Parents Makes Therapy Work*. Northvale, NJ: Jason Aronson.

Office for National Statistics. (2006). Work and family (Focus on Gender Archive) [http://www.statistics.gov.uk/cci/nugget_print.asp?ID=436].

Olds, D. L., Sadler, L., & Kitzman, H. (2007). Programs for parents of infants and toddlers: Recent evidence from randomized trials. *Journal of Child Psychology and Psychiatry, 48*(3–4), 355–391.

Palfreeman, S. (1982). Mother and toddler groups among "at risk" families. *Health Visitor, 55*, 455–459.

Parsons, M. (1999). The logic of play in psychoanalysis. *International Journal of Psychoanalysis, 80*(5), 871–884.

Parsons, M. (2007). Raiding the inarticulate: The internal analytic setting and listening beyond countertransference. *International Journal of Psychoanalysis, 88*, 1441–1456.

Pastorova, A. (2002). *Non-Disabled Children and Full Inclusion*. Prague: RSS.

Phillips, A. (1992). Learning not to talk. In I. Ward (Ed.), *The Psychology of Nursery Education: Papers Presented at the Anna Freud Centenary Conference, November 25, 1995* (pp. 27–42). London: Karnac.

Pleshkova, N., Muhamedrahimov, R., & Crittenden, P. (2008). *Quality of attachment in St. Petersburg (Russian Federation) sample of family and orphanage children*. Paper presented at the 1st Biennial Conference of the International Association for the Study of Attachment in conjunction with the University of Bologna, Bertinoro (October).

Power, T. G., & Chapieski, M. L. (1986). Childrearing and impulse control in toddlers: A naturalistic investigation. *Developmental Psychology, 22,* 271–275.

Pretorius, I. M. (2004). The skin as a means of communicating the difficulties of separation-individuation in toddlerhood. *The International Journal of Infant Observation and its Applications, 7*(1).

Radina, N. K. (2004). *Ressotsializatsiya i adaptatsiya vypusknikov detskih domov i internatov.* Nizhniy Novgorod: Nizhniy Novgorod University.

Radke-Yarrow, M., Cummings, E. M., Kuczynski, L., & Chapman, M. (1985). Patterns of attachment in two- and three-year-olds in normal families and families with parental depression. *Child Development, 56,* 884–893.

Repacholi, B. M., & Gopnik, A. (1997). Early reasoning about desires: Evidence from 14- and 18-month-olds. *Developmental Psychology, 33,* 12–21.

Reynolds, D. (2003). Mindful parenting: A group approach to enhancing reflective capacity in parents and infants. *Journal of Child Psychotherapy, 29*(3), 357–374.

Roberts, V. Z. (1994). The organization of work: Contributions from open systems theory. In A. Obholzer & V. Z. Roberts (Eds.), *The Unconscious at Work* (pp. 28–38). New York: Routledge.

Rudestam, K. E. (1982). *Experiential Groups in Theory and Practice.* Monterey: Brooks/Cole Publishing Company.

Rycroft, C. (1968). *A Critical Dictionary of Psychoanalysis.* London: Nelson.

Sandler, A.-M., & Hobson, R. P. (2001). On engaging with people in early childhood: The case of congenital blindness. *Clinical Child Psychology and Psychiatry, 6,* 205–222.

Sandler, J. (1965). The Hampstead Child Therapy Clinic. *Aspects of Family Mental Health in Europe, 28,* 109–123.

Sandler, J., & Freud, A. (1985). *The Analysis of Defences: The Ego and the Mechanisms of Defence Revisited.* New York: International Universities Press.

Sandler, J., & Rosenblatt, B. (1962). The concept of the representational world. *The Psychoanalytic Study of the Child, 17,* 128–145.

Schore, A. (1993). *Affect Regulation and the Origin of the Self: The Neurobiology of Emotional Development.* Hillsdale, NJ: Erlbaum.

Searles, H. (1963). The place of neutral therapist-responses in psychotherapy with the schizophrenic patient. In *Collected Papers on Schizophrenia and Related Subjects* (pp. 626–653). London: Hogarth Press.

Seigal, D. J. (1999). *The Developing Mind: Towards a Neurobiology of Interpersonal Experience.* New York: Guilford Press.

Simpson, D., & Miller, L. (2004). *Unexpected Gains: Psychotherapy with People with Learning Disability.* London: Karnac.

Sinason, V. (1992). *Mental Handicap and the Human Condition.* London: Free Association Books.

Slade, A. (2003). Holding the baby in mind: Discussion of Joseph Lichtenberg's "Communication in Infancy". *Psychoanalytic Inquiry, 23,* 521–529.

Slade, A. (2005). Parental reflective functioning: An introduction. *Attachment and Human Development, 7*(3), 269–281.

Slade, A., Aber, J. L., Berger, B., Bresgi, I., & Kaplan, M. (2003/2005a). *PDI-R2-S Parent Development Interview Revised Short Version.* New York: The City College of New York.

Slade, A., Aber, J. L., Berger, B., Bresgi, I., & Kaplan, M. (2003/2005b). *PDI-R2 Parent Development Interview Revised*. New York: City College of New York.

Slade, A., Aber, J. L., Fiorello, J., DeSear, P., Meyer, J., Cohen, L. J., et al. (1994). *Parent Development Interview Coding System*. New York: City University of New York.

Slade, A., Bernbach, E., Grienenberger, J., Levy, D., & Locker, A. (2004). Addendum to Fonagy, Target, Steele, & Steele reflective functioning scoring manual for use with the Parent Development Interview. Unpublished manuscript. New York: The City College and Graduate Center of the City University of New York.

Slade, A., Bernbach, E., Grienenberger, J., Wohlgemuth Levy, D., & Locker, A. (2005a). *Addendum to Reflective Functioning Scoring Manual for Use with the Parent Development Interview, version 2.0*. New York: The City College of New York.

Slade, A., Grienenberger, J., Bernbach, E., Levy, D., & Locker, A. (2005b). Maternal reflective functioning, attachment and the transmission gap: A preliminary study. *Attachment and Human Development, 7*(3), 283–298.

Slade, A., Sadler, L., Dios-Kenn, C. D., Webb, D., Currier-Ezepchick, J., & Mayes, L. (2005c). Minding the baby: A reflective parenting program. *Psychoanalytic Study of the Child, 60*, 74–100.

Smith, J. A., & Osborn, M. (2003). Interpretative phenomenological analysis. In J. A. Smith (Ed.), *Qualitative Psychology: A Practical Guide to Methods*. London: Sage.

Smith, J. A., Osborn, M., & Jarman, M. (1999). Doing interpretative phenomenological analysis. In M. Murray & K. Chamberlain (Eds.), *Qualitative Health Psychology: Theories and Methods* (pp. 218–240). London: Sage.

Solnit, A. J., & Newman, L. M. (1984). Anna Freud: the child expert. *The Psychoanalytic Study of the Child, 39*, 45–63.

Steele, M., Steele, H., & Fonagy, P. (1996). Associations amongst attachment classifications of mothers, fathers and their infants. *Child Development, 67*, 541–555.

Stern, D. N. (1985). *The Interpersonal World of the Infant: A View from Psychoanalysis and Developmental Psychology*. New York: Basic Books.

Stern, D. N. (1995). *The Motherhood Constellation: A Unified View of Parent-Infant Psychotherapy*. New York: Basic Books.

Tewkesbury, J. (2006). *The Hampstead Child-therapy Course and Clinic. A film compiled and directed by Joan Tewkesbury (1976) and produced by Sidney Pollack*. London: The Anna Freud Centre.

Thomas, D. G., Whitaker, E., Crow, C. D., Little, V., Love, L., Lykins, M. S., et al. (1997). Event-related potential variability as a measure of information storage in infant development. *Developmental Neuropsychology, 13*, 205–232.

Thomas, K. R., & Garske, G. (1995). Object relations theory: Implications for the personality. Development and treatment of persons with disabilities. *Melanie Klein and Object Relations, 13*, 31–63.

Thomas, K. R., & McGinnis, J. D. (1991). The psychoanalytic theories of D.W. Winnicott as applied to rehabilitation. *Journal of Rehabilitation, 57*, 63–66.

Tulkin, S. R., & Kagan, J. (1972). Mother-child interaction in the first year of life. *Child Development, 43*(1), 31–41.

Tyson, P., & Tyson, R. L. (1990). *Psychoanalytic Theories of Development: An Integration.* New Haven and London: Yale University Press.

Weise, K. (1995). The use of verbalisation in the management of feelings and behaviour: A therapeutic intervention in the nursery. *The Bulletin of the Anna Freud Centre, 18,* 35–47.

Wellman, H. M., & Phillips, A. T. (2000). Developing intentional understandings. In L. Moses, B. Male & D. Baldwin (Eds.), *Intentionality: A Key to Human Understanding.* Cambridge, MA: MIT Press.

Wills, D. M. (1965). Some observations on blind nursery school children's understanding of their world. *The Psychoanalytic Study of the Child, 20,* 344–364.

Wills, D. M. (1979a). Early speech development in blind children. *Psychoanalytic Study of the Child, 34,* 85–117.

Wills, D. M. (1979b). The ordinary devoted mother and her blind baby. *Psychoanalytic Study of the Child, 34,* 31–49.

Wills, D. M. (1981). Some notes on the application of the diagnostic profile to young blind children. *Psychoanalytic Study of the Child, 36,* 217–237.

Wilson, P. (1980). The use of observation in the Hampstead Clinic Nursery School. *The Bulletin of the Hampstead Clinic, 3,* 29–47.

Winnicott, D. W. (1945). Primitive emotional development. In *Through Paediatrics to Psychoanalysis.* London: Hogarth Press, 1975.

Winnicott, D. W. (1949). The world in small doses. In *The Child and the Family* (1957). London: Tavistock.

Winnicott, D. W. (1957). The child's needs and the role of the mother in the early stages. In *The Child and the Outside World.* London: Tavistock.

Winnicott, D. W. (1960a). Ego distortion in terms of true and false self. In *The Maturational Processes and the Facilitating Environment* (1965) (pp. 140–152). New York: International Universities Press.

Winnicott, D. W. (1960b). The theory of the parent-infant relationship. In *The Maturational Process and the Facilitating Environment* (pp. 37–55). New York: International Universities Press.

Winnicott, D. W. (1963a). The development of the capacity for concern. In *The Maturational Processes and the Facilitating Environment* (1965) (pp. 73–82). New York: International Universities Press.

Winnicott, D. W. (1963b). From dependence towards independence in the development of the individual. In *The Maturational Processes and the Facilitating Environment* (1965) (pp. 83–92). New York: International Universities Press.

Winnicott, D. W. (1966). The child in the family group. In C. Winnicott, R. Shepherd & M. Davis (Eds.), *Home is Where We Start From* (1986) (pp. 128–141). London: Penguin.

Winnicott, D. W. (1967). Mirror-role of the mother and family in child development. In P. Lomas (Ed.), *The Predicament of the Family: A Psycho-Analytical Symposium* (pp. 26–33). London: Hogarth Press.

Winnicott, D. W. (1968). Sum, I am. In C. Winnicott, R. Shepherd & M. Davis (Eds.), *Home is Where We Start From* (1986). London: Penguin.

Winnicott, D. W. (1969). The use of an object and relating through identifications. In *Playing and Reality* (1971) (pp. 86–94). London: Tavistock.

Winnicott, D. W. (1971). *Playing and Reality.* London: Tavistock.

Winnicott, D. W. (1988). *Human Nature.* London: Free Association Books.

Wittenberg, I. (2001). The transition from home to nursery. *Infant Observation*, *4*(2), 23–35.

Woodhead, J., & James, J. (2007). Transformational process in parent infant psychotherapy: Provision in community drop-in groups. In M. Pozzi-Monzo & B. Tydeman (Eds.), *Innovations in Parent Infant Psychotherapy*. London: Karnac.

Wright, K. (1991). *Vision and Separation: Between Mother and Baby*. London: Free Association Books.

Young-Bruehl, E. (2004). Anna Freud and Dorothy Burlingham at Hampstead: The origins of psychoanalytic parent-infant observation. *Annual of Psychoanalysis*, *32*, 185–197.

Young-Bruehl, E. (2008). *Anna Freud: A Biography* (2nd edition). New Haven and London: Yale University Press.

Zamaldinova, G. (Ed.). (2000). *Mamy-vypusknitsy detskih domov. Problemy, opyt podderzhki i soprovozhdeniya*. St. Petersburg: Korchakovskiy Centre of youth programmes "Realniy putj".

Zaphiriou Woods, M. (2000). Preventive work in a toddler group and nursery. *Journal of Child Psychotherapy*, *26*, 209–233.

Zaphiriou Woods, M. (2005). The Anna Freud Centre Parent-Toddler Groups. Unpublished paper, presented at the Toddler Symposium, Anna Freud Centre. London.

Zaphiriou Woods, M., & Gedulter-Trieman, A. (1998). Maya: The interplay of nursery education and analysis in restoring a child to the path of normal development. In A. Hurry (Ed.), *Psychoanalysis and Developmental Therapy*. London: Karnac.

Zigler, E., & Styfco, S. J. (Eds.). (1995). *Head Start and Beyond: A National Plan for Extended Childhood Intervention*. New Haven: Yale University Press.

Index